LOVED

BY THE

LIGHT

Endorsements

"Is there meaning in life? Is there continuity of life after death? In *Loved by the Light*, John Audette shares the extraordinary and compelling experiences that changed him from an agnostic to a believer. Whether or not you believe in God as some great spiritual power you cannot fail to be fascinated by this book."

Jane Goodall, PhD, DBE
Founder, the Jane Goodall Institute and UN Messenger of Peace
New York Times best-selling author of *Reason for Hope; The Book of Hope: A Survival Guide for Trying Times* and *Local Voices, Local Choices*

"It's rare to read a book that you honestly cannot put down, but *Loved by the Light* is one of these remarkable treasures. I have always believed the mystical truth that angels assist us and yet authentic stories still fill me with awe. And if ever there was a need to connect with the mystical reality of how intimately we are watched over by the divine, it is now. And John Audette has given us this gift through sharing his personal spiritual journey."

Caroline Myss, PhD
Five-time *New York Times* best-selling author of *Anatomy of the Spirit* and *Intimate Conversations with the Divine*

"*Loved by the Light* is a masterpiece! This book is a treasure trove of wisdom about God and an evidence-based spiritual path. John Audette's personal spiritual experiences are as gripping as they are insightful. This book is a sentinel event in providing evidence that allows anyone to affirm God rationally. You won't want to miss this vitally important book! I enthusiastically recommend this exceptional book as essential to everyone interested in spiritual experiences and spiritual enlightenment."

Jeffrey Long, MD
New York Times best-selling author of *Evidence of the Afterlife: The Science of Near-Death Experiences* and *God and the Afterlife: The Groundbreaking New Evidence for God and Near-Death Experience*

"*Loved by the Light* presents amazing heartfelt accounts of authentic life changing encounters, honoring the mysteries of life and death along with exploring the realms of visions, divine intervention, angels, a near-death experience and out of body travel. An invaluable and enlightening resource. Much wisdom is found in this extraordinary book. A must read!"

Anita Moorjani
New York Times **best-selling author of** *Dying to Be Me* **and** *Sensitive is the New Strong*

"John Audette has spent his life as a true idealist, focused on achieving the best of all possible worlds. His book, *Loved by the Light,* is an exciting and refreshing expression of the wondrous reality enabled by taking seriously the myriad modern examples of humans experiencing God through near-death and similar spiritually transformative experiences, beginning with his own remarkable encounters. The Introduction eloquently synthesizes how recovering knowledge of a loving God offers the potential to mitigate humanity's most urgent challenges. Audette's approach of inviting people to share the unconditional love of God for others by emulating God (even if just for a day!) is a brilliantly simple approach that might just help save the world."

Eben Alexander, MD
Neurosurgeon and *New York Times* **best-selling author of** *Proof of Heaven, The Map of Heaven* **and** *Living in a Mindful Universe*

"John Audette has been a vital force directing spiritual, social service and healthcare organizations for the past half century. In his book *Loved by the Light,* John bares his soul in revealing his gradual awakening through a series of close brushes with death. This intimate account of his spiritual awakening will inspire readers to reimagine their connection to the divine. John's compelling message of a holistic spirituality comes at a critical time for humanity as we face an uncertain future, offering us a more meaningful and fulfilling vision of life."

Bruce Greyson, MD
Carlson Professor Emeritus of Psychiatry and Neurobehavioral Sciences
Division of Perceptual Studies
University of Virginia Health System
New York Times **best-selling author of** *After*

"In this book, John finally has come forth to tell his personal story, which has plainly been of a life marked by a staggering number of mind-boggling events that clearly show the hand of a divine providence in orchestrating John's path. The stories he relates in *Loved by the Light* are absolutely riveting. Prepare to be amazed and inspired by what John relates about his God-centered journey and quest to realize his life-affirming vision for our world."

Kenneth Ring, PhD
Author of *Lessons from the Light* and *Blogging Toward Infinity* and *A Near-Death Researcher's Notebook: What I have Learned about Dying, Death and The Afterlife*

"*Loved by the Light* is one of the most original and creative books ever written. Inspired by the "life review" reported by many people who have had a near-death experience, it describes numerous methods we can use to hasten our spiritual awakening and transformation. The author challenges us to live our lives based exclusively upon kindness, compassion, and unconditional love - agape love - so we'll learn how to create heaven on earth."

Bill Guggenheim
Co-Author of *Hello from Heaven!*

"The poignant, compelling stories in *Loved by the Light* make it crystal clear: we live in a Universe that absolutely treasures and adores us. This book will reacquaint you with the sanctity and miraculous nature of life in general and life on earth in particular."

Rob Schwartz
Between Lives Soul Regression Hypnotist
Author of *Your Soul's Plan, Your Soul's Gift* and *Your Soul's Love*

"Anyone who doubts the validity of spiritually transformative experiences and the immortality of the soul will be spellbound by the author's numerous and enlightening insights, which taken together form a well-conceived urgent rescue plan for humanity. With no attempt at hyperbole, this book is a brilliant masterpiece that deserves to be read by every thinking person on the planet."

Joe St. Clair
Author of *The Seven Stages of the Soul, The Path to Indra, The Feather and the Stone* and *Contentment: 100 Keys to Total Life Fulfilment*

"In an age where most wonder if God's presence is real, *Loved by the Light* reveals His miraculous hand is always present and ready to intervene. In 2014, I was captivated when John shared several of his angel encounters with me and insisted that he share these incredible experiences with the world. Prepare to be astounded and deeply moved by riveting stories of divine intervention and John's vision to create a more loving and compassionate God-centered world."

Virginia Hummel
Author of *Cracking the Grief Code, Orbs and the Afterlife* and *Miracle Messenger*

"In a field rich with the writings of people who have had near-death experiences (NDEs), John Audette substantially enriches the literature by reporting in this book an extraordinary parade of spiritually transformative experiences (STEs) he has encountered through his lifetime to date. Audette is above all a big-picture author. His highly readable book wanders deeply into under-attended corners such as our collective responsibility to understand the implications of these spiritual experiences for human mindsets, including those that manifest as world religions."

William D. Coffey
Author of *RENEWAL: Old Stories, a Godly Algorithm, and Choices for the Earth Today*

"I couldn't put this delightful book down. I was captivated by its deep exploration into one of the most mysterious places we humans dare to explore. John is an elegant storyteller who brings the miraculous to light and ends this thoughtful book with lessons of hope."

Jane Tobal, PhD
President and CEO, Visionary Alternatives

LOVED

BY THE

LIGHT

TRUE STORIES OF DIVINE
INTERVENTION AND PROVIDENCE

John R. Audette
Eternea, Inc.

Published by Eternea, Inc.
102 NE 2nd Street, Ste. 331
Boca Raton, FL 33432
(561) 868-6880 Telephone/Fax
Editor@Eternea.org

LEGAL DISCLAIMER: The author of this book does not dispense medical or mental health advice or prescribe the use of any method, technique, exercise, drug, medicine or psychopharmaceutical agent as a form of treatment for any physical, psychological or emotional problem, or to obtain spiritual enlightenment, either directly or indirectly. Please seek advice and consent from licensed physicians, psychologists or other trained professionals for all such personal issues or matters. The intent of the author is to offer information of a general nature to help people in their quest for spiritual well-being. In the event any of the information in this book is used or acted upon by any reader or readers for this expressed purpose, which is their constitutional right, the author and the publisher neither bear nor assume any responsibility for their actions in this regard or the actions of others in relation with or in response to any of the contents provided in this book.

Audette, John R. – Loved by the Light: True Stories of Divine Intervention & Providence

Library of Congress Control Number: 2022921912

Hardcover ISBN   979-8-9872633-9-6
Paperback ISBN   979-8-9872633-0-3
Digital   ISBN   979-8-9872633-2-7

Cover & Interior Design: Virginia Hummel
Cover Photo © h4ackermodify/iStock
Graphic Artist: Fiver/Cal5086
Author photo: Fabrice Ziolkowski

Dedication

Lovingly dedicated to dearest life-long friends and colleagues, all progressive forward-thinking pioneers of the ever-evolving global spiritual awakening movement: Dr. Kenneth Ring for inspiring me to write this book and for his ceaseless efforts to quicken the evolution of human consciousness; Dr. Raymond Moody for innumerable and unfathomable contributions to expanding the boundaries of science into the metaphysical realm, surpassed only by his magnificent intellect and humor, and for enabling me to hear the ring of destiny only once in February 1974; and William Guggenheim III for a lifetime of constant service to the greater good, giving so much to so many, including me. Also dedicated to Dr. Steven Jarecki, (1948-2022), a gifted healer and kind-hearted soul, whose abundant charm, charisma, humor and "je ne sais quoi" was outshined only by his compassion for and generosity to others.

Contents

"We have come to know and to trust in the love that God has for us. For God is love, and he who abides in love abides in God, and God in them."

1 John 4:16

LOVED

LIGHT

Foreword

John Audette is one of my dearest friends. I tell people who inquire about him that he is by far the most idealistic person I know, and the purest of heart too. This has been true consistently throughout the entire course of our special friendship which began in February 1974.

My high regard for John notwithstanding, I believe he has written a seminal work on the topic of progressive spirituality. *Loved by the Light* is truly a one-of-a-kind book in terms of the spectrum of peak experiences it addresses and the crystal-clear message points it delivers. It telegraphs an urgent clarion wake-up call to humanity, as well as a simple, straight-forward but brilliant "rescue plan" for our species that could lead us to the shores of an optimal future.

This powerful gem is in a class all its own. Along with its uniquely holistic and integrative approach, it offers practical strategies to help people awaken spiritually, buttressed by a realistic plan for constructive transformational social action. John bears his soul to the world to help humanity evolve "from great to greater to greatness," and none too soon as rumors of a potential World War III abound.

Expect much wisdom to be revealed on these pages, including John's deeply personal stories about life-saving angel encounters, near-death and shared-death experiences, bona fide after-death communication, personal sacred epiphanies, as well as several other extraordinary events. He also discusses mystical synchronicities such as the intriguing story about how he and I came to meet. All this information is presented in a smartly organized and riveting manner. It affirms that God is real and so too is survival of human consciousness after bodily death.

As a psychiatrist and professor of philosophy, I have naturally become a lifelong observer of human beings. During that time, I noticed a remarkable trend that deserves serious consideration. Namely, as people age, an increasing percentage of them have had the experience of stepping over into some other realm or sphere of existence. This is precisely what John describes in this fascinating book.

Many people are afraid they are alone in having stepped across the threshold into another level of reality. But no! They are actually in the ever-expanding company of countless others. It is increasingly clear to me that as we age, glimpses into other realms of spirit are a normal and natural occurrence. Knowing the truth of this observation, I feel justified in concluding that what has been previously known as the realm of the afterlife is rapidly seeping into or meshing with ordinary waking reality.

The increasing amount of aging that is occurring in the world right now has spawned the emergence of a new "Generation of Elders" and a fresh wave of stories to share on par with John's trans-dimensional accounts. So, I suspect that even though he waited decades to finally share his "Elder wisdom" and compelling stories, this is indeed the perfect time for publication of *Loved by the Light*.

John has written a timely and powerful book, a genuine page-turner, one that compulsively engages the reader from start to finish. I am confident that many will be comforted by the conclusions he espouses, and by the recognition that they themselves have had similar kinds of experiences. They may even have been puzzled by them as John was at first, not knowing what to think.

So, prepare to be deeply inspired by this wonderful book and soulfully enriched by it too. Reading it might just take you on a life-changing transformative journey of your very own. I feel sure it will inspire many others to enjoy their very own voyage of spiritual awakening.

Raymond Moody, MD, PhD
Author of *Life After Life* and many other best-selling books

Introduction

For a man of his time, (470-399 B.C.), and even by the standards of today, Socrates had a commanding intellect and a brilliant mind. He knew a great deal about a great many things. Yet, one of the most profound things he ever said, which sparkles brightest in an ocean of the profundity he espoused throughout his 71-year much-heralded lifetime, was this: "I know that I know nothing."

Mind you, this statement was not an attempt at insincere humility or false modesty. If indeed Socrates made this statement, as Plato claimed, I find myself in full agreement with him over 2,400 years later. I totally share this candid transparent sentiment.

Like Socrates, I know that I know nothing. Truly, I am constantly humbled by what I do not know. But I am in good company in making this admission. Not one ordinary human being on this earth, living or dead, has come close to scratching the surface of all there is to know. We actually know so very little, and as the old adage states, "The more we learn, the less we know." How true.

But, that said, I hasten to point out that there are a few exceptions to this otherwise foolproof observation. There are a few basic things that I claim to know based on direct first-hand experience. First and foremost, I know that I am deeply and unconditionally *Loved by the Light* and will be for all time. I know you are too, and so is everyone and everything throughout the cosmos. I also know God is real and so too is the afterlife.

Yes, these are blockbuster claims, all of which I offer not as conjecture, but rather as statements of fact based on my experiences.

How do I know these things for certain? How can I be so sure? I wrote this book to answer that very question.

To be sure, some people may not accept that what I claim to know for sure in this book is true in any objective sense of the term. But for those who are willing to venture forward with an open mind and a receptive heart, I am optimistic that my conclusions may resonate with many readers after careful contemplation of the wide array of compelling evidence offered, some of which is corroborated by either testimony or the eyewitness accounts of others.

The "Light" I am referencing, of course, is the Light of God, the magnificent loving Creator and Source of all that is, or ever was, or ever will be. And the evidence I provide herein, hopefully, will be sufficiently credible to convince many, if not most, that God exists and so does the reality of God's unconditional love for all things.

To commence what promises to be a fascinating journey through this evidence, please know that on seven separate occasions, I came perilously close to death. Seven times I narrowly escaped its clutches. But instead of meeting a tragic and violent fate, I was miraculously saved by God's angels. In each instance, they promptly intervened to spare my life.

These interventions, which I believe were all acts of God, make me both a witness to and a recipient of God's amazing grace and bountiful love. Multiple times, I was literally rescued by the Light and *Loved by the Light*, the glorious divine Light of God.

Could there be any greater expression of love, grace, mercy or compassion than to have one's life saved miraculously, not once or twice, but seven times? It renders me thunderstruck, humble and extremely grateful. The familiar 23rd Psalm, Verses 5-6, describe it so eloquently: "My cup runneth over. Surely goodness and mercy follow me in all the days of my life."

My first angel encounter occurred in 1960 at the age of eight. It was the only encounter that was not of a life-saving nature. The last one took place in 1993 at the age of 41. These unforgettable experiences are deeply meaningful to me. After all, in seven of the eight angel encounters, I nearly died, traumatically and violently. Each time, my life was in great danger, but instead of being killed, which was the most probable outcome, my life was divinely spared.

I cannot comprehend why the hand of God reached out to protect me from certain death in these instances through angelic intervention, but this is precisely what happened. Across the full spectrum of my many amazing experiences, there is no other plausible explanation for it. Yet, in all humility, I cannot fathom the reason. Surely, I do not remotely qualify as an indispensable or irreplaceable member of the human race.

However, I know it was the hand of God that saved me. I know with every fiber of my being that I was *Loved by the Light* beyond measure in each of these instances. This much seems indisputable to me. In my mind, even with all due scrutiny, it is an inescapable conclusion. To lend even more credence to this assertion, I offer objective validation of my claim in the form of eyewitness testimony where available.

This book is divided into three parts. In Part I, all eight angel encounters are described in as much detail as can be accurately remembered. In Part II, other kinds of experiential evidence are offered to include afterlife communications; deathbed visions; near-death and shared-death experiences; mystical synchronicities; a vision quest epiphany that occurred in the Mojave Desert which involved the spontaneous manifestation of a physical object that literally appeared from out of nowhere; verified channelings; and a powerful lucid dream which also resulted in a spontaneous physical manifestation soon after. Moreover, I share a deeply personal story about miraculous divine intervention *in utero* that saved my life as a young embryo from multiple abortion attempts by my mother, which she later personally confirmed directly to me.

Finally, in Part III, the overarching meaning and significance of all these experiences are explored together with various methods that can be considered for bringing about a firsthand spiritual awakening in a direct manner by engendering one's own epiphany or peak breakthrough event. Moreover, a practical structured exercise is introduced and explained in an effort to apply the knowledge gained from experiences such as these in grounded, pragmatic ways. They are aimed at helping improve the quality of life for all things to advance the cause of achieving an optimal future for earth and all its inhabitants.

Although I did not have a personal near-death experience or out-of-body experience or past-life regression, all of the things that did happen to me as described in this book were enormously powerful and life-changing, fully on par with these other kinds of compelling phenomena. What's more, during the past 48 years of my career, I encountered hundreds of people throughout the course of my work who reported exceptional peak experiences comparable to my own. These were credible people who gave very credible accounts of extraordinary love-filled divine happenings in their lives, all of which reinforce the central premises of this book.

In nearly all such cases, including the many exceptional experiences I personally encountered as detailed in this book, there are two main commonly reported recurring motifs. The first is that experiencers feel a profound sense of peace and acceptance about what is happening to them during their close encounters with death. There is no fear, angst or trepidation.

It is indeed fascinating to hear people consistently report that during their experiences, they felt cradled in the arms of the universe, suspended outside of time and space, floating in some kind of divinely created womb or bubble. They felt no anxiety whatsoever, only joy and a strong sense of euphoric anticipation about what might come next during their other-worldly adventures.

The second commonly reported element is that they experience a glorious overpowering love like none they have ever felt before. It shines forth in powerful undulating rays of golden-white light gloriously emanating from an effulgent deity or Supreme Being. They invariably perceive it to be an indescribable canopy of unconditional love and compassion. It is extended equally to all regardless of who they are or what they may have done during their lifetimes. In the sacred presence of this transcendent deity or Supreme Being, who many identify to be God or Christ, all are uniformly and equally *Loved by the Light.*

Some report visual perception of this divine presence, but others simply feel it energetically deep within the core of their being. It manifests in waves of engrossing, captivating, mesmerizing, awesome energy. But always, nearly everyone is at a loss for words to accurately describe the fullness of what they experienced during their journey to the other side.

Typically, they say they lack the vocabulary to do justice to what they encountered. They report that what happened to them cannot be adequately explained in words. But all agree that they were *Loved by the Light,* like they have never experienced love before. I am no exception.

In all my miraculous experiences, the very same thing happened to me. I encountered the same exact feelings. Thus, I am as resolute in my convictions as anyone who had a bona fide near-death experience, or out-of-body experience, or who accurately recalled a past life in a highly evidential manner such as Jenny Cockell does in her wonderful book *Across Time and Death,* and she did so spontaneously, interestingly, without the use of hypnosis.

Now some will say that my combined spectrum of metaphysical experiences are merely the result of accidental random events or fortuitous coincidence. This could be a plausible theory to explain away perhaps a few incidents, but taken altogether as a whole, it is inconceivable that the sum of all my exceptional experiences in life could be readily dismissed or explained away in such a fashion. The odds of that would be beyond astronomical.

Looking back on these life-saving angel rescues and many other kinds of extraordinary experiences throughout my life, a child-like sense of awe and wonder has preoccupied me for decades about what it all might mean. After spending almost five decades reflecting on this question, the time for wonder and reflection has been replaced in my mind by certainty and conviction, reinforced by accounts from millions of other people around the world who have been blessed to experience various mystical events like my own.

I am not a religious person. I have no affiliation with any religion. Rather, I am a dispassionate observer of what enters my life; that is to say what happens around me and to me. I keep an open mind, a "beginner's mind," in Zen speak. My nature is guided by logic and deductive reasoning in the formulation of objectively defensible conclusions. I endeavor to be scholarly and academic in my analysis of data and events. I form grounded opinions, but they are subject to change if and when new credible information arrives.

I freely admit I was an agnostic about the matter of God…that is up until the time that I could no longer be. I evolved from shallow half-hearted beliefs based on tenuous religious faith, to becoming an avowed agnostic, to holding firm abiding convictions derived from knowledge acquired through direct personal spiritual experiences as detailed and discussed in this book.

Frankly, I outgrew agnosticism when compelling evidence in support of God's existence and the continuation of human consciousness after physical death became so overpowering and undeniable, I could reach no other defensible conclusion.

I am one who is extremely reticent to presume or proclaim firm sweeping conclusions. Yet, all these sacred events taken together as described in this book now compel me without reservation, trepidation or equivocation, to wholeheartedly affirm the certainty of God's existence, God's unconditional love for all things, God's omnipresence throughout creation and the reality of an afterlife.

There is no other satisfactory explanation I can offer for all the mystical events in my life, much as I have tried, certainly not one that would do full justice to all I have experienced. For me, the evidence is overwhelmingly convincing that God is indeed real, and so too is the afterlife, and so too is God's infinite love and grace for us all.

Please understand that this work is not a personal memoir. If it were, there would be so much more to tell. While it may seem like an autobiography in places, it should not be construed as such. Yes, I do tell my life's story to some extent, but only in the context of sharing many remarkable events throughout my life which brought me to the firm conclusion that God exists and so too does survival of human consciousness after physical death of the body. This is the recurring message in all the stories I share.

After many decades of personal debate and vacillation, at the encouragement of a few close friends, I finally decided to write this book, not only to share my eight angel encounters, but also a wide variety of other extraordinary sacred experiences that personally happened to me, all of which are veritable instances of unmistakable divine intervention and providence...all of which prove how very loved I am by the Light, and by extension, you too!

To my academically trained mind, these experiences are evidential confirmation of God's existence and God's love. But in making this declaration, I rely not just on my own personal experiences, but also on the exceptional experiences of millions of other people all over the world throughout recorded history.

One example of an independent account such as this comes from my dear friend Virginia Hummel, who made enormous contributions to this book's development. She is the author of several books, including *Cracking the Grief Code,* in which she wrote about her own amazing experience of being "Loved by the Light," which I share here with her kind permission:

> "In the thick of grieving the loss of my youngest son Chris, I dealt with intense emotional pain that at times became unbearable. On one of

those days, I happened to be driving in my car on the way to pick up my daughter at her elementary school.

Suddenly, I felt my heart chakra open wide. Then, spontaneously, I experienced an overwhelming connection to divine love. I had a sustained vision in my mind's eye of Jesus. He was surrounded by a luminous aura of love and golden-white light. It was as if I had a direct link to Him. He offered me the great gift of divine unconditional love, so genuine and pure that one could only feel it in His presence.

The only way I can describe it is to imagine a stream of golden-white light brighter than the sun starting at the center of my chest and reaching directly into the entire being of Christ. It was filled with extraordinary, indescribable love, so much so that I became overwhelmed with absolute joy and euphoria. Endless tears of exaltation ran down my cheeks.

For the next twenty minutes or so, I found myself in a profound state of grace as though the highest form of divine Love had filled every part of me. I felt safe and protected, cradled in this Love. It healed and restored me almost instantly.

Somehow, I managed to end up safely in the school's parking lot, but I surely don't remember most of the drive there. All I remember is feeling overwhelming love from God. During this profound event, I had a powerful epiphany. I remembered what it felt like to be in the presence of Christ, connected with pure unconditional divine love and my authentic self. I remembered what it feels like to be loved by God."

Now, kindly imagine if we all could experience something on the order of what Virginia described. Imagine if we all knew for certain there was something more than this world and this single lifetime, and that God exists, and that we are loved beyond measure by God.

With that as my overriding goal, I decided to write and publish this work to help convince more people that experiences like mine and Virginia's are real and inarguably evidential. It is the most important thing I can do during this distressing time when huge challenges are ravaging humankind.

Simply put, the many miracles I have been blessed to encounter throughout my lifetime have inspired me to share what I have learned with the whole of humanity. My sole motivation for doing so is to help improve the quality of life for all people and all other living things by engendering widespread belief in God, not on the basis of faith, but rather on a firm empirical foundation buttressed by credible evidence.

By revealing my highly personal sacred experiences for the first time to the public, I hope many more will embrace the certainty of God's existence and God's unconditional love for everyone. Moreover, I hope it will give more people unwavering knowledge about life after death, filling them with an abiding peace of mind that the afterlife is indeed real, more real than our lifetime here on earth.

PART I

Eight Angel Encounters

Angel Encounter One

In recent decades, scores of people around the world have shared stories about personal encounters with divine beings, usually referred to as angels. The literature is replete with fascinating accounts on this subject. A basic internet search about angel encounters or angel rescues and cases of divine intervention will yield a deluge of firsthand accounts.

Typically, these stories describe divine intervention of one kind or another during times of great danger or dire need. Generally, people talk about how they were healed or rescued by an angel or a divine being of some kind. They often report their lives were unmistakably saved by divine intervention. Well, add my name to that expansive, growing list.

I am only one among a throng of people all over the world who has been blessed to have amazing experiences of this kind. I know beyond any doubt that my life was saved at least seven times by divine intervention. God as my witness, I survived seven close brushes with death thanks to help from above. There is no question in my mind that I narrowly escaped being killed in each of these instances. Most assuredly, I would have been if not for the timely arrival of divine assistance.

I recall these seven life-saving events as vividly as the day they happened, literally as though they happened just yesterday. That goes for my first angel encounter too, the only one that was not of a life-saving nature. They are indelibly etched in my mind.

I discuss these seven angel encounters and one more that was not lifesaving, in sequential chronological order, not in order of substance, magnitude or importance. While I can offer no irrefutable scientific proof or evidence that my life was saved by angel encounters or divine intervention, it is my strong personal opinion reinforced by compelling independent corroboration in some instances. And while I am not a scientist, I am trained in the scientific method, so I approach matters such as these with the clinical objectivity of a trained scientist and the scholarly discipline of a diligent ethical academician.

Only after carefully exploring all other conceivable options, I arrived at the personal conclusion that I experienced multiple life-saving angel encounters. I simply cannot explain these things any other way except to label them examples of divine intervention. If other information comes to me in the future that would cause me to reverse my opinion or explanation, then so be it. But, for the moment, I would be hard pressed to account for these events in any other manner.

At the time these incidents occurred, I did not define them or view them as encounters with angels or other-worldly divine beings. Only three of these instances involved a physical meeting with an angel. Each time the angel manifested in human form, not in stereotypical angel form with wings and a bright halo. I was not convinced these were angel encounters until many years later after independent third-party corroboration was provided either by eyewitnesses or gifted shamans and mediums who described some of these occurrences with impressive accuracy in private sessions.

Most of these stories have not been shared before publicly. There was truly no conceivable way these psychics and mediums could have known about these events or been able to share with me such precise details of what transpired other than by means of their special gifts.

More about this later, lest I get way ahead of myself in the chronology of seminal events.

As for the most obvious question of all, I can only wonder myself why my life was miraculously saved seven times by angels. I have no special gifts, talents or abilities. I am not of any strategic importance to planet earth or humankind, so I cannot discern why I was divinely rescued on many occasions when countless other humans involved in mishaps or accidents clearly were not spared and tragically died as a result of their misadventures.

Honestly, I do not know why I was saved and others were not. Fatal accidents happen all the time all over the globe. Surely, those who died in these incidents were no less worthy of being rescued than me and they were no less loved by God than me. They were no less worthy of a miracle than me. Why I was spared and they were not remains a totally imponderable mystery to me. Perhaps it involves that enigmatic concept called fate, but who can say for sure?

I could flippantly remark that "nobody dies before their time," or "it just was not my time," or "I have some special destiny still to fulfill," but this would be false reliance on popular clichés.

It is impossible for me to accept the notion that my life was spared many times by divine intervention and providence because I have a special destiny to fulfill or some super important contribution to make to the advancement of human civilization. I have no evidence to support an explanation such as this.

Moreover, many people with critically important destinies well beyond my own (whatever it may be) have had their lives cut short when there was still so much left ahead of them that they desperately wanted to accomplish. Yet the opportunity to do so was denied to them.

If this reasoning about fulfilling a special destiny is valid to account for my life being divinely saved multiple times, then why was there not divine intervention to save the likes of Abraham Lincoln, Gandhi, JFK, RFK, MLK, Malcolm X and John Lennon, among so many others?

I am not in their league, not even close, yet their lives were not spared. So, I simply cannot accept the special destiny theory. Frankly, I don't have an explanation. It becomes even more baffling to me when I acknowledge the unwavering fact that we are all equally loved by God, unconditionally, and as such equally eligible recipients of astonishing amazing grace.

My first fascinating angel encounter took place in early 1960. I was eight years old, sound asleep in my bed inside our home in Fort Lauderdale, Florida. Of all eight angel encounters, this one did not involve saving my life. It is the sole exception in that regard because my life was not in any danger on this occasion, none whatsoever. Also, it was one of only three angel encounters out of eight total that involved the manifestation of an angel in physical form.

I am normally a very sound sleeper, all my life. Once I fall asleep, I am down for the count until the next morning. There are a few rare exceptions to this general rule, and one of the most memorable was my first angel encounter. I do not remember the events of this day before turning in for the night, but I feel safe in saying it was completely unremarkable. If anything out of the ordinary had occurred that day, it would be stored in my memory.

There were two twin beds in this room, one for me and one for my middle brother Henry. Our youngest brother, Ronald, had a room to himself. There was a bunkbed in it and a twin bed too with a nightstand in between. Ron liked to sleep on the bottom bunk. Henry would sometimes sleep on the top, but rarely. He had a bad habit of rolling out of his bed and suffering a scary fall to the floor. On this particular night, Henry and I followed our normal routines. We both went to bed right around the same time in the same room. Ron went to sleep in his room by himself.

It was a mildly cool winter night as winters go in Fort Lauderdale. Our bedroom window was left open so that we could enjoy the brisk fresh air that blew the white lace curtains back and forth, rhythmically. I remember looking outside our window that night before going to bed. The night was unusually aglow courtesy of a big bright full moon.

As was my custom, within a matter of minutes after climbing into bed, I fell fast asleep, tired from a full day of non-stop locomotion typical of an energetic eight-year-old. Henry conked out before me. I remember seeing him sleeping soundly in his bed just before I fell asleep.

I never have nightmares or scary dreams, quite the opposite in fact, always pleasant. On this night, I do not recall dreaming at all. What I do remember vividly is somehow being awakened from a deep sleep during the wee hours by something or someone, I know not what. I just remember being roused into full high alert waking consciousness.

As I laid in bed wide awake on my left side, I gazed at the patterned wallpaper on the east wall of my bedroom. I recall sensing another presence in the room. It was just a feeling, like the kind one gets when hair stands up on the back of one's neck. But I was too perturbed about whatever interrupted my normal sleep pattern to give it much thought.

I was not sure what woke me or what I would do with myself now that I was wide awake, but I was not happy about the interruption. Feeling restless and annoyed, I rolled over onto my right side. I looked over to check on Henry, but he was no longer sleeping in his bed. His bed was empty, to my surprise. He was gone. He had left me all alone.

Then I cast my gaze toward the south wall of my bedroom, where the entrance door was located. It was closed tight. To my amazement, directly in front of the door stood an imposing figure of a tall adult male Native American Indian, 50-60 years old I would guess. My eyes grew as big as silver dollars. They nearly popped out of their sockets. I literally pinched myself to make sure I was fully awake and not dreaming. I was awake all right, and petrified too. I was not imagining this. It was real.

This figure of an older male Indian was dressed in buckskin with fringe on both legs and arms. He was wearing deerskin moccasins too. Strangely, his left arm was fully extended in front of him parallel to the ground. He kept moving it from side to side, slowly and deliberately in what seemed to be a mesmerizing manner.

I stayed awake the whole night watching him do it. I said nothing to him. I was too frightened. He said nothing to me, probably not wanting to frighten me further. I rolled back over on my left side ever so gently, pretending to be asleep. I was scared that he might come over, take me out of my bed and steal me away.

I tossed and turned all night long. When morning came, none too soon for me as a terrified little boy, the Indian was gone. He had vanished in the morning light. I immediately leapt out of bed and ran as fast as I could into my parents' bedroom. They were still sleeping. I woke them up with a shrill voice that expressed my holy terror.

"Mommy! Daddy! There was this spooky Indian in my room last night, waving his arm back and forth, all night long. I did not get any sleep."

"You just had a bad dream son," Dad replied. "It's early still. Go back to bed."

"No, Dad. I saw him. He was standing near the doorway to my bedroom all night long. He was blocking my door."

"Go back to bed, Johnny, before you wake up the whole house," Mom commanded.

Well, I did not go back to bed. I went outside and searched the ground directly below the windows in my bedroom. I was looking for footprints or some sign of forced entry. I was looking for proof of my claim that this Indian had somehow gained entrance into my bedroom the night before. To my deep disappointment, I found nothing. Not one single piece of hard evidence was present, not there and not inside my bedroom in the spot where this Indian was standing all night long!

But to this day, I know I saw that Indian. I know he was real. No one could ever convince me otherwise, especially not after I became the proud owner of a pen and ink etching/print of the same face of this same Indian. I found it at an art show I visited on impulse one day in 1982 in

East Hartford, Connecticut, not far from St. Francis Hospital, the place of my birth. Now how odd is that? And how odd is it that I look at it nearly every day when I am home? It is print 22/500 by the artist Joyce Moninger. Please visit *AffirmingGod.com* to view this image.

Several times throughout my adult life, I have had readings with shamans, mediums and psychics. Several consistently mention this cornerstone experience from my childhood. How they can see it in such detail, or pull it out of my psyche, or come to know about it in such detail is a mystery which baffles me even now. But they do see it and quite often they uniformly tell me about its significance.

I am told this Indian is one of my principal guardian angels who is always with me. I am told he came to visit me that night to perform a purification ceremony and protect me from anything that might interfere with my life's destiny. I am told that this night was a milestone event for me, a major rite of passage in my spiritual unfoldment. This came to have even deeper meaning for me many years later during a vision quest in the Mojave Desert consistent with the rituals and traditions of North American Indian cultures, but more about that later.

After Henry had awakened the next morning, I asked why he left our bedroom and why he felt the need to sleep in Ronald's bedroom on the top bunk. He had not done that in a very long time. He said something woke him up in the middle of the night, but he did not know what. He could not get back to sleep, so he walked over to Ron's room and climbed up the ladder to the top bunk where he quickly fell back to sleep.

I asked Henry if he heard or saw anything unusual like a Native American Indian older adult male dressed all in buckskin. He told me he had not seen a thing. When I told me I had, he called me a fruitcake. I wondered if he might be right up until the first time a seer told me otherwise and set me straight about what really happened that night. When other psychics agreed with this assessment, I finally gave this encounter the credence it deserved.

Angel Encounter Two

My second angel encounter occurred in 1961 when I was nine years old. When it happened, I was walking through a wooded area in what was then an undeveloped part of northwestern Fort Lauderdale. With me were three boyhood friends. We rode our bikes several miles from our homes to what was then our favorite wilderness area. We went off in search of a suitable tree in which to build our fort.

After walking half an hour or so along the beaten path, I stopped beside the trunk of a fallen tree to remove sandspurs or "stickers," as we called them, from my socks. Part of the fallen tree trunk was hollowed out from rot. My friends kept walking ahead of me. I intended to catch up with them after I finished the task at hand.

I sat down on the log and then bent over. I extended my left hand to my left ankle to remove the sandspurs from the sock on my left foot. I had removed three or four stickers when all of a sudden, I heard a resounding voice yell out to me, "Watch out for the snake!"

I looked up to see who was yelling at me. It was a young brown-haired, brown-eyed Caucasian boy about my age, weight and height. He was about ten feet or so behind me on the same path that my friends and I had traveled just a few moments before.

I did not recognize this boy. He was completely unfamiliar to me. As we made eye contact, I noticed his right arm was raised. He was pointing toward the bottom of the tree trunk where I was sitting near my right leg. I turned my head quickly to look in the direction where he was pointing.

No sooner had I fixed my gaze in the direction of his pointed finger then I leapt about two feet away from where I had been sitting to avoid being bitten by a colorful coral snake that had reared up fully positioned in a ready-to-strike pose. It was aiming directly for the mid-calf region of my right leg.

I was solely focused on the ankle of my left leg removing pesky sandspurs. I did not have my right leg in sight, not even remotely in my peripheral field of vision. If the boy had not alerted me to the snake's presence, it would have remained undetected and surely would have bitten me, injecting its highly poisonous venom into my bloodstream, killing me most likely within an hour or so.

In the instant before I jumped, the snake and I made eye contact for a split second. Reflexively and instinctively, in one fast continuous movement, I stood up and jumped away from the log in the opposite direction of the snake. I did not think about it. I did not hesitate, not for a moment. I just jumped.

Simultaneously, when I made eye contact with it, the snake immediately relaxed its strike pose and withdrew quickly in the opposite direction. It rapidly slithered into some nearby high grass out of sight. As soon as I realized that I was out of danger, I began to shiver as if feeling the chill of cold winter weather. A flood of emotion came over me. First was profound fear, but that was quickly replaced with surprise and bewilderment.

"Why would that snake want to bite me?" I thought. "I did not do anything to it," I reasoned. "I did not even know it was there!" I exclaimed. I then felt shocked, startled and aghast all at once. I could not believe what had almost happened. I was nearly bitten by a highly poisonous coral snake. A bite from a coral snake can be fatal in a matter of thirty minutes or less. The coral snake is one of the most venomous snakes known. Its bite can be deadly in no time.

I looked back to thank the boy who had yelled to me only a few moments before. He was not there. I ran down the same path he was on in both directions, but he was nowhere to be found. I looked all over for him with no success. He vanished almost as quickly as he first appeared. I wanted to profusely thank him for the warning. I wanted to meet him. I wanted to ask his name. But he was nowhere in sight. It seemed as if he just disappeared into thin air.

After I caught up with my friends a few minutes later, I told them what just happened to me. I asked them if they had seen the coral snake that almost bit me, or the young boy who warned me about the pending attack. They said they had not seen the snake or the boy. Since they were close enough to have heard the boy's yell, I asked them whether they heard anyone scream, "Watch out for the snake!" They said they had not seen or heard anything. We all were extremely puzzled.

One of the friends with me that day knew a lot about snakes. He said I must have been sitting near a nest of eggs. He felt sure the coral snake that almost bit me was probably a mother snake acting aggressively to protect a nearby nest.

Since I was not a threat to the snake itself, and did not even know it was there, I figured I had inadvertently frightened the creature. But Roy explained that these snakes are creatures of the night and are rarely seen in the daytime, giving more credence to his nest theory.

One of my friends asked me how I knew it was a coral snake and not a non-venomous scarlet king snake. The two species look very much alike. They are often confused for each other. I quickly recited a simple poem I learned in cub scouts in reference to the snake's colorful rings: "Red touches yellow kills a fellow. Red touches black a friend of Jack." My friend nodded in approval. He was glad I knew how to tell the two species apart.

But truthfully, all I saw at that precise moment was an angry snake preparing to bite me. I immediately sensed danger and reflexively jumped away in a quick single leap. It was only after the snake withdrew from its strike pose and rapidly slithered away that my brain processed the fact that this snake had a black snout and tail, with red rings touching yellow rings. It was not until then I remembered that coral snakes have a black tail with yellow rings and a black snout. King snakes have a red or scarlet snout and tail. Indeed, it was a few minutes after the fact when I realized that I was almost bitten by a highly poisonous coral snake.

One of my friends commented that without a doubt I had just received the luckiest break of my life. Then we continued our adventure through the woods as though nothing much had happened. We did not know what more to make of it at that time, so we forgot about it and resumed our search for the perfect tree. We found it after an hour or so of walking, but we never built our fort. Turns out we never could figure out a way to transport all the lumber we would need for the project, so it just never happened.

Later that night, in my prayers, I thanked God for that little boy, whoever he was. In my heart of hearts, I know he saved my life on that out-of-the-ordinary afternoon. At the time, I did not think he was an angel. But today, deep down inside, I know he was an angel, a guardian angel of some kind, watching over me to keep me from dying before my time. If he had been a real live human being, I suspect he would have hung around to be showered with praise. But not this young man. He appeared and disappeared as fast as that coral snake.

I had been raised in the Roman Catholic faith and received Roman Catholic indoctrination as a young boy, as well as the sacraments of baptism, communion and confirmation. I prayed to God often as a young boy. Sometimes, I did the Stations of the Cross at church. Being a dutiful Roman Catholic to please my father, I often said the Rosary too.

As a family, we went to church nearly every Sunday and to confession nearly every Friday. We never ate meat on Friday, like all good Roman

Catholics, nor did we ever step foot inside a Protestant church. Such transgressions were labeled "mortal sins," and if we should die with a mortal sin on our souls before a priest could forgive us at confession through penitence, then God would send us straight to hell forever in a fit of cold-hearted rage.

According to our faith, there could be no reprieve, no redemption and no other fate for such sinners other than eternal damnation. For grievous offenses against the church such as these, we would burn forever in the bowels of hell. Our souls would be eternally damned.

With fairy tales such as these to create weighty doubts about my religion, God was not real to me either back in those days, except in an abstract conceptual sense. I certainly never felt the presence of God during Mass or Communion, and never while saying the Rosary or praying at the Stations of the Cross. I wanted to feel God's presence during these times, but I never did. The notion of a Supreme Being remained abstract and doubtful in my mind.

To be sure, the coral snake incident made God seem real to me. Looking back on it as I now understand it in retrospect, I felt like I was walking in a pure state of grace right after the event happened. I felt God must have saved me. I truly believed the hand of God reached out to shelter me from harm and spared my life. Indeed, that is exactly what happened, but I did not have the words for it then in my formative vocabulary as a young boy who was just beginning to comprehend the world. This was the first real evidence in my life that God was in fact real.

When I reached the age of 18, I became disillusioned with teachings of the Roman Catholic Church's teachings. So when I left home in 1970 for military service right after high school graduation, I also left the religion, never to return.

I experimented with other religions for a few years, mostly the protestant faiths, but by age 20 with the snake incident in my distant past, I became a self-proclaimed yet short-lived agnostic. Back then, at the height of the Vietnam War, I felt disconnected from God. I questioned everything and believed in very little, but more about this later.

My dismay with the Roman Catholic Church began one Saturday morning in Catechism class at Saint Clement's Church in Fort Lauderdale. I was eight years old. We were studying the Bible from beginning to end, starting with Genesis, of course. The nun read passages from the Holy Book. We, her students, followed along obediently by reading the same passages from our own Bibles.

When the nun told us about the Garden of Eden, Adam and Eve, and also Cain and Abel, I was fascinated. But then later on in the story she read that Cain and Abel went off to the "Land of Nod" to acquire wives. Well, when she read that, it stopped my reading dead in its tracks. I promptly raised my hand with a question. The nun soon recognized me.

"Sister, I do not understand," I said. "God created Adam, then Eve and then they had two sons, Cain and Abel. So, there were only four humans on earth at that time, right?" I asked.

"Yes, Johnny," she replied. "That is correct."

"Well, Sister, then I am confused," I responded. "Where did the wives come from in the Land of Nod?"

"You're a sarcastic disrespectful troublemaker John Robert Audette!" she barked angrily as she walked briskly over to my desk. She grabbed me by the ear and hauled me off to the office of the head priest.

"Father, John Audette is being a wise-guy. He's disrupting my class. He needs to be disciplined," she insisted. "He is asking silly nonsense questions." With that, she left hurriedly to return to her class. The priest looked sternly at me and asked me to confess what I had done and I did.

The priest blurted out that I was a real smart aleck and ordered me to say ten "Our Father" and ten "Hail Mary" prayers while he called my father at home to inform him about my offensive behavior and to demand that he pick me up immediately. He wanted me off church grounds as soon as possible. Wow. I could hardly believe my ears as the angry priest conveyed his feelings to my father.

Within twenty minutes or so, my dad came into the priest's office looking rather red-faced. "I am sorry Father," my dad said to the priest. "My son will be properly disciplined. This will not happen again."

Dad said nothing to me as we walked to his car, nor all the way back home. But when we arrived home, he ordered me into the garage, removing his black leather belt from his waist as we walked. A few moments later, I received a vigorous spanking from him, and all for nothing. It was not my first experience with receiving punishment for committing no offense whatsoever, nor would it be my last.

Surely, I did not deserve the belt-lashing from my father or the reprimand from the priest or the nun. My only offense was asking a simple logical question, but it was a question that drew their ire. I told my dad what happened after I stopped crying. He admonished me to keep my mouth shut in Catechism and at all other times too.

"You deserve what you got for opening your mouth," he said. "Don't ask stupid questions again."

Well, frankly, that confused me even more. "Why was it a stupid question?" I asked.

"Because there is no answer for it," he replied. "Because they can't answer it. You made them look stupid by asking them a nonsense question they could not answer," he explained. "Nobody wants to look stupid. Don't be precocious, son. If it's not in the Bible, then they don't' know the answer. You embarrassed them."

Needless to say, this incident was the start of my gradual departure from the church. But I could not officially part company with the religion until I moved out of my father's house right after high school graduation. While I was under his roof, I had to do as he commanded, and he was adamant that his family would consistently behave as devout Roman Catholics. So when I left home in the summer of 1970, I also left the religion. I told people I gave it up for Lent. It always got a good laugh.

Angel Encounter Three

The third angel encounter in my life took place in the fall of 1968. I was 16 years old and a junior at Ft. Lauderdale High School. A few months before, I had received my Florida Operator License, which granted me full driving privileges.

I borrowed my dad's 1954 Studebaker Commander and drove from Ft. Lauderdale to Perrine, Florida, south of Miami. It was about a two-hour haul. My girlfriend lived there. She had just moved there after transferring from Ft. Lauderdale High School to Palmetto Senior High School. Kristine and I had a lovely date that night. It consisted of dinner at a Chinese restaurant and then a movie, *The Detective*, starring Frank Sinatra.

Afterwards, I took Kristine home around 11:30 p.m. and then began the long trek back to Ft. Lauderdale. It was late and I was very tired. I was also a newly licensed inexperienced driver. I entered the Palmetto Expressway (Florida State Highway 826) and proceeded northbound headed for home. Before long, my eyes began to close, but just momentarily. I was falling asleep behind the wheel of a car traveling at about 65-75 MPH. I thought nothing of it, much to my shame, and later, much to my chagrin.

At first, my eyes would close infrequently, but only for a few seconds. I would quickly reawaken from my brief slumber and resume complete control of the vehicle. As I drove farther into the night, apparently my periods of intermittent dozing became longer and more frequent. While fully asleep at the wheel, I began to run off the shoulder of the road. I would right the vehicle seconds later, quickly maneuvering back onto the road.

At some point along the way, I must have been swerving into other lanes of traffic while sound asleep at the wheel of a car speeding down the expressway. Although I had no conscious awareness of it, I ran many cars off the road that night. Soon enough, I noticed the blue lights of a determined Florida Highway Patrol car flashing behind me. There was a thundering voice over a loud speaker. I was commanded to pull over in a stern and angry voice, which I did of course, immediately.

The trooper pulled his car up behind me. In front of me, a 1968 Volkswagen Fastback parked on the shoulder with a family inside. Out jumped a justifiably enraged middle-aged man who was shouting all kinds of nasty things at me, including threats of bodily harm. I noticed that his wife and children were sitting in the car. The trooper ordered him to return to his vehicle. The trooper said, "Get back in your car before I arrest you too." The man complied with his instructions to my great relief.

"Arrest you too?" I thought. What did he mean by that I wondered? Was I about to be arrested? Why? What had I done? I had no idea who this man was in the Volkswagen Fastback or why he was so angry with me. The trooper then ordered me to present my driver's license and registration. I did so, of course. The trooper then ordered me out of the car. He told me to place both hands on the hood and separate my feet wide apart. Then he frisked me.

After that, he shined his flashlight in my eyes and asked me if I had been drinking. "No," I replied, "I do not drink. I am only 16, not 21." He then ordered me to walk a straight line, which I did, with no problem at all. Next, the trooper searched my car, obviously in search of alcoholic beverages or drugs I suppose. He found none. There were none to be found. He also smelt my breath.

Next, the trooper asked me if I knew why he had pulled me over. "I have no idea," I replied. He said "You were running off the road and swerving in and out of traffic. You ran a dozen cars off the road including that man in front of you. You almost killed him and his family. You almost killed yourself too, dummy, several times over in fact. I'm amazed you are walking away from this alive and unhurt."

I was shocked and aghast to learn this but remained in a state of firm denial. I told the trooper he was mistaking me for someone else. I was a law-abiding Boy Scout with several merit badges. I could never have done such a thing. I had no recollection of it whatsoever. I explained I worked part-time for the Fort Lauderdale News as a staff writer and was President of Fort Lauderdale Young Americans for Freedom and a member of the Fort Lauderdale Police Youth Auxiliary, as well as Public Relations Director for the Ft. Lauderdale Junior Theater. All true, but he was totally unimpressed.

"Son, I followed you for over ten miles," the trooper said. "I tried everything I knew to get you to pull over, but you stubbornly kept right on going. I sounded my siren, flashed my lights and blew my horn, but you were oblivious and unresponsive. You were dead to the world. Young man, you were asleep at the wheel. You remained asleep through all of this craziness for quite a long distance. I have been a trooper for over 20 years now and I have never seen anything like what I just saw tonight with you and this car of yours."

"No sir," I replied. "Not me. That could not have been me. Sure, my eyes closed now and then but only for a few seconds, no longer," I insisted.

"Sorry, son, you were asleep for a whole lot longer than that. But I'll be damned, no one was hurt and no damage was done. I don't believe my own eyes, but by God, it happened. I witnessed a genuine miracle. I really did. You may not know it, but you must be someone really special in

God's eyes. That's why no harm came to you. God was surely watching over you."

The trooper said he was off duty and on his way home, but he had to pull me over because I was such a threat to public safety and my own welfare. He said he could not comprehend how no one had been injured or killed and that no accidents had occurred. He said it was astonishing.

I remember his words as though they were spoken yesterday. "Son," he said, "What I witnessed tonight, I have never seen anything like it in my life. Your car was about to hit the guardrails on the N.W. 103rd Street overpass. You were about to go over those guardrails and nosedive off the overpass. Your car would have fallen over 30 feet down to the road below. You would have died a gruesome death. But, miraculously, at the last second, your car jumped over about ten feet and continued heading straight down the expressway like nothing out of the ordinary had happened. It was like something or someone levitated your car and moved it over back onto the road. You're damn lucky to be alive, son," he said.

Then, the trooper said something more which resonated through me like shivers from a cold, wet wind. "You must have a powerful guardian angel watching over you. That angel was surely with you tonight," he said. "I cannot explain how your car jumped back onto the expressway, or how all those people you ran off the road did not meet with any harm. God above must have protected you and all the other drivers. That's all I can figure. I witnessed many miracles tonight. I will never forget it, but I'll deny it if you quote me, so don't."

Upon hearing the trooper's words, I felt God truly saved my life that night and the lives of those around me that I had inadvertently impacted. Then I knew why the man in the Volkswagen Fastback wanted to do me bodily harm. I did not blame him. I went up to him after the trooper had finished with me and apologized profusely, but to no avail. He was boiling mad. He called me all kinds of foul names. I fully understood. I deserved his wrath. In his place, I would have been sizzling mad too.

The trooper apologetically issued a traffic citation to me for reckless driving. He really did not want to issue the citation. I honestly believe he wanted to let me off with a warning ticket, but could not. He had no choice in the matter because the man in the Volkswagen Fastback insisted that the trooper give me a ticket for the most serious charge possible. That is what the trooper did. He was right to do so.

Toward the end of our encounter, the trooper treated me like someone special, like someone saintly who had been anointed or touched by God. After giving me the citation, he released me and admonished me to drive straight home. His parting words to me were, "After what I just saw, I have no doubt you'll arrive home safely. Take good care of yourself."

Months later, I made a mandatory appearance in a Dade County court before the Honorable Judge William J. Piquette. Joining me for the hearing was the state trooper and the man who owned the Volkswagen Fastback. Yep, sure enough, he was there too and still mighty angry as he should have been. Being a minor, my mother was required by law to accompany me. The judge quickly ordered me to leave his court room and not to come back until I had a lawyer. We left immediately and returned a few months later with counsel.

At the second hearing, my lawyer asked for understanding and leniency since I was a new inexperienced driver. Judge Piquette granted his request. He suspended my license for just six months but granted permission to drive back and forth to work and school. He also levied a fine of $200. This was the least he should have done.

I paid the fine from my meager savings, which I had accumulated from years of part-time jobs that paid me $1.25 per hour. That was the minimum wage back in those days. I also paid $300 to the lawyer, which he said was a 50% reduction from his normal fee. All totaled, this deeply regrettable incident cost me $500, which amounted to 400 hours of my labor working as a bus boy, dishwasher, paper boy, copy boy at the Ft.

Lauderdale News then later a staff writer, shoeshine boy, lawn care service helper, bag boy at A&P, McDonald's cashier and other odd jobs.

These two expenditures wiped out my savings, so there went my dating money. In 1968, it was the custom for the guy to pay for everything when taking a lovely lady on a date. Due to the geographic distance between us, and a suspended driver's license for six months and no money for dates, Kristine and I were forced to break up. She was my first love. It broke my heart that our relationship had to come to an abrupt halt, but such was life.

Trust me when I say that this incident cost me dearly. But I deserved all of the consequences I suffered for my irresponsible actions. I do not fault the state trooper or Judge Piquette for their part in this matter. To this day, I believe they both gave me every consideration they could under the strange circumstances.

For Judge Piquette's part, by ordering me to leave at the first hearing and return later with a lawyer, he was able to exercise leniency toward me at the second hearing, which he surely could not have shown during the first hearing in the presence of the livid man whose family I nearly killed.

At the first hearing, the man from the Volkswagen Fastback gave his account of what had happened that night. He told the judge that I had almost killed him and his family when I ran them off the road. He wanted his pound of flesh even several months after the incident. He was right to feel the way he did. I fully appreciated where he was coming from, even at my young age.

Still, even now as I write this account, I have absolutely no recollection of running him or anyone off the road that night or running off the road myself. Apparently, I did, several times. Fortunately, God intervened, and as the state trooper said, brought forth powerful guardian angels who no doubt saved my life and the lives of all those around me. With and through God, all things are possible. Let there be no mistake about that.

When I drove away from the FHP trooper that night heading back home, I was more than wide awake. I was fully energized with a heightened sense of awareness. My entire body was engulfed by goose bumps. An electrical current swept through me from head to toe. I was euphoric, giddy in fact, about what the trooper told me earlier about my guardian angels. I felt truly loved and protected by God. I felt "loved by the light" in demonstrably tangible terms.

I remember feeling fully immersed in intense gratitude. All I could think about was that angels miraculously came to my rescue and to the rescue of all the other drivers I unknowingly ran off the road that night. According to the trooper, angels literally had taken control of my car to save my life and many other lives as well. And even though I had no awareness of it in real time, who was I to doubt him?

As I drove home, the car radio was turned on, tuned to my favorite rock 'n' roll station at the time, WQAM, 560-AM on the dial, one of just a few choices back then. Guess what song came on soon after I drove away from the scene? Clearly, God and the angels have a terrific sense of humor. It was the perfect song for the occasion, one that brought me much needed comic relief. After all, I had just been issued a traffic citation for reckless driving, my first citation ever, being a newly licensed driver. It was a real doozy of a charge, but one of which I was both guilty and ashamed.

The song that was playing on the car radio at that moment was "Baby, You Can Drive My Car," written by John Lennon and Paul McCartney, performed by The Beatles, one of the selections on their album entitled *Yesterday and Today*, released in the U.S. in 1966.

So, comic relief was exactly what I needed at that very moment. I guess the angels knew that too. You see, without the prompt delivery of timely comic relief, I am certain I would have engaged in brutal self-flagellation all the way home. I am sure I would have castigated myself mercilessly. Even now, to this day, it's hard to forgive myself for carelessly endangering myself and so many others.

Back then, I loved playing with words and rhymes. In 1967, I began writing simple poetry. One of my first poems was inspired by and dedicated to Kristine. So, as this song by The Beatles played on the radio, I was spontaneously inspired to change the lyrics to correspond to the amazing experience I just had as described to me by the state trooper.

I sang out the changed lyrics at the top of my lungs as the tune played on the radio, chuckling the entire time. With profound apologies to Lennon/McCartney, here are the modified lyrics I sang:

"Angels, you can drive my car. With you I can travel far. Angels came to drive my car. And, angels, I love you. Toot-Toot, Toot-Toot, yeah! I told the angels they could start today. They said right John, God thinks you're okay. Asleep at the wheel and that's not good, so we'll take over now, from trunk to hood. Angels you can drive my car. With you I can travel far. Angels came to drive my car. And, angels, I love you. Toot-Toot, Toot-Toot, yeah!"

The song changed my mood completely. It shifted my emotions dramatically from self-loathing, regret and guilt to a profound sense of peace, acceptance and gratitude. I had been lovingly showered with God's grace, not just in saving my life, but also sparing all the other drivers and their passengers too. If any serious harm had come to anyone else due to my reckless negligence, knowing my inner mental circuitry, I might have become seriously suicidal, especially if someone else had been killed by my actions. I doubt I could have lived with myself in that event. I think the angels knew this too.

Judge Piquette died in August 2006 at the age of 84. He was a graduate of the University of Miami School of Law. He served on the bench in the 11th Circuit Court for Miami-Dade County from 1964-1975 and then as a senior judge up until 2002. I shall remain forever grateful to him for the leniency he extended to me, which I believe was a further expression of the divine grace that was showered upon me and all those who were saved from harm or death by divine intervention during that not so proud moment in my life. I shall also remain forever grateful to that very understanding state trooper. He helped me all he could.

To that man and his family in the Volkswagen Fastback, and to any others my actions adversely impacted that night, words cannot express the remorse I feel to this day for the trauma I unknowingly caused. My profound apologies. I thank God no one was hurt.

I do not remember the name of the state trooper who pulled me over that night, or his badge number. I doubt he is still alive today because at the time of the incident in 1968, I would guess his age then to be about 45 years old. He would be 99 years old today if he was still alive. Odds are, like Judge Piquette, he is no longer with us.

To obtain a copy of the citation the trooper wrote back then, I wrote to Harvey Ruvin, Clerk of Court in Miami-Dade County and to the Florida Department of Motor Vehicles, Driver's License Division and to the Florida Highway Patrol, Troop E, in Miami-Dade County, all to no avail. I was told their records do not go back that far.

I look forward to my life review after I leave this world when "all things shall be known." Among other things, I am most eager to see a replay of this incident from a birds-eye heavenly perspective. I would love to see that Studebaker Commander about to crash through guardrails at high speed, then rescued by angels and levitated back onto the expressway. What a sight that must have been. Only the state trooper witnessed it. I surely did not. I was fast asleep at the wheel, dead to the world. I would also like to know how many cars I ran off the road that night and how all the people affected by my reckless actions were saved from harm, thank God.

During my second appearance before Judge Piquette in the fall of 1968, after my sentencing had concluded, the FHP trooper who issued the citation came over to me and placed his hand on my 16-year-old shoulder, as if to comfort and reassure me. He told me not to feel bad about the suspension of my license. He said Judge Piquette gave me a huge break and was as lenient as he could have been with me. Then he turned his gaze toward my mother. I remember vividly what he said to her like it was yesterday.

"Mrs. Audette, you have a very fine son here. I hope you and your husband will go easy on him. After what I witnessed that night just before I pulled your son over, he must be someone really special in the eyes of God. That your son and all the people he ran off the road that night were unharmed despite his reckless driving, that no accidents occurred, and that no property damage took place, is way beyond miraculous.

"I saw firsthand many miracles that night. It was the biggest and happiest surprise of my life. I felt blessed to witness it. Now I know beyond any doubt that God and the heavenly angels are real, that they watch over us and protect us the way they did your son and all the other affected drivers that night. So, praise God and amen."

As the trooper uttered those words in the courtroom, all I could think to do was to sing to myself silently, "Angels, you can drive my car. With you I can travel far. Angels came to drive my car. And, angels, I love you. Toot-toot, toot-toot, yeah!"

Angel Encounter Four

The fourth angel encounter I experienced occurred in early 1971. I was serving in the U.S. Army, stationed at Fort Gordon, Georgia, near Augusta. I went to Fort Gordon for Advanced Individual Training (AIT) in the Signal Corps.

A three-day holiday weekend was approaching. So, Will, a fellow student in my AIT program from Louisiana, proposed that we should drive his brother's new Volkswagen bug from Augusta to Cocoa Beach, Florida. Previously, I had told him a good friend of mine from high school days lived there near the ocean. Her name was Cheta Johnson. We agreed to leave following evening formation, after retreat was sounded at the lowering of the flag.

Cocoa Beach was about a seven-hour drive from Augusta. Will and I took turns driving. We were both dog-tired from a long week of training and the overall rigors of Army life during the Vietnam era. So, one of us slept while the other one drove. Will drove first. Later in the evening, around 10 p.m. or so, it was my turn to drive. Will woke me up from a sound sleep and I got behind the wheel.

Heading south on I-95 at about 65 MPH, I did my best to remain alert and stay awake. Will quickly fell asleep right after settling into the passenger seat. He was snoring within moments. Both of us had no business driving an automobile as tired as we were, but we could not afford a hotel, so we just kept going. That was penny-wise and pound-foolish thinking in retrospect. One night in a hotel would have cost me much less than the cost of totaling Will's brother's car.

We were only 20 miles or so from the Cocoa Beach exit, so the end of our journey was in sight. I thought I could go the whole distance, but my eyes grew heavier and heavier. Before long, I fell asleep at the wheel, yet again. The car ran off the shoulder of the road and slid into the median, which was a "V" ditch. No sooner had I applied the brakes then it began to roll over and over and over, at least five times. If the car had seat belts, we were not wearing them.

Ahead of us was a culvert or concrete embankment. The car was rolling over heading straight for it on a direct collision course. I thought we were goners for sure. In that instant, a profound peace settled over me. As we rolled over and over, I felt a deep acceptance of what was happening. Strangely, I felt comforted, like I was floating in the air inside the car, protected from harm. I actually felt like I was inside of a bubble or a womb, cushioned on all sides. I knew that no matter what the outcome was going to be, everything would be fine…everything would be all right, even if Will and I were to die. I knew instinctively that I should just relax and be unafraid. I had lost all control of the vehicle anyway, so there was nothing I could do but surrender to the void…to the unknown…to the divine.

The rolling car seemed to be somehow positioned outside of time. I had no temporal awareness while we were rolling over and over and over. It could have lasted a few minutes or an eternity. I had no way of knowing because it seemed like time had been suspended.

When the car finally stopped rolling, it came to rest right side up just before impact with the culvert. By now, Will was wide awake. He asked what had happened. I told him a deer had run out in front of the car and I swerved to miss it, which caused me to lose control of the car and run off the road. I was too ashamed and embarrassed to tell him the lame truth that I had fallen asleep at the wheel.

We opened our doors and walked outside. We were shaken up, but not hurt. We circled the vehicle and surveyed the damage. It was considerable. The car had been mangled like an aluminum soda can that someone had crushed underfoot. The front and back windshields were now spider webs. Both had popped out and one of the tires was flat. The roof above our heads was so caved in one would think the occupants inside must have been seriously injured. But we were fine. Not even a scratch had befallen us.

A middle-aged black man, driving with his family northbound on I-95 in a late model station wagon, witnessed the roll over. He pulled his vehicle off to the side of the road and ran over to us, wide-eyed, to offer assistance. We told him we were fine. He could not believe it and kept insisting that we must have been badly injured from what he had observed. "No one walks away from an accident like this," he said. But we assured him we were all right.

He then asked if he should go to the nearest phone and call the Florida Highway Patrol. We politely asked him not to do that. We told him that no other vehicles were involved and there was no property damage other than our own vehicle, so we did not see any practical reason to inform the Florida Highway Patrol. We explained that we were both in the U.S. Army and would face a heap of trouble if this incident were to be reported to the authorities. I pleaded further with him that I did not want this mishap to be entered into my driving record. Sympathetic to our situation, this kind Good Samaritan got back in his car and drove away into the night.

Will and I changed the flat tire and pushed the mangled VW bug out of the ditch and back on to the shoulder of the road. We then turned the key in the ignition. Would you believe it, much to the credit of VW, the car actually started! So, we drove it at 10-15 MPH to my friend's house in Cocoa Beach, which was only about 15 miles away or so from the scene of the accident. The car was not capable of going any faster. It was sputtering the whole way.

I remember that drive very well. We both were on pins and needles. We did not know one minute to the next if our car would go the distance, but it did, again to the credit of VW engineering. We pulled up to Cheta's house after midnight. We parked in front along the side of road so as not to block the other vehicles in her driveway. We walked up to the front door and knocked ever so lightly since it was quite late. Cheta opened the door and greeted us. She asked us to be super quiet because her parents were both asleep.

After exchanging pleasantries and cordialities, we told Cheta that we were desperately in need of sleep. She showed us to the guest room equipped with two twin beds. We quickly climbed into our beds and fell fast asleep. We never said a word to Cheta about the car accident we had just survived, not until the next morning. We were just too exhausted to have any further conversation.

Cheta's father, who was an active-duty Air Force colonel, made breakfast for the whole family and for us. Over our delicious meal that next morning, we told everyone what happened. I stuck to my story about the leaping deer being the cause. After breakfast, we all went outside to inspect the car in the daylight. It looked much worse than Will and I originally thought, much worse.

Colonel Johnson just shook his head in a state of sincere disbelief. He could not believe we survived the crash. He was even more amazed that we were able to drive that mangled car from the crash site to his home. I think he was more astounded by that than by the fact that both Will and I seemed to be completely unhurt.

Yet, in a commanding stern voice, Colonel Johnson reminded us that we were U.S. Government property. He ordered us to accompany him to the nearest military hospital facility at Patrick Air Force Base, which was not very far away. He wanted us to have x-rays and other tests just to make sure we were truly all right.

We did not want any official record of the incident, but an order is an order, and we were not about to disobey. So, the colonel drove us to the base hospital. We presented our Department of Defense active-duty military identification cards and got thoroughly checked out on orders from the colonel. Air Force doctors confirmed that we were fine without even so much as a minor contusion from our harrowing ordeal. They marveled, just as our Good Samaritan did at the scene, that we escaped injury.

Colonel Johnson drove us back to his house, and that's when we had the crippled bug towed to a nearby VW dealer for an estimate on repairs. We told the dealer that some drunk driver ran us off a nearby local road the night before. Will explained that his brother was the owner and he had no insurance. He also explained that no other people or vehicles had been involved in the mishap.

The service manager examined the vehicle carefully. He told us it was a total loss and could not be repaired because the frame was badly twisted and bent. None of the mechanics could figure out how we had been able to drive the vehicle to Cheta's house in the shape it was in. They were amazed. We could not believe it either.

The dealer offered Will $250 for salvage parts. Then and there, Will called his brother to tell him what happened and to convey my offer to fully reimburse him for the cost of the vehicle. Without any other realistic choice, Will's brother accepted my offer and the dealer's offer for salvage rights.

After that, Cheta drove us to the Greyhound Bus Terminal. We bought two one-way tickets to Fort Lauderdale, where my parents lived at that time, which was my military home of record. My dad picked us up at the bus station and then let me borrow his car. We dropped him off at my boyhood home and then drove over to visit another close friend from high school days. His name was Tim.

Tim came from an affluent family. He was the only person I knew in those days whose parents had plenty of money. Nearly all of my other friends came from blue-collar working-class families like mine, whose parents survived one paycheck to the next, just like mine.

I confided in Tim about the accident and asked his permission to seek a $2,000 emergency loan from his well-to-do parents. He consented and even offered to speak to his parents on my behalf. The cost of a new VW was $1,995 in those days, so that's what I needed to reimburse Will's brother for the loss of his car.

Tim spoke with his folks right away. God bless them, Bob and Betty kindly made the loan to me there on the spot. To this day, I am so grateful to them for entrusting me with their money. Honestly, I had nowhere else to turn.

I gave Will the cash then and there and he sent a money order in that amount to his brother via Western Union straight away. His brother bought a new VW bug soon after, which was delivered to Will at Fort Gordon about a week later on loan from his brother.

On Army pay back then, it took quite a while to repay that loan, but Bob and Betty were patient. They were in no hurry to be re-paid, thank God. It took me a few years to satisfy that loan, but I eventually paid it off along with my deepest gratitude. They refused to accept any interest on the loan, bless their hearts.

Will and I flew Delta Airlines from Fort Lauderdale to Augusta after that, reporting back for duty as though nothing had happened. Suffice it to say that we never made it to the beach that weekend, which had been our original plan. But we were not crestfallen about that, nor was I lamenting losing $2,000. All we could think about was how lucky we both were to still be alive.

Ironically, that very next year on Mother's Day weekend 1972, Tim was killed instantly in a tragic roll-over automobile accident. He was driving his fiancée's convertible sports car in South Carolina on his way to Charleston. The top was down. He took a sharp curve going way too fast. The car flipped over and killed him instantly.

All of us who knew Tim and loved him were grief-stricken. He was my closest and best friend at that time. I often wonder why God saved me from certain death, but not Tim. Our accidents both involved vehicular roll-overs, strangely. It baffles me even now.

Tim and I served on the staff of *The Navigator*, which was the Fort Lauderdale High School newspaper. I served as the editor-in-chief during my senior year. Tim served as a sports writer. We collaborated on several articles, including an award-winning story about the "Bermuda Triangle" that we both enjoyed researching.

Right after high school graduation, I enlisted in the U.S. Army. One day, I came home to Fort Lauderdale on leave. I visited Tim while dressed in uniform. Within days after seeing me in my "dress greens" back then, Tim impulsively decided to join the Army too. He later told me I looked "dazzling" in my uniform. He said it had impressed him greatly and inspired him to join the Army as well. He never asked for my advice about it. He just did it one day on a whim, spur of the moment. And as fate would have it, after he finished AIT at Fort Sam Houston in Texas, he too ended up being stationed at Fort Gordon where he served as a medic.

A few days before he was killed, I begged Tim to come with me to Fort Lauderdale to surprise his mother for Mother's Day. But instead, he and his fiancée, Eileen, decided to drive her Fiat Spider to Charleston for the weekend. Eileen served in the Women's Army Corps. Amazingly, she was completely unhurt in the accident.

Tim's family requested that I serve as the military escort to accompany the casket containing his body home. They wanted me to be the Army's representative at the funeral. It was my honor, but I hated every minute of it. It was the most difficult assignment of my entire enlistment, especially the part where I was ordered to identify the body as a formality. To see Tim that way for the last time broke my heart into a thousand pieces. I thought about how hard it must be for combat soldiers to lose friends in battle. There was a lot of that happening back then because of the Vietnam War.

I hated that we lost Tim. He was a dear and precious soul, barely 20 years old. He had just earned his private pilot's license and planned a career in aviation, one that never happened. I grieved his loss deeply in 1972 and still do. A photo of him taken shortly before he died remains on display in my study. It always will until I am no longer here to keep his memory alive.

Betty, Tim's mother, lost her son, her husband Bob, and her mother, Mrs. Hayes, all within six months of each other. But she was a lady of great strength and dignity. She somehow gathered the inner resources to bravely carry on, which she did gallantly until death from natural causes claimed her in July 2009 at age 90. I was honored to be treated like a surrogate son by her, but hard as I tried, no one could fully replace Tim. His loss left a gaping hole in everyone's heart, as sudden tragic deaths of loved ones usually do.

Later, I asked Will what he was feeling during the time our vehicle was rolling over. He described feelings and sensations similar to what I experienced. Looking back on it, in today's vernacular, I can say that it was as if the entire interior of the vehicle had been encased in bubble wrap, or giant air bags like the landing apparatus on the Mars rover that deploy on impact.

Whatever it was, I know for certain that it truly cushioned the impact and spared us from sustaining any injury whatsoever. It had to be the work of angels. What else could account for it? Again, I thank God for my good fortune, but in light of it, how can Tim's misfortune be explained or reconciled? I should have been killed instantly in that roll-over accident, but I was not, nor was Will. Yet, a little more than one year later, in May 1972, Tim was killed in a similar vehicular roll-over accident. Why him and not me? Words fail. It remains a great lingering mystery.

Angel Encounter Five

The fifth angel encounter in my life, and perhaps the most dramatic (to be explained later), took place in the spring of 1976 in southwestern Virginia. I was a full-time graduate student at Virginia Polytechnic Institute and State University in Blacksburg. My studies focused on thanatology, which is the study of death and dying, along with gerontology and medical sociology.

The year before, I had the great pleasure of meeting and befriending Dr. Elisabeth Kübler-Ross, the late prominent Swiss-born psychiatrist who single-handedly revolutionized treatment and care of terminally ill patients in the U.S. and abroad. She also pioneered the hospice movement in the United States and elsewhere. I had read her books and attended several of her workshops and lectures during that time. I deeply admired and respected her. She was a true force of nature, a real dynamo, a high voltage powerhouse and a genuine agent of profound social change.

One day in early 1976, Elisabeth called to tell me that she would be flying into the Tri-Cities Regional Airport in Blountville, Tennessee, in a few weeks. It was about 130 miles from where I lived at the time, a little more than a two-hour drive. Elisabeth was to be the keynote speaker at a gathering of nurses there. She was also to receive an award for her work.

She was an advisor to my thesis project, entitled "Proximity to Death and Physicians' Attitudinal Disposition Toward Patients and Their Families."

Elisabeth asked me to pick her up at the airport, which I was more than pleased to do. Spending time with Elisabeth was a true honor, so much so that I was willing to skip classes for a couple of days and drive better than two hundred miles roundtrip for the privilege of having some private time with her, which was hard to come by in those days as she was very much in demand. We agreed it would be a good time to discuss the proposed design for my thesis research.

Her plane was due to arrive from O'Hare early in the morning, around 8 a.m. That meant I had to set my alarm for 5 a.m. to allow enough time for the drive and other things that needed to be done. The night before, I didn't get to sleep until well after midnight. I had stayed up later than usual to finish a term paper that was due the very next day.

When the alarm rang, I reached over in my sleep to turn it off. I then started to drift back to sleep once again. After a few more moments of light dozing, I finally roused myself and struggled to get out of bed. After a fast shower and a quick bowl of cereal, I ran out the door and jumped into my white mist-covered Austin Marina. I headed to my first stop, which was the mailbox of a fellow graduate student who had agreed to deliver my term paper to our Social Theory professor. It was a paper about the work of Dr. Alvin Gouldner, a sociologist whose writings I much admired. It was entitled *The Art of Making Waves in an Era of Receding Shorelines.*

The morning was a chilly and foggy one in the Blue Ridge Mountains of rural southwest Virginia. I entered I-81 southbound and found visibility to be quite limited due to the fog. In 1976, streetlights were not in place along Interstate 81, so the highway in front of me was quite dark. But despite the poor driving conditions, I was determined to get to the airport on time for the arrival of Elisabeth's plane. There was hardly any traffic heading southbound or northbound, so I mostly had the entire interstate to myself.

After an hour or so of driving, my eyes began to close. Tired from not getting much sleep the night before, I began the dangerous practice of falling asleep at the wheel of my car (yet again). More than a few times, my eyes would close completely, and my head would drop, whereupon my car would veer over to the right shoulder of the roadway.

The sound of gravel hitting the undercarriage of my vehicle would abruptly awaken me each time. It was a God-awful sound, frightening to say the least. Upon hearing it, my eyes would open wide and I would quickly pull back on to the pavement. This happened several times in fast succession. Each time I'd hear my inner voice warning me to pull over and sleep for a while. But I stubbornly ignored that voice, bound and determined to arrive on time to meet Elisabeth. She was counting on me to arrive on time. I was not about to let her down. She had a tight itinerary during this visit and I would not be responsible for getting her off to a late start.

About 75 miles or so from my destination, I could no longer keep my eyes open. I was running off the road with much greater frequency. One time I can vividly recall, I nearly lost control of the car. I had a knee jerk reaction and turned too sharply in an effort to bring my car back onto the pavement. It was scary.

I tried everything I could think of to keep myself awake, but to no avail. No matter what I did, my eyes kept closing. Still, I foolishly continued down the interstate. I knew instinctively that the next time I heard that horrible sound of gravel hitting my car's undercarriage, it would be my demise. I was certain of it.

This part of Virginia is quite hilly and mountainous. Steep drop offs, ravines and gullies were commonplace all along both sides of I-81. There were no guardrails in place at that time to stop a wayward car from going over a cliff. I knew that I could easily kill myself if my car was to crash into one of those ravines or gullies. I knew I would be a sure traffic fatality if I continued to drive half asleep at the wheel. I knew better than to continue, but I did anyway.

My inner voice grew louder and louder. "Pull over and go to sleep for a half hour or so, dummy, before you kill yourself!" But I kept turning a deaf ear to it. In desperation, I even slapped myself in the face several times in a vain attempt to wake up, but to no avail. I also played the radio at full blast and opened my windows all the way, hoping that the cool early morning air would wake me up.

But still my eyes kept closing, even though I sensed that my life was in peril. I admonished myself. I gave myself stern warnings, thinking I could somehow scold myself into staying awake. "Next time you fall asleep you're going to run off the road and nosedive into one of those deep ravines down there," I told myself. "You'll die a horrible, ugly, nasty, gross death in that dark, black void down below. They won't even find your body. WAKE UP!"

I fully expected that the next time I fell asleep, it might be permanent. Nevertheless, foolishly, I kept on driving, tenacious as ever about making it to my destination on time. Sensing the hopelessness of my careless attitude, and the immediate prospect of certain death, I believe God intervened in a deliberate effort to save my life yet again.

Half asleep at the wheel, with eyes mostly closed, I barely noticed a man with long black wavy hair, wearing an all-white suit with his thumb outstretched, hitchhiking alongside of the road, mostly obscured by thick mist. I zoomed by him in a rather oblivious state, half asleep. When my brain finally registered his presence there, I pulled over onto the shoulder of the road better than 150 feet in front of him. Yes, my reaction time was that bad because I was so very, very drowsy.

I stopped the car and sat for a moment to absorb what I had just seen. I could hardly believe my eyes. For an instant, I wondered if I was imagining the sudden appearance of this man. I thought to myself, 'That guy seems to have just materialized out of thin air. What's he doing out here in the middle of nowhere hitchhiking?' I mean, there was no one around. No other cars. Nothing but nothingness, and not even close to an exit off the interstate. I could not understand how he got way out there in the middle of nowhere. The scene was weird and eerie. In fact, it was surreal. It was so surreal I thought I was dreaming the whole thing.

I wondered whether it was safe to offer this guy a ride, but then I realized that his company would keep me awake. It occurred to me in no uncertain terms that if I didn't pick him up, some terrible fate might befall me because I would probably continue falling asleep at the wheel and eventually kill myself. So, reasoning that I had nothing to lose and everything to gain, I put the car in reverse and backed up to offer this strange man a ride.

By now, he was running toward my car as I was backing up to meet him. But I did not have to back up very far because surprisingly he was right there already beside my car. I could not figure out how he got up to my car so fast, but in my half-asleep brain-dead state of being, I did not seriously question it or think too much about it.

He came up to my car door on the passenger side. I turned on the dome light and rolled down the window of the passenger door. He politely bent down with one hand on the door. He asked if I would give him a lift. I asked him where he was going. He said he was going to Reno, Nevada. I told him I could only take him as far as the exit for the Tri-Cities Airport near Johnson City, Tennessee and Abingdon, Virginia. He said that would be fine, so I invited him to join me.

We quickly introduced ourselves. He told me his name was Michael. He said he was a minister. Surprisingly, he told me he was going to Reno on instructions from God to raise money for his church. He said that his fledgling church in Woodbridge, Virginia needed funds to pay for renovations. He went on to say that God had told him where to go in Reno and what to do when he got there to procure the needed funds. He said God instructed him to visit a certain casino there, the Cal Neva, and to play "blackjack" at a certain table. He was convinced that God was guiding him to the right place for the right reason. He had total fullness of faith.

Michael was about 35 years old, best guess. He was approximately 5' 11" and weighed about 175 pounds or so. He had collar length wavy black hair, black eyebrows and piercing soulful brown eyes. He was wearing an all-white suit. Even his belt and shoes were white. All he carried with him was a Holy Bible with a black cover. But he had no luggage, not even a toothbrush or shaving kit.

Michael and I talked and talked, non-stop. We spoke about God, about religion, about good and evil, about forgiveness, as well as social theory and my studies in graduate school. We also spoke about Dr. Elisabeth Kübler-Ross and her work. Inspired by her, I told him I was in the process of forming an international association for the scientific study of near-death experiences made popular by the recent publication of a book called *Life After Life,* written by Dr. Raymond A. Moody, a close friend of mine.

The conversation was enlivening. Suddenly, I was stimulated and wide awake. The sleepy feeling that clouded my brain earlier was gone, long gone. Michael's company was invigorating and strangely comforting, like having a reunion with an old friend. His presence quickly put an end to the driving equivalent of Russian roulette that overtook me in my drowsiness behind the wheel not long before.

I became most intrigued when Michael told me that the work I was doing was very important. He said I should press forward no matter what and never allow discouragement to get the better of me. At the time, I thought his words were rather odd, but I just figured that this was typical banter for a minister. We had driven for more than an hour together, but it seemed timeless. As I looked into his eyes, I felt a certain recognition, almost at the soul level, like we had met before, or like I knew him from some other place, perhaps some other time. Truly, it was a very spooky feeling.

Soon, the sun rose and the new day had begun. Before I knew it, we arrived at the exit for the airport. I liked Michael and was not ready to say good-bye. So, I invited him to join me in meeting and greeting Elisabeth. Politely and graciously he said, "No thanks. I don't think that's going to work out." I thought who in their right mind would turn down an opportunity to meet Dr. Elisabeth Kübler-Ross at the height of her fame and popularity? Well, Michael did. I was about to find out why.

Just before the exit, I pulled off onto the shoulder of the road and stopped the car momentarily. I asked Michael for his address. I told him I would write him soon to find out how his trip to Reno turned out. He obliged my request and wrote down his name, address and phone number. He handed me the paper with this information. I glanced at it and then placed it in the glove box of my car. I also gave him my contact information at the same time.

As he was exiting my vehicle, I wished him lots of luck. We shook hands and said goodbye. I pulled away and headed up onto the exit ramp, watching Michael in the rear-view mirror for part of the time, feeling grateful for his company, which saved me from catastrophe.

As I turned left onto the overpass from the exit ramp, I lost sight of the place where Michael was standing, but only for a few moments. When that spot came into my view again just a minute or so later, Michael was gone. He was nowhere in sight. He could not have walked under the overpass so quickly. It was too far away from where he was standing to have walked or run there in the short time that he was out of my sight. And no other car could have picked him up so quickly without me seeing it.

I drove slowly along the overpass looking for Michael. I surveyed the median and the shoulder of the interstate, up and down, through and through, but he was nowhere in sight. I searched around to discern where Michael might have gone, I did not see any place for him to go. His only option was to keep walking straight ahead along the shoulder of the road toward the overpass.

Puzzled by Michael's disappearance, I made a mental note to write him as soon as I returned to Blacksburg to inquire about where he went once I drove away from him. I then parked my car in the airport parking lot and proceeded into the terminal. Once inside, I quickly made my way to the gate designated for Elisabeth's arriving flight. I arrived there ten minutes or so before the plane pulled into the gate, right on time.

All of the deplaning passengers strolled by me, every single one of them, all except Elisabeth. Then the procession stopped. A few moments later, the flight crew walked by me. I asked them if any other passengers were on board. They said there were none. I went to the ticket counter for the airline she was supposed to have flown and asked the agent to page her. The nice lady at the ticket counter obliged by paging her three times for me, but all was for naught.

Around that time, a supervisor then returned from break, and said "Are you Mr. Audette?" How did she know my name? I wondered.

"Yes, that's me," I replied. She said Dr. Kübler-Ross left a message that I was to call her at home in Flossmoor. She did not make her flight due to a sudden onset of illness.

I changed dollars for quarters and then made a long-distance call to Elisabeth from a nearby pay phone inside the terminal. She was home sick in bed. She had taken ill at the last minute and could not make the trip. She canceled her flight and her appearance. She had tried to reach me at my home before I left for the airport, but apparently, I had already begun my journey when she called. She apologized of course, but I said no apology was needed. I then wished her a speedy return to perfect health and said good-bye.

As I walked through the terminal on the way back to my car, I stopped in the gift shop to buy a post-card and a stamp to send a note immediately to Michael. Now my mind was really racing. How did he know that this was not going to work out before I knew it was not going to work out? I asked myself. Who was that guy and how did he know Elisabeth was not coming? I wondered.

The first thing I did when I returned to my car was to open the glove box to retrieve the paper with Michael's address on it. I wanted to send him the card right away as my curiosity had gotten the better of me. There was only one problem. The piece of paper which contained his address that I had carefully placed in the glove box maybe an hour or so before was not in there anymore. It too had vanished, just like Michael. Just like Michael, it was nowhere to be found. I looked through everything in that glove box, including each and every one of the pages in my car's owner's manual. Not there. Gone. Vanished. I checked around the passenger seat for it too, but it was nowhere to be found.

As quickly as Michael had appeared, he disappeared. As quickly as the paper with his address appeared, it too disappeared. This is really strange, I thought. Could he have been another guardian angel sent by God to keep me from being killed just like the previous angel encounters? I wondered. Perhaps. No other explanation makes any sense, but I did not form any firm conclusion about it until much later.

At that time, I really did not know what to think about my encounter with Michael. I was just puzzled by it, no less than the puzzlement I felt about similar events in 1960, 1961, 1968 and 1971. I did not connect these events in my mind until much later in my life, not until January 28, 2014, surprisingly. That was when I met a very talented medium. I have had the good fortune of meeting many gifted psychics and mediums during the course of my life. They were mostly consistent in what they told me.

So, when I heard similar information during my medium session in January 2014, I became annoyed. Honestly, I was tired of hearing the same thing without proof or corroboration. I was frequently told some pretty amazing things, but I had no means to verify any of it. I never accepted what they told me as true, nor did I dismiss any of it as false and fantasy. I simply kept an open mind about it, not rejecting it, but not accepting it either.

This particular medium came highly recommended by a university professor who made it a practice to scientifically study mediums. But, during this particular reading, I became somewhat feisty. For the first time, I actually began to challenge what was being said to me. I did not accept these psychic observations at face value, which had been my customary practice in previous readings. Politely, I began to ask questions to challenge the information I was being given at the time.

I will not share most of what I was told at that time, or most of what other gifted psychics have said to me in years past, because I have no way to confirm or challenge its validity. However, I will share that this particular medium accurately answered all of the challenging questions I asked her, all except one.

This medium claimed to be channeling Archangel Michael (Michael). This came as no real surprise to me. I am often told by psychics that Archangel Michael had intervened to save my life many times and is my primary guardian angel. But when this medium answered nearly all of my questions accurately, my skepticism quickly retreated. In fact, I was left thunderstruck.

Other psychics told me in the past that my life had been saved many times by divine intervention. Most told me it was Michael who had saved my life many times in his role as my primary guardian angel. So, when the medium I consulted in late January 2014 brought up the name of Michael yet again in relation to these claims, I simply had to ask a number of challenging questions.

I began by asking Michael (through the medium) if we had ever physically met in this lifetime. The answer was yes. I asked him to name the year we first met physically. I asked the circumstances of our initial meeting. I asked about the color of the clothing he was wearing at that time. I asked what he was carrying with him. I asked what we talked about during our meeting. I went on to ask many more similar questions. I was astounded and astonished then as I am now that I received fully accurate replies to my many questions, all except one. The odds of this happening are truly astronomical.

This remarkable exchange blew me away and the medium too. Telepathy or mind-reading could not account for the amazing accuracy, which was outrageously impressive, way off the charts. The reason for ruling out telepathy as an explanation is that I was resolutely thinking the wrong answer each and every time I asked her a challenging question.

If telepathy was involved, I would have been given the wrong answer each and every time. But instead, with one minor exception, what I received from the medium was the right answer each and every time. How can that be? How is that possible? Pure coincidence as a matter of random events? The odds are way against it.

Note that the encounter with Michael was in 1976. The reading with this medium took place in January 2014. Nearly 38 years had passed since one event and the other. I hardly ever spoke about it to anyone, and then never in great detail, nor did I ever write about it. In short, none of my angel encounters were in the public domain. They were not known at the time and were not discoverable.

As the session continued, Michael went on to say that he and other angels had saved my life many times, even times of which I was unaware. Then the medium told me something truly mind-blowing. I was told that there was a split-second moment during my time with Michael when we gazed intently into each other's eyes.

At the mere mention of it, I remembered that moment in time instantly. I remember feeling a powerful soul connection with Michael in that moment. It happened, undeniably. But how could the medium know this? It was just a brief fleeting moment in time. I never spoke about it to anyone before. I hardly believed it myself when it happened, but I clearly remembered that it happened.

At the time it took place, I chose to pretend that this amazing split-second energy connection with Michael had not happened. I did not want the encounter to be uncomfortable for Michael or me. I did not want to blow his cover. I do not know what the protocol is for angel meetings, but since we seemed to be playing a mutual game of pretend, I thought it best in that moment to keep up the same game of pretend, and so I did.

Frankly, I did not know for certain Michael was an angel at the time of our interaction. I really was not sure what was happening in that moment. What I do know is that our meeting had a very surreal quality about it. But how could I know for sure that the man riding with me in my car was a celestial being descended from heaven who physically manifested to rescue me? How could I know this at that point in time? I merely suspected it, but it was only a fleeting mild suspicion. I chose instead to consider it a normal interaction with another human being while it was happening in real time.

That all changed on January 28, 2014 when the medium confirmed for me psychically that my 1976 encounter with the fortuitous hitchhiker dressed in all white clothing was something entirely different, something that was truly other-worldly.

Angel Encounter Six

My sixth angel encounter took place in the winter of 1978 on I-74 in route to Davenport, Iowa from Peoria, Illinois. I was working as a health planner for the Illinois Central Health Systems Agency at that time. I had been asked to attend a meeting in Davenport and decided to drive rather than fly to minimize the expense to my employer. Although it was winter, the weather that day was superb. It was clear, cold and crisp. Not a cloud in the sky. There was a slight accumulation of snow on the ground, but no snow falling. The air temperature was in the teens.

The interstate highway was in good shape. No snow on the roadway. All would be clear sailing so far as I could tell. I was traveling westbound about 70 MPH in my new Toyota Celica listening to a cassette of Jimmy Buffett songs. I was happy, relaxed, wide awake and feeling quite content. As I passed over the span of a bridge, suddenly, without warning, my car began to spin in 360-degree circles. Apparently, I came upon a patch of black ice, which caused me to lose complete control of the vehicle.

Behind me was a tractor-trailer (18-wheeler semi-truck) carrying a load of automobiles. CB radio enthusiasts would call this vehicle a "portable parking lot." The driver could not brake. There was not adequate distance between us. If he had applied his brakes, his truck would have fishtailed right into me with a broadside impact.

My car, spinning in circles, stretched over both lanes of the interstate. It left no room for the truck to maneuver through. His vehicle was headed straight for me and there was nothing either one of us could do to avoid a collision, which to me at the time seemed like an absolute certainty.

As I caught a fleeting glimpse of the approaching tractor-trailer, it occurred to me that death by trauma was a distinct likelihood. I truly believed I was going to be killed on impact. I felt sure the truck was going to slam into my car and flatten it like roadkill. There seemed to be no other alternative and no means of escape for me or for the driver of the truck.

In that instant, as I accepted the inevitability of my pending death, a profound peace settled over me. As I spun about in circles going over that bridge, I felt a deep acceptance of my fate. I felt comforted just as I felt in the VW roll-over accident in 1971. I knew that no matter the outcome, everything would be fine…everything would be all right, even if I were to die. I knew instinctively that I should just relax and be without fear. I knew I should just surrender to God, whatever will be will be.

I closed my eyes tightly, but I did not brace for impact. I just let go in full acceptance of my fate. I felt my car lurch forward but was not sure what caused it. When I opened my eyes seconds later, my car had stopped spinning and was occupying both lanes of the interstate, smack in the middle. Cars were lined up in front of me blowing their horns. So, I started my stalled vehicle and drove it over to the shoulder of the road on the other side of the bridge. The tractor-trailer was long gone, way in front of me by that time.

Two other motorists pulled over their vehicles to see if I was all right. I stepped out of my car and began to shake all over. The peace I felt moments before had left me. Trembling from head to toe, all I felt now was fear, terror, shock and disbelief, but yet I was no longer in any danger. It took me several minutes to collect myself. I was in an obvious state of distress.

The two motorists who had stopped were two Midwestern gentlemen traveling by themselves. They looked puzzled. They asked me how in the world I managed to move my car out of the path of the oncoming truck. They said they saw my car jump forward about five feet or so.

I told them I felt my car lurch forward, but that I did nothing to make it happen. Like the Florida State Highway Patrol trooper, they both thought it must have been the hand of God reaching down to save me. I wasted no time agreeing with them. Once more, I was "Loved by the Light." Once again, angels came to drive my car.

After waiting silently for a half hour or so off on the side of the road, I continued my journey and arrived safely in Davenport in time for my meeting. I thanked God the whole way there for rescuing me once more and for protecting me like so many times before. Why? I have no clue. I pray for an answer, but one never comes.

In the winter of 1976, a similar "black ice" event happened traveling southbound on I-81 from Charlottesville, Virginia, to Wentworth, North Carolina. There was no snow on the ground, but temperatures were in the teens. Traffic was light as Dr. Raymond Moody and I drove along in my car in route to Rockingham Community College. He was to give a lecture about near-death experiences and his new hot-selling book called *Life After Life*.

Midway in our journey, my car passed over a fairly long bridge which was, unbeknownst to us, laden with black ice. The moment the vehicle made contact with the black ice, it began to spin wildly in full circles. I lost total control of the car which had been traveling about 70 MPH at that point.

"Watch it!" Raymond exclaimed. I thought he was talking to me.

"I cannot help it," I replied. "I cannot control what's happening here. We hit a patch of black ice."

"Oh, I am sorry John," Raymond said, as we continued to spin wildly. "I am not talking to you. I am talking to them," he commented, as he pointed his index finger upwards toward heaven.

"Who is them?" I asked.

"Oh, you know, our guardian angels. I asked them to step in to protect us," he explained.

Just then, the spinning stopped and I regained full control of my vehicle. We came close to hitting the guardrail once and running off the road into the median, but neither happened, thank God. I mean that literally. This too was a miracle. Raymond agreed. There and back, we encountered no further difficulties.

I do not count this incident as one among my personal angel encounters because it seems to have involved Raymond's interaction with the angelic realm more so than mine. Yet, it is an interesting story worth noting. It does add more evidence in support of the grounded conclusions I offer in this book based on the many miracle experiences.

Angel Encounter Seven

In 1988-1990, I had the good fortune of being employed by Dwina Murphy-Gibb and her late husband, Robin Gibb, of the Bee Gees. I managed a start-up merchandising company for them called Aniseed, Inc. I worked from their palatial residence on North Bay Road in Miami Beach, which they sold many years later.

Often times, I slept over in one of their guest rooms rather than make the long trek back to my home near the beach in Lake Worth, about a 90-minute drive north in good traffic. Other times, I would commute. Sometimes I drove my 1982 Toyota Supra, but other times I would drive their staff vehicle which was a 1989 brown Toyota van.

One day in early 1990, I was driving the staff van from Lake Worth on my way to the stately Gibb home, which boasted a gorgeous panoramic view of beautiful Biscayne Bay. As I neared their residence mid-morning, traveling northbound on Alton Road just shy of the signal light at 47th Street, a rather large frond from a tall palm tree fell from the tree-top onto the roadway about 20 feet or so in front of my vehicle, just shy of the intersection. It caused me to make a sudden stop to avoid hitting it.

I could have proceeded along my way. No harm would have come to the vehicle if I had chosen to just run over it. But a soft gentle voice inside told me to be a good Boy Scout and remove the frond from the roadway. So, I put the van's transmission in park and then turned on the emergency flashers. I got out of the vehicle and walked over to the fallen palm frond.

As I bent over to lift it up and move it off the road, I noticed a speeding full-size late model four-door black sedan, possibly a Lincoln Town Car, going eastbound on 47th Street. The driver aggressively ran through the red light at the intersection traveling at no less than 35-40 MPH.

An older Caucasian male was driving. He appeared to be in distress considering the reckless way in which he was operating his vehicle. To give him the benefit of doubt, it could have been a genuine medical emergency. He could have been driving himself to nearby St. Francis Hospital for urgent medical care. Surely, he was quite agitated about something from the contorted look on his face. It is also possible he was intoxicated.

Tires screeching, the distressed driver then made a dangerously sharp left turn onto Alton Road heading northbound. He fishtailed wildly as he proceeded on Alton Road, swerving in and out of both lanes. Fortunately, traffic was very light and there were no cars in his way at that time. However, I noticed two cars heading southbound on Alton Road had slammed on their brakes at the 47th Street signal light. They narrowly avoided a collision even though they clearly had the right of way.

I continued to watch the distressed driver speed north on Alton Road until he was no longer in sight. His impaired state caused him to lose control of his vehicle. I thought for sure he would run off the road and strike a tree or a utility pole, or crash through one of the homes along the eastern side of Alton Road. Fortunately, nothing like that happened, at least not as far as I know. It was remarkable for all involved that a collision was avoided.

What was that soft voice inside me that beckoned me to stop and remove the frond from the roadway? It was this action that delayed me from entering the intersection at the exact same time as the distressed driver. I believe it was an angel who implanted the thought or inclination in me to stop. What was it that caused the frond to fall when and where it did? Once again, I believe it was that very same angel.

If that fortuitous palm frond had not fallen exactly when and where it did, I suspect the car that ran the red light would have struck me broadside causing serious injury to me if not sudden death. I cannot know this for certain, but the timing of it all seemed to generally support this likely conclusion.

I consider this event further evidence that angels watch over us constantly to help us if and when they can. I believe an angel caused that palm frond to fall when and where it did and subtly beseeched me to stop my vehicle to remove it from the roadway. The timing was much too fortuitous to be mere happenstance or coincidence. I believe it saved my life.

Angel Encounter Eight

In the summer of 1993, I worked as Executive Director of the Foundation for WLRN Public Radio & Television in Miami. In that position, and the one I held previously, which was Director of Development for Friends of WLRN, I traveled all over our service area from West Palm Beach to Key West to meet with major donors, as well as large corporate underwriters and sponsors. At that time, I drove a 1982 Toyota Supra with a manual five-speed transmission.

Late one afternoon, after finishing a successful meeting with a planned gift prospect in Miami Gardens, I began my journey home. I was stationery waiting at a red light in the inside lane of Highway 441 at the intersection of Ives Diary Road, not far from Hard Rock Stadium. I was preparing to go straight southbound on 441 to 125th Street headed to my apartment on Biscayne Bay near the Broad Causeway, at a place called the Mid-Bay Club, in the Sans Souci neighborhood of North Miami.

When the light turned green, I proceeded to slowly release the clutch as I had done successfully thousands of times before. But something odd happened this time…something that rarely happened in the many years I owned that car. Clumsily, I popped the clutch and stalled the engine. So, I placed the transmission in neutral and turned the key in the ignition to start the engine again, all the while listening to the sweet sounds of annoyed impatient drivers behind me blowing their horns.

Once the engine started up again, I put the transmission back into first gear and proceeded into the intersection. But before I ventured no more than five feet ahead, a super-sized construction dump truck carrying a load of gravel came barreling into the intersection, making a left turn onto 441 from westbound Ives Dairy Road. He was traveling way too fast for the turn considering the size of his truck and the weight of his load, but such was his conduct as he carelessly ran the red light. A car heading southbound on 441 from the outside lane had to swerve to miss the truck which turned wide into both southbound lanes. That it did not collide with the truck was a miracle too.

The truck driver was either in a hurry to catch the green turn signal or else could not stop in time for the red light given the size of his truck and weight of his load. Surely, if I had not popped the clutch when and where I did, this formidable giant-sized dump truck would have slammed broadside into my car, causing me serious injury or instant death. There could not have been any other outcome.

I caught up with this truck as I sped down 441 southbound to express my outrage at his reckless driving. But when I caught up with him, with our two vehicles parallel to each other, I thought better of it. Road rage incidents in South Florida seldom end well, so I let it go. Yes, sometimes discretion is the better part of valor.

Yet again, I believe an angel saved my life. No, an angel was not driving my car at the time. No, an angel did not pop the clutch of my car at that crucial moment. Rather, I speculate that my watchful and ever vigilant guardian angel subtly influenced my central nervous system to slightly alter my reflexes, as well as the muscles in my left leg and foot with the intended result of having me pop the clutch to cause my car to stall. This is what caused me to avoid a certain collision with the dump truck.

Are these eight angel encounters proof of God's existence? No, they are not. They do not prove angels exist. These accounts are purely subjective and anecdotal. They are only one man's report of what happened to him. And even though I would swear to their validity on a Bible under oath in a court of law, they do not constitute scientific proof of anything.

Yet, taken together with millions of other similar angel encounters and other related evidence, they affirm for me that God is more real than life itself and so too are angels. They watch over us and protect us as a matter of divine providence. Angels rescue us even when we do not realize we are in danger.

But sometimes, as in the case of Tim, my high school friend and Army buddy, death comes to stake its claim. At times such as these, fate takes its course and destiny plays out as it does. We do not know when we will be called home or how, but when we are, I have no doubt that our angels will be on hand to show us the way.

It is reassuring to know that we are always "Loved by the Light," no matter what course our lives take and no matter when or how death comes about. We can take solace in the fact that God's love is an invariable universal constant to cushion us and ease our burden.

Dr. Kübler-Ross was fond of saying that "no one ever dies alone." Even when no one else is around or with us in close physical proximity, she frequently observed we benefit from the company of angels, as well as loved ones who crossed over before us.

Interestingly, in her public interviews, lectures and workshops, Kübler-Ross often commented that God's amazing love for us goes so far as to instantly extract our souls from our physical bodies whenever violent or traumatic death is imminent. Based on her research, she was firm in her conviction that we are divinely spared the horror and psychic distress of a brutal death by compassionate angels who facilitate an instant separation of our souls from our bodies before tragedy actually strikes.

Kübler-Ross was not alone in asserting these reassuring conclusions. Many other researchers concur that this is indeed what happens. In fact, there are many cases found in the literature where near-death experiencers who were brought to the brink of death by violent or traumatic means describe this very process.

They uniformly report that they were removed from their physical body before the violence or trauma occurred that brought them into a near-death state. Many claim that they witnessed the violence or trauma from up above in an out-of-body state of being without fear, pain or psychic distress of any kind.

To be clear, three out of my eight angel encounters happened because I almost killed myself, and others as well (in two of the three incidents), by carelessly driving an automobile while falling asleep at the wheel. I am terribly ashamed about this. I would never deliberately do anything to intentionally harm myself or endanger public safety. Yet, in these three instances, I did just that. This was completely out of character for me and I deeply regret these incidents.

From personal experience, I caution readers never to drive while fatigued or even slightly tired. Sudden onset of sleepiness while driving is not uncommon. It is also referred to as drowsy driving, excessive daytime sleeping, sleep apnea, narcolepsy and highway hypnosis. In my case, it was plain exhaustion while driving a car.

The National Highway, Transportation & Safety Administration estimated 90,000 crashes in 2017 involved drowsy drivers injuring some 50,000 people and causing nearly 800 deaths. But experts think this is a gross understatement of the problem.

As in my case, these episodes often occur between midnight and 6 a.m. or late afternoon when people experience dips in their circadian rhythm, the human internal clock that regulates sleep. And just like me, the driver is often alone and is usually driving in a rural area or on a highway. So be forewarned, it is no less dangerous than drunk driving.

PART II

Divine Intervention and Providence

An In Utero Divine Intervention

As powerful as my eight angel encounters may be, other true stories of divine intervention and providence have occurred in my life no less compelling. These include personal experiences of deathbed visions or nearing-death awareness (as it is sometimes called), along with after-death communication or contact, as well as near-death and shared-death experiences.

Also discussed are mystical synchronicities and serendipities, an *in utero* divine intervention event and a powerful story about the divinely orchestrated spontaneous manifestation of a physical object in the Mojave Desert during a vision quest. I also discuss a cogent lucid dream from September 2017 in South Florida right after Hurricane Irma with after-the-fact physical validation.

From common experience, we know that tomorrow is promised to no one. Most assuredly, it is not. Tomorrow never knows if it will find any one of us still here living on earth in physical form to enjoy the company of our loved ones and the things we cherish in this plane of existence.

As The Buddha once said long ago, "things appear only to disappear." To quote another popular cliché that conveys the same insight: "We're here one minute and gone the next."

To be sure, death of our physical form can come at any time, for some with warning or advance notice, and for others with none. Death stalks us moment to moment, hovering like the proverbial sword of Damocles, lying in wait for the time when time runs out on our physical existence. Whether we live here for a short while or a long while, our lifetime in physical form on planet earth still races by from start to finish like the blinking of an eye.

The recognition of this fact has preoccupied me since early adulthood, if not before, and placed me firmly on a life-long spiritual path to find truthful evidence-based answers about the meaning and purpose of human existence. To call it a hobby or an avocation would not be accurate. Rather, it was and is an all-consuming drive to become reliably enlightened about these matters. This penchant even worked its way into the whole of my professional career.

To cite just one example, in connection with my job as Associate Administrator of JFK Hospital in Atlantis, Florida, just west of Lake Worth (yes, there really is a town called Atlantis), I spent a good part of the summer of 1984 in Los Angeles, California. I traveled there to meet with various celebrities and spiritual luminaries of the so-called New Age Movement, sometimes called the Human Potential or Spiritual Awakening Movement, which supposedly launched what was purported to be the "Golden Age" or the "Age of Aquarius."

During this time, I also met with a colorful assortment of healers, holistic health practitioners and highly progressive non-traditional health care professionals on the so-called fringe or cutting edge, in addition to several top psychics, channels and mediums. It was all in connection with my job. My primary responsibility at JFK back then was to oversee construction of a "holistic" Comprehensive Cancer Treatment Center and to develop a visionary concept I had conceived called the Center for Optimal Health (COH). (Please view concept at *AffirmingGod.com.*)

COH was a politically sensitive hush-hush project that only a few top people knew about because it was deemed to be far ahead of its time. I was admonished by my superiors that if word should get out prematurely about COH, it would cause a mass exodus of the entire medical staff. They would never tolerate such a thing.

I understood completely, so I reported strictly to the CEO, James K. Johnson (Jim) and Chairman of JFK's Board of Trustees, Generoso Pope, Jr. (Gene), who was also the hospital's founder. He had achieved substantial wealth and fame as founder and editor of the *National Enquirer* based nearby in Lantana, Florida.

Gene often featured stories in the *Enquirer* about miracle cures and spontaneous healings. Rarely was there an issue that did not reference some shaman, healer, medicine man or purveyor of medical miracles that led to improbable recoveries from serious or terminal illness. He gave credence to many of these stories. He wanted JFK Hospital to offer all of these things under its rubric.

Gene wanted "his" hospital to be an "east meets west flagship" medical center, the first truly holistic hospital in America. He wanted the very best practitioners of non-traditional or unconventional health care to be assembled there offering all modalities under the sun to prevent, diagnose and treat illness, and he wanted me to be the guy to bring it all to fruition.

Jim Johnson, JFK's CEO, was also a member of the Board of Directors at Hospice of Palm Beach County, which is where and how I originally met him. He commiserated with me when its Board of Directors turned down my proposal to transform the program into a Center for Conscious Dying. I also had many chats with Jim about the COH vision. Upon my resignation, he offered me a job at JFK as Associate Administrator, largely to develop the COH vision, including the Center for Conscious Dying idea, and to oversee development of a comprehensive cancer treatment center.

I developed a graphic for both Jim and Gene to consider at our first meeting of the minds. They loved it. Our initial meeting was a big success. It could not have gone any better. We quickly achieved full consensus about the project and could hardly contain our shared excitement about creating something historic, all under JFK's auspices.

We truly envisioned sparking a sea-change in health care and the complexion of modern medicine, inspiring both to become more embracing of the holistic approach, and to reform healthcare insurance at the same time by offering a convincing demonstration of superior clinical efficacy and cost-effectiveness.

I advised Jim and Gene to separately incorporate COH and position it as a "research and demonstration project" to test the efficacy of experimental modalities and compare them to traditional medicine. I also advised them to build COH on a 13-acre oceanside tract of land in Manalapan, Florida, where the Eau Palm Beach Resort & Spa is now located, only five miles from the JFK campus.

My strong feeling was that COH should be managed separately and apart from the hospital, but that both should cross-feed and cross-fertilize one another, giving the two distinct cultures ample opportunity to merge and assimilate over time. They concurred.

Gene knew many celebrities because of the *Enquirer,* most all of whom wanted to stay on his good side to avoid being the subject of controversial front-page headlines in some future issue, whether true or not. So, my first job was to cultivate celebrity support for the project. At the same time, I was to hand pick an award-winning clinical team to do justice to the magnificent concept we would soon be bringing to fruition with mega-fund-raising help from Gene's collection of celebrities, all eager to please.

During my visit to LA that summer, through several fortuitous happenings, I was introduced to a gifted psychic named Stephan. He insisted upon meeting as soon as possible, declaring that it was of the utmost importance. He somehow knew, psychically perhaps, that I was the co-founder of the International Association for Near-Death Studies, (*IANDS.org*) and that I recently resigned my position as Executive Director of Hospice of Palm Beach County.

Surprisingly, Stephan also knew that I had resigned because my plan was not approved to transform the program into a Center for Conscious Dying. He knew I was greatly disappointed about it because I had pledges of support from nationally known experts such as Dr. Richard Alpert (Ram Dass) and Stephen Levine, as well as Dr. Elisabeth Kübler-Ross and Dr. Raymond A. Moody. What's more, financial support for the project had been promised by Henry Rolfs, a Palm Beach millionaire who really loved the idea of taking the hospice concept to its fullest expression.

But what Stephan also conveyed to me was that my life had been saved repeatedly by angels coming to my rescue, as well as several other forms of divine intervention, including an event I learned about for the first time from him. He told me about a providential *in utero* miracle that prevented a determined abortion attempt by my despairing mother, one that surely would have ended my life then and there if she had succeeded. My heart was crushed upon hearing this news.

Well before meeting Stephan, I learned I was a "love-child," born out of wedlock. Narrowly escaping abortion, I was born in May 1952. But my parents did not marry until December 1953. I know this because one day in 1968, I was sorting through my father's papers in the top drawer of his dresser. I was looking for my birth certificate to prove I was 16 years old in order to obtain my Florida Operator Driver License.

While shuffling through the stack of papers and documents, I found my parent's marriage certificate. When I saw the date of their actual marriage, I was shocked to discover that they did not become legally married until 18 months after my birth.

I did not blame my mother for the abortion attempt. I understood her extreme desperation at the time. She grew up in a very large dirt-poor family in Brooklyn, NY. Her parents were unskilled Italian immigrants who barely spoke English.

As the oldest daughter, she was forced to quit school to help support the family. She married in 1939 at the age of 18 and delivered her first child, a boy, that same year. She gave birth to three more children by the same husband, one right after the other, all girls. I am the oldest of five from her second "litter," which consisted of three boys and two girls.

Soon after mom's first four children were born, her first husband heartlessly abandoned her for another woman who happened to be affluent. He left my mother with four young children and no payment of alimony or child support. She quickly began working three jobs to support herself and her young children. Her younger sisters helped out by watching her children while she worked three demanding jobs. It was an extremely tough time for her all around.

One of these jobs was working as a waitress at a diner. One day in September 1951 when he went there to eat, my father befriended my mother. He was married at the time to a nice demure woman named Helen. They had a lovely young daughter named Sandra, my half-sister, as it later turned out.

Dad frequented this diner specifically to see mom. Each time, he went there to flirt with her. These were tempting flirtations to which my mother eventually succumbed, not knowing he was a married man. A steamy affair ensued, and soon after, mom became pregnant with me, being the extremely fertile woman that she was. The last thing my struggling mother needed at that time was another mouth to feed, so she tried to abort me, without my father's knowledge, I later learned. The attempt was self-administered of course because in those days abortion was not legal.

When I walked into Stephan's office in the summer of 1984, he greeted me with a warm gregarious hug, as if greeting an old friend he had not seen in a very long time. I was taken aback by it because to me he was a complete stranger. I did not sense anything familiar about him, nor did I sense that our meeting was somehow written in the stars.

I was also taken aback by the amount of background information he had accessed about me. I was puzzled about how he knew so much. All I knew about him was that he had been struck by lightning twice and was twice rendered clinically dead with two extensive near-death experiences as a result, both of which blessed him with a powerful psychic gift.

I was told by the mutual friend who introduced us that he also had the ability to engage in astral projection and remote viewing at will through out-of-the body travel. It was all I needed to know about Stephan to welcome a meeting. Still, when I agreed to meet with him, I had no inkling that he was about to blow my mind with startling revelations about my history that were later independently corroborated, hence validated as factual and genuine, first-hand.

"John, my brother, we meet again," Stephan said. "It is God's will that we have been finally reunited. We have much to discuss and much important work to do together, but before I tell you anything, I must first convince you that my near-death experiences blessed me with powerful psychic abilities. You are very analytical, intellectual and scientific in your approach to things. If it cannot be validated, you will not accept it as true. So, I must begin by telling you something about yourself which you could not possibly know which can later be verified directly by you."

"Stephan, I understand you were struck twice by lightning and that you were declared clinically dead both times," I replied. "I realize you had two amazing NDEs as a result which blessed you with psychic talent, but you are wrong to say that we are meeting again. We are only just now meeting for the first time. I have no history with you. None whatsoever."

"Yes, John, that is true for this lifetime, but we led many other lifetimes together always in dedicated service to God," Stephan remarked. "Now we will do so again. We've been brought together again to do some very important work in service to the divine. You know, John, you are God's dedicated servant. You always have been, consistently, one lifetime to the next. You have never faltered. You will never fail God. You're as true and pure of spirit as humans come, but first things first because you will not believe anything I tell you until I firmly convince you that what I tell you can be trusted."

"Okay, Stephan, I am all ears," I replied. "Tell me something I don't know that I can later validate."

"This might hurt John, so brace yourself for a major emotional jolt," Stephan advised. "I know you love your mother very much. I know you're very devoted to her, but my friend, near the end of 1951 when you were only about 3.5 months along in your embryonic development floating around in her womb, she tried to abort you rather aggressively, several times, all in one sitting.

"Now, I know you don't believe me, so you must call your mother to ask her if this is true. She will deny it, of course, three times. She'll make light of it until you tell her specifically how she tried to go about aborting you. She used a coat hanger, castor oil and quinine. It did not work, but she kept trying to make it happen. It never succeeded thanks to divine providence. God intervened to save your embryonic life. Use my phone. Call your mother now and ask her. She will confirm that what I just told you is true."

I remained silent for a few minutes collecting my thoughts about what I would say to mom to reassure her and put her mind at ease. Stephan was right. I did not believe his story. I doubted my mother would have tried to abort me. I expected her to prove Stephan wrong. Then I dialed her number. She answered after a few rings.

"Hey mom, it's me. How's everything?"

"I'm fine, sonny," she said, "but I really miss you. When are you coming to see me?"

"Soon, mom, real soon, a few weeks after I return home from California," I replied.

"Mom, I am calling now to ask you a very important and difficult question. You know I love you very much. Nothing will ever change that. Nothing. No matter what your answer is to my question, it will not change anything between us. I would never judge you harshly because of it nor will it dampen my love for you in any way. It will not cause me to lose any respect for you either. It's important to me that you believe me. Do you?"

"What's this all about?" she asked. "Why are you acting so strange? What's going on?"

"Mom, there is a psychic here with me," I explained. "His name is Stephan. He told me something about my past, when I was just an embryo in your womb. I need to know if it is true because I need to determine whether he has genuine psychic ability. I must do this for my job. Do you understand?"

"Yeah, yeah, yeah. What do you want to know?" she asked.

"Mom, did you try to abort me in late 1951?" I queried.

"I tried to abort all of youse," she answered, verbatim, in relation to all nine of her children.

"Mom, seriously, I need to know. Did you try to abort me back then?"

"Who in the hell remembers!" she exclaimed.

"Mom, I will ask you once more. Did you try to abort me?"

"Go scratch your ass!" she declared.

"Mom, did you use a coat hanger, castor oil and quinine? Did you make several repeated attempts, none of which succeeded, obviously?"

It was clear to me that Mom was completely stunned and psychologically immobilized by my question. She did not know what to say, so she said nothing. For several minutes, there was nothing but dead silence on the line. I knew she was processing internally and giving intense thought about she would respond.

Then, finally, after a long pregnant pause (pardon the irresistible pun), she replied. "How in the hell do you know that?" she retorted in a shocked and dumbfounded tone of voice. Then she repeated the same question again. "How in the hell do you know that? No one knows about that, no one but me."

"Stephan, the psychic, mom," I answered. "He saw it all. Is he correct?"

"Yes, son, it's all true," she responded. "That Stephan is a really good psychic. I'm so sorry Johnny. You know I love you deeply."

"It's okay mom," I replied. "There's no need to apologize. I understand completely. I understand what you were going through back then. Don't worry about it. Don't give it another thought. I love you very much. Please don't fret about this. I'll see you soon. I've got to get back to work. Bye for now."

"Now, will you trust what I tell you, John?" Stephan asked.

"Let's say you have my full undivided attention Stephan, and yes, let's say I am eager to hear what more you wish to share with me," I answered. "I cannot say I will believe or trust everything you tell me henceforth because how am I to know if it's true?

"Yes, the information about the abortion attempt is true, for sure, but that does not mean everything else you will tell me from this point forward is also true. You could be wrong about other things, so all of what you tell me is subject to independent validation by me. Let's just take it as it comes, step by step. Please proceed," I requested.

"You know the issues and problems you have with your cervical spine? They are all congenital, are they not?" he asked. I nodded in the affirmative. "Well, the repeated abortion attempts with the coat hanger are what caused all of that. And now you're afflicted with relentless chronic pain and extremely limited range of motion all life-long because of it, as well as other issues too. Pretty raw deal for a Golden One, don't you think?"

"What's a Golden One?" I asked.

"You are a Golden One, John, always in service to God's will. Your guides and comrades are all archangels. You volunteered for this incarnation to help bring more divine love and light to a dark place. You always voluntarily come into this world from the realm of Spirit, from the highest reaches of heaven, during pivotal times in the spiritual evolution of humanity to help move things forward. This is what makes you a Golden One, John. You are stalwart in your convictions about God, unassailable, full of integrity, impeccable and incorruptible.

"You and I worked together as brothers in many of these incarnations. You and I followed The Buddha. You were a Bodhi Sattva, one of his favorites, and so was I. We were also together during the life of Christ, but Spirit will not allow me to share any further information with you about these incarnations or others. Just know and trust that they happened.

"You are a highly advanced soul. You came here in this lifetime to fulfill a very important and powerful destiny. This is why your life has been divinely spared so many times in holy demonstrations of great providence, beginning way back when you were developing in your mother's womb.

"Humanity is in deep trouble, John. You know this. They need to be showered in God's love and light. They need to be reminded that God is real and that they are ultimately eternal spiritual beings. Most have succumbed to greed, materialism and egocentrism. They are lost in the illusion that this body and this lifetime is all there is. You and I are here to help them awaken spiritually before they blindly self-destruct in a sea of suffocating ignorance.

"I know about your project at JFK Hospital. I know what you are trying to accomplish. I want to work with you on this. I want to help you hand-pick the clinical team, as well as the celebrities you are attempting to recruit to support this project. You must be careful here. There are many wolves in sheep's clothing all around you who will try to sabotage and circumvent you. They will talk a good game, but they really do not want to see you succeed.

"This is why you need me. Spirit wants me to be your chief oracle for this project. You must include me in all your meetings. I can help you ascertain who brings wind into your sails and who is dead-weight."

"I hear you Stephan and I promise to give careful consideration to all of your comments," I answered. "I cannot make any commitments to anyone about this project without the blessings of my superiors. So, for now, let's stay in touch. I will keep you apprised of my progress as things move forward. More than this I cannot say."

"Fair enough John," Stephan replied. "But do not try to go it alone. You will crash and burn if you do. This project is much too important for that to be its fate. I will leave you with one head's up before you go. I know you have been talking with Dr. John Upledger (the founder of Cranial Sacral Therapy). If things don't work out well at JFK, you could consider going into partnership with him."

"How do you know about John Upledger?" I asked. "And how did you learn about what happened at Hospice of Palm Beach County?"

"The same way I knew about the abortion attempt and your past lives, John," Stephan remarked. "I am inside your head. I can see inside your soul. I am a remarkable seer, better than most you'll ever meet. This is why you need me. This is why Spirit wants us to work together. Don't be apprehensive. COH will be better off for it."

Stephan and I said good-bye to each other with a sustained hug. But something just did not feel right about his energy. It felt a bit creepy. I left his office feeling very unbalanced and off-center, which was not customary for me. He spooked me and gave me great pause. I thought perhaps I was reeling from the revelation about the abortion attempt, but that was not the basis for my vexations. Rather, it was more of an ominous feeling that Stephan was abusing his gifts to further his worldly ambitions.

Through me, I felt he might be opportunistically trying to meet the celebrities I was recruiting for the project and the prospective clinical staff members too, including Dr. John Upledger, whom he repeatedly expressed a desire to meet. Something just did not feel right about the situation, so I distanced myself from Stephan thereafter. I kept him at arm's length after that first meeting.

Weeks later after our initial meeting, Stephan asked me if I was being distant because of the shame I felt about the abortion attempt and his knowledge of it. I told him I felt no shame about it at all. If anything, I explained that I felt bewilderment about why I chose to enter this world under such challenging circumstances.

Stephan's remarks about me being a Golden One with a special destiny aroused considerable doubt within me. If that were true, I said, and if it is true that we choose our parents, then I could not fathom why I chose my parents and the abysmal circumstances into which I was born. Such a choice seemed to belie the special destiny he said I was to fulfill. None of it felt right to me, certainly not the part about divine intervention saving my life so many times because I had a special destiny.

I explained there was no evidence to conclude that I was somebody special in the eyes of God, no more than any ordinary person. But he kept trying to persuade me otherwise, which I interpreted as gratuitous behavior as if to beguile me into naming him the chief oracle and gatekeeper for COH. That just did not feel right either, so I introduced him to a gifted shaman named Spirit Storm for a second opinion.

I met Spirit Storm around that time through a mutual friend. Back then, he divided his time between Hollywood Hills and Mill Valley doing group and individual sessions, as well as sweat lodge ceremonies and vision quests. He would later supervise my own vision quest in 1988 in the Mojave Desert. Spirit Storm had a good reputation. I had confidence in his discernment ability, as well as his prowess as a shaman.

So, one day, I brought him to Stephan's office in Santa Monica for a meeting. After introducing these two spiritual titans, I excused myself so the two of them could have complete privacy. I do not know what they discussed or what transpired or how they got along. I only know that about an hour and a half later when their meeting ended, I returned to pick up Spirit Storm and then drove him home.

During the drive to his home, we talked about several subjects, but Stephan was not one of them. However, when I dropped Spirit Storm off at his home that day, he did say that Stephan would not bring good medicine to me or my project. That was my sense of it too. Nothing more needed to be said on the subject. From that point on, I distanced myself from Stephan and had scant communication.

For that matter, as the months went by during the remainder of 1984 and into 1985, things just did not feel right at JFK Hospital either. The more I saw there, the less I wanted to see. There seemed to be blatant corruption, malfeasance and financial improprieties rising all the way to the top. I had no hard evidence of anything, only deep suspicions. It all culminated in an unavoidable crescendo one day in 1985 when I met with Jim Johnson urgently for the purpose of tendering my resignation.

"What's this all about John?" Jim asked.

"Well, Jim, I told you and Gene from the outset that we were embarking on a sacred mission to bring spirituality into medicine and health care. We talked about all disease and illness having its causal origins in the realm of Spirit, as well as its antidotes. We talked about the role of mind and spirit regarding their effects on the body, hence the holistic model. We also talked a lot about respecting the sacred and approaching this undertaking with the utmost reverence, not as some kind of superficial marketing gimmick.

"So, Jim, it should come as no shock to you when I tell you that you cannot plant a sacred garden in sour secular soil. The soil here is sour. Nothing will grow. I think you know what I mean. Aside from that, someone leaked the COH diagram and related plans to the Chief of the Medical staff. He's up in arms about it. You will soon have a revolution on your hands if you do not quickly abandon the project and sacrifice me on the altar reserved for what some would consider foolish dreamers and utopian visionary thinkers. I wish you the best of luck, Jim. Give my regards to Gene. Please tell him I said no hard feelings."

About two years later, a mega-storm of nasty headlines surfaced in local newspapers. Derogatory stories on morning and evening news programs were broadcast by local television stations. It was quite messy and much more than a black eye. It was all about the trials of JFK's senior management unfolding in federal court.

Some of the corruption I had warned Jim and Gene about before my resignation, but I had no conclusive proof. It was discovered much later by the IRS and Medicare officials. It led to criminal charges against the CEO, the COO and the CFO. At the conclusion of the criminal trials, all three gentlemen were given lengthy sentences in federal prison. It was heartbreaking indeed.

As magnificent as the JFK story could have been, to honor the tragically slain President for whom it was named, there would be no happy ending here. It was clouded even further when Gene died unexpectedly of a heart attack in October 1988 at the young age of 61 soon after the trials ended. Many speculated that it was the stress and shame of the JFK scandal that triggered his unexpected and tragic demise. He died in an ambulance on the way to JFK Hospital's emergency room from his oceanside mansion in Manalapan, not far from the site I had chosen to house our COH project.

As though Stephan had seen the whole thing unfold way before the fact, soon after the news of my resignation was publicly known, John Upledger, D.O., approached me about partnering with him to bring the COH project to full fruition. He assured me that he fully shared my vision. He also said a wealthy patient he was treating had offered to donate $14 million to the project to help us get started. So I agreed to collaborate with him. Soon after, we formed the Resonance Foundation and the Upledger Institute in Palm Beach Gardens, Florida. They were the initial stepping stones, I thought, in our quest to bring COH back to life in the aftermath of the scandalous JFK debacle.

But as time went on, Dr. Upledger's actions and decisions plainly revealed that his primary interest was to build a large clinical operation and teaching program focused solely on Cranial Sacral Therapy, nothing more. This was not my vision and so I resigned from this effort as well in 1986. When we parted company, John was well on his way to building a global clinical practice and educational institute that generated many millions of dollars in annual revenue, bearing his name as the sole proprietor. Many years later, he succumbed to dementia and died at the age of 80 in October 2012.

COH went onto the shelf where it has remained to this day, as yet another un-manifested progressive vision. As for me personally, the corruption at JFK and the subsequent parting with Dr. Upledger persuaded me to leave health care entirely and shift my career into performing arts management, which is when I began directing the Palm Beach Festival of the Performing Arts in 1986.

A few weeks after my return from Los Angeles in September 1984, I went to visit my mother for healing and closure. After all, the abortion revelation was a ton of bricks falling down on both of us. She was in Augusta, Georgia, where she and my father were living at the time. They moved there from Fort Lauderdale in 1975 after several visits with me there during my days as an undergraduate student at Augusta College, and before that when I was active-duty military stationed at nearby Fort Gordon. My two younger brothers, Henry and Ron, followed them to Augusta soon after they moved there.

When I arrived at my parent's home, mom was alone. Dad, now retired, was out bass fishing, his favorite hobby. It was the first time I saw mom since news of the abortion attempt had been conveyed to me by Stephan. She was standing there to greet my car when I first pulled into the driveway of their home on Oakridge Drive. I emerged from the car and we gave each other a long, tight hug. She was crying. "What is it mom?" I asked. "What's wrong?"

"Please forgive me, son," she said. "Please forgive me. I am devastated that I tried to abort you. How could I have done such a thing? And to see you standing here, to see how you turned out and what you've done with your life, it just tears me apart. To know I almost killed you is more than I can bear. I have been tormented with guilt all these years, torn apart by the guilt. I could never tell you, but I am glad the truth of the matter finally came out. A load was lifted from my heavy heart. I am so sorry."

"Mom, there is nothing to forgive," I said. "I came here to give you a big hug and thank you for being such a wonderful mother. I know you tried to abort me, and I know why and I understand. It does not change a thing. Don't give it another thought. I love you deeply and I always will. You're a really good person and a wonderful mother. Dreadful circumstances dictated your actions back then. What you did could not be helped. But now it's time to let it go. Forget about it. Let's move on with life. No need to dwell on it or discuss it further. Let it go, please."

"Thank you, son, for your forgiveness and understanding," Mom said. "It really touches my heart."

"You're welcome mother, but you don't need to thank me for anything," I replied. "You don't need to be forgiven either. All you need is compassion and understanding. It is I who should thank you for carrying me in your womb for nine months and for going through the painful ordeal of giving birth to me, and for your generous expression of forgiveness. Don't you see, mother, by giving birth to me, you forgave me for further complicating your already very complicated life."

We humans come into this world one way, born of a woman, to experience the great gift of physical life. Yet, this gift comes with only a finite number of heartbeats and breaths. One day in the not too distant future, whether it is one year from now or ninety years, it will seem too soon when the rise and fall of our breath and the steady beat of our heart cease to be.

In this sense, every single one of us suffers from a terminal condition called physical existence. Life as we know it in the body will surely end, predictably and invariably. This holds true for all matter throughout all physical creation, even for our planet, our sun, our solar system, our galaxy and the entire cosmos too. It is all to say that what is physical and seen is not really the domain of enduring essence. It is not the place to store your treasure. That which is unseen and un-manifest is what deserves emphasis and focus, but it is that which is also the most elusive and enigmatic.

Deathbed Visions, Shared-Death Experiences and Terminal Lucidity

Eventually, all things must pass and transcend material form. But it is this finiteness that gives meaning and purpose to physical existence, for each incarnation has its beginning and its end. This finiteness qualifies our temporal existence on earth to be nothing more or less than a proving ground for one's eternal spirit. Death challenges us to make life meaningful, and in that sense, all of physical life should be a continuous preparation for death, one incarnation to the next.

Most assuredly, our physical existence will end one day and that end could come about in any number of ways from any number of causes, some horrific and unthinkable, others comparatively benign and uneventful. But no matter how we meet our physical demise, meet it we will, all of us, without exception.

This qualifies death to be the great common denominator…the great equalizer, for it affects us all equally and renders us all equal when we pass on, reducing our once vibrant physical form to an unremarkable lifeless corpse. The sooner we acknowledge this fact to ourselves, the sooner we can begin the very important inner work of discovering our larger spiritual identity beyond the body that temporarily houses our eternal essence.

Of course, we can delude ourselves into thinking otherwise. Many of us do by denying the prospect of our own death. We can and do fool ourselves into thinking, "To thee and to thee and to thee but never to me," as Kübler-Ross would often say in public lectures.

Eventually, however, death will find each one of us, like it or not, with a rude command to "shuffle off our mortal coil" in the famous words of William Shakespeare. When that time comes, it will teach us in visceral terms the meaning of the poet John Donne's famous observation, "And therefore never send to know for whom the bell tolls. It tolls for thee."

There is a Native American Indian expression that was commonly used among some tribes to convey their philosophy of life and death: "Today is a good day to die" so the saying went, as a recognition that any given day could be one's last on earth in the body. It was an expression to acknowledge their association with or belonging to "the Great Spirit." It was reflective of their understanding that this earthly existence was temporal and transient. To say it another way, "life is but a dream."

Even though death is always lurking and looming, many of us in Western culture do not think about it. We busy ourselves with mundane earthly pursuits, dramas and distractions that keep us quite preoccupied, all the while pretending we will live forever in this body and in this world. But such an attitude keeps us from confronting our own mortality and from asking ourselves the deeper questions about life's true meaning and purpose. We can play this game of pretend only for so long, and then, like all games, it must come to an end.

Many of us lead relatively superficial lives transfixed by pursuit of the things of this world: material possessions, sports, romance, sex, wealth, fame, power, personal beauty, anti-aging strategies, popular entertainment, drugs, alcohol and the like. In the end, none of these things hold any meaning for us whatsoever. One day, we will come to view them as imposters and dead ends.

Still, many individuals will avoid life's deeper questions until the proverbial hand grenade is in the trench. Only when the death of a close loved one occurs or a personal terminal illness strikes, will they begin a deeper thought process in an effort to discover what more there may be to reality and to themselves apart from the body and the things of this world.

When this happens, which it will for many of us sooner or later, it often can be an opportunity for profound personal growth. Typically, this is when the search for deeper meaning begins, often very late in life for the average person. Sometimes it happens much too late for a person to die with one's inner house fully in order, too late to mitigate the choking fear that can occur when we meet our physical demise.

Dr. Elisabeth Kübler-Ross would often remark in her lectures and interviews that, "Dying patients are the greatest teachers in the world if we would only put aside our own fear of death long enough to listen to them and learn from them."

In her classic work from 1969, *On Death and Dying,* Elisabeth conceived the well-known five psycho-emotional stages that most dying patients experience when they face death: Anger, Denial, Depression, Bargaining and Acceptance.

Elisabeth would frequently comment that many of us in Western culture have "a very erroneous view of death." She would often observe that, "If we truly understood death and what it means to die, we would lose our fear of it. We would live our lives very differently and treat one another very differently." She could not have been more right then, or now, or a thousand years from now.

In 1977, Kübler-Ross not only inspired the thesis I wrote for my Master of Science degree at Virginia Tech, but she also advised me on the design of my thesis research at the Medical College of Georgia in Augusta. What's more, she influenced me to become involved with hospice early on in my career in health care administration.

Thanks to Elisabeth, I had the privilege of directing two non-profit hospice programs, including Hospice of Palm Beach County (now known as Trustbridge), which today may have one of the greatest endowment funds in the world in part due to key accomplishments made during my tenure. My thesis research and subsequent involvement with hospice brought me into direct contact with dying patients, some of whom I would counsel during their final days.

As Elisabeth predicted, I learned a great deal from these encounters. One of the most important things I discovered is that some dying patients go through an intense mental meltdown or emotional breakdown related to an identity crisis that shakes them to the inner core of their being. It is a time when all the facades come crashing down, when the game of make-believe is no longer tenable. It is the time people get very honest about who they really are in the spiritual sense if they had not done so already.

When some individuals come to full recognition that their body is dying, and when they come to accept the absolute finality of that fact, it can trigger a flood of deeply disturbing realizations. This process can cause great internal confusion and despair because these individuals no longer have a basis or foundation from which to form a mental construct of their own personal ego-identity. The ego props and pretenses used theretofore no longer work.

When people who lack spiritual depth or conviction come to grips with their own impending death, they realize they can no longer define themselves in familiar customary terms. Their long-held ego-identity begins to quickly disintegrate under the weight of so many long-harbored false illusions and assumptions concerning physical existence. They realize that it is no longer possible to define themselves as the sum of their physical body, or net worth, or material possessions, or accomplishments in life, or the social roles they played in this lifetime (husband, wife, sister, brother, father, mother). This is when the social construction of reality implodes.

Moreover, some among the dying realize that they are losing their citizenship status, in effect, as well as their physical presence on planet earth because soon they will die. All they will leave behind as a trace of having been here at all is their mortal remains or cremains. All the anchors of personal identity disintegrate, one by one, even the association with species Homo sapiens.

Stripped to the core, reduced to nothing but their eternal soul, people can no longer relate to themselves in the conventional material terms they once used to define themselves. It is not a pretty picture, for it provokes psychic angst in magnitudes never felt before. These realizations spark an identity crisis of the first order and give rise to a series of gut-wrenching questions. They ask themselves, "If I am no longer any of these things, then who am I? What am I? What will become of me?"

It is indeed painful to bear witness to this mental meltdown process, although not nearly as distressing as actually experiencing it firsthand for oneself. Those who are not acquainted with their inner eternal essence, who lack solid spiritual bedrock and moorings, can indeed have a very difficult time during what can be a rather intense end of life struggle.

They will cling to the physical body as long as they can because it is the only reality they know, that is, until the time comes when they begin an intriguing interface with the other side, with the spiritual dimension, with the larger greater unseen reality. Hospice workers call this phenomenon "nearing death awareness." It is also referred to as "deathbed observations" or "deathbed visions."

Amazing things can happen at the bedside of dying patients as they begin to make their final transition and in preparation for it. Several good books have been written on the subject, including *Final Journeys* and *Final Gifts* by Maggie Callanan, a former hospice nurse. To illustrate this phenomenon, I offer five examples from personal experience, three of which are curiously related.

Catherine Cambria Audette

My mother, Catherine Cambria Audette, died at age 85 on November 19, 2006 at Hospice by the Sea in Boca Raton, Florida, in room S-102. She and I were very close. We remain so across time and death. I took care of her in the last few years of her life when she could no longer live independently. It was my honor and privilege to do so. I would gladly do it again for as long as she required.

I agreed to arrange inpatient hospice care for my mom with great reluctance. I did so only after several of her attending physicians insisted. I did not want to let go. I visited mom every day during her hospice stay. I used the opportunity to acquaint her with what little I knew about the transition called death. She knew her body was giving out. She could feel it. After nine children and a challenging life, she was worn out. She was ready for a new body.

Mom was a simple woman. She was the child of immigrants from Sicily who arrived through Ellis Island around 1912. Her parents, Sal and Jenny, had 10 offspring, all raised in Brooklyn, New York, on the meager income of a baker and later a longshoreman. They all spoke fluent Italian. I met my maternal grandparents once, but they spoke little English. Obviously, we did not have much to say to each other.

Mom had very little formal education, so when I attempted to explain things to her, I did so in the simplest terms possible. Her favorite expression, which she declared frequently with conviction was, "I want a new body."

So, one day when I was visiting her at hospice, I explained she had to give up the body she was in to get a new one. I told her that the physical body does not represent who she is as an eternal spiritual being. I explained that she was in a body, her body, at the present time, but that her body does not define or represent who she is from a spiritual perspective. That last part really confused her. She replied, "Well, son, if it's not my body, then whose body is it?" Her very serious quizzical reply gave me a really good laugh.

Several times, I alerted mom to expect the arrival of her "Welcoming Committee" one day soon. I explained that this was a term I invented during my hospice work. I added that it happened frequently to many hospice patients as they were about to cross over to the other side. I said that her Welcoming Committee, like all others, would consist of friends and family who died before and were now on the other side. I told her they would come to help her make the journey from her body to the world of Spirit. I advised her not to be afraid, but to embrace it and enjoy. I also remarked that everyone is blessed to have a Welcoming Committee when they cross over. I remarked that no one dies alone.

About two weeks before mom passed, her Welcoming Committee showed up. She began talking in Italian to her deceased parents and siblings. In the days that followed she had chats with her two former husbands and her firstborn son, all on the other side. She was very happy about it. She said it was good to see them all again and to talk with them. She said they wanted her to go with them, beckoning her to follow, but she told them she was not ready yet. I think she was holding on to life until all of her children living out of state could arrive to see her and say their farewells.

I witnessed some of these exchanges with mom's deceased loved ones. Typically, mom would be looking over toward double French doors that led out to a lovely terrace. She relished sitting outside on that terrace to enjoy the morning sun. She loved the warmth it cast on her face, arms and legs. She also enjoyed watching all manner of birds and squirrels in the lush landscape behind the terrace. Occasionally, she would spot a raccoon.

During these surreal exchanges, usually mom would be conversing in Italian. It was as if she was having a conversation with another person or with other people who were unseen and imperceptible to all but her. She would even pause in between her statements presumably to listen to what was being said in response by her invisible friends. I took these exchanges to mean that mom's Welcoming Committee had arrived.

When these conversations ended, I asked her who she was speaking with just then. Usually, she said it was her mother and father. But sometimes it was one or more of her siblings who had crossed over. But no matter who it was, the message was always the same. "Come with us. It's beautiful here. There's no reason to have any fear. You're going to be very happy here with us."

When her time came, mom was ready and totally unafraid of impending death. In fact, she told me the day before she died that she was really looking forward to her new adventure on the other side. She said she welcomed it. She had no fear.

When she was admitted to hospice in early September 2006, the medical director examined her and told me she would pass within 72 hours. She lived much longer than that and mystified everyone by having many successive valleys and rallies, in the vernacular of hospice workers. Her length of stay in hospice extended beyond two months to everyone's utter amazement, but several times during the course of these two months, the medical director and attending nurses felt sure her time was at hand. Mom fooled them all by extending her life as long as she did.

On November 19, 2006, I was in a state of high anxiety and absolute dread. I had been at the bedside of many others during their passing, but with my mother, it was completely different. She raised me. I was inside her womb. She sacrificed so much for me and gave me all she had. No one had ever loved me like my mother. No one. I was choked up with emotion, even knowing what I know about life after death and even after seeing all the mystical events I have witnessed on so many deathbeds.

When mom's time to leave neared, I left her room. I went to the chapel to pray and collect my emotions. Actually, I went there to hide and be alone. It was very hard for me to let her go. I did not want my energetic presence at her bedside to hold her back or impede her transition in any way. I knew it was her time and I knew I had to let her go, hard as it was. It was emotionally overpowering for me, so I had to escape and find solitude. I also did not want to lose control of my emotions in front of others.

In her room with me at that special time were my sister Rebecca and half-sister Dorothy, a hospice nurse named Anita, and my dear close friend since February 1974, Dr. Raymond Moody.

Raymond happened to be in town to speak at a conference in Fort Lauderdale. He preferred staying in my home instead of a hotel. I was pleased to have him around during this very difficult time. He was delighted to be with me to help me through the ordeal. He knew my mother. They had met and conversed several times over the many years of our strong enduring friendship.

After ten minutes or so of alone time spent praying and deep breathing, Anita and Raymond left mom's room and came looking for me. Soon enough, they found me hiding in the chapel. "It's her time," Anita said. "She wants you in the room by her side. She will not cross over until you are there with her."

"Anita is right, John," Raymond said. "You have to come with us now. I know it's hard for you, but you must come with us now to be with your mother."

Begrudgingly and really having no choice, I left the chapel and walked toward my mother's room with Raymond by my side holding one arm and Anita on the other side holding the other arm. Thank God for their physical support on both sides of me. I probably would have fainted or fallen without it.

I entered her room and then dropped down on both knees at the foot of my mother's bed with my arms extended over her legs. I closed my eyes and went quickly into a deep meditative state to try to calm my emotions and attune to my mother who was clearly in the final stages of leaving this world for the next. I connected with mom energetically within a few moments. I could feel her love, and she could feel mine. It was overpowering. Even with my eyes closed, I could tell when she took her last breath of earthly air.

"She's gone," Anita said, a few minutes later. Becky and Dorothy began to sob. I did too, with my face nestled in between my Mother's lower legs. I stayed there bent over resting my head on her legs for what seemed to be an eternal moment. It could have been hours or days, or just a few seconds. I was outside of time. I had no concept of it. I was there in that room, but I was elsewhere too, somewhere in the twilight zone no doubt.

I placed my arms under Mom's legs and hugged them, still sobbing uncontrollably and inconsolably. It was then I suddenly realized what I had said before so many times in leading bereavement support groups: "You do not do grief. Grief does you."

I pride myself on always being in control, but then and there I lost control. My emotions overtook me, probably for the first time in my life in those surreal moments after my mother passed. It was God-awful, but also bittersweet.

I opened my eyes and quickly noticed that mom's face was all aglow, as if a heavenly light was shining down upon her. She looked so incredibly peaceful, almost happy, that her long journey in her worn out body had finally come to an end. She also looked quite beautiful, amazingly so, as though she had been kissed by God.

After a long while, I stood up and regained my composure. I stroked mom's face and kissed her forehead. Then, I took notice of Raymond sitting behind me in a Queen Anne chair with his head bowed in what seemed to be prayer. He was wearing a New York Yankees' baseball cap, which was not characteristic of him. I walked over to the other side of the room and hugged my sisters, trying in vain to comfort them. Then I hugged Anita while thanking her profusely for all she did. I thanked all the hospice staff for giving superb care to mom. She deserved the very best and so much more.

Raymond and I then left the hospice facility to be on time for a pre-planned dinner engagement with Dr. Edgar Mitchell of Apollo 14 fame at nearby Mizner Park in Boca Raton. After I parked my car, Raymond and I walked arm in arm to the restaurant. He had the presence of mind to support me physically. He saw that I was unsteady on my feet.

When Edgar saw me initially, he knew I was clearly not myself. He asked if I was okay. I told him I was emotionally shaken because my mother had just passed away at hospice. He expressed his condolences and empathetically asked if we should reschedule. I thanked Edgar for his kind offer but insisted that we proceed.

The truth is, I should have accepted his gracious invitation to reschedule. During the whole dinner, I hardly spoke a word. I was there in physical form only. A huge part of my consciousness was elsewhere. I was not all there. Both Raymond and Edgar knew it. Everything seemed surreal to me at that point. I was somewhere else, completely gone, somewhere in deep space.

The next day I received a phone call from a dear friend, a precious soul blessed with many spiritual gifts and talents. We met at a conference in Houston, Texas just a few months before Mom died. A deep instant spiritual connection occurred from the moment we met. She said I needed healing and offered to do a session with me in my hotel room, gratis. I accepted and was very glad I did.

Her skills were impressive as a shaman and energy healer. When she finished her session with me that day, she told me I needed more work and asked my permission to connect with me energetically for distance healing. I quickly agreed because I knew she had a very powerful skill which would bring great benefit to me.

A few months later, to my great surprise, my friend reached out to connect with me the day after my mother died. She knew Mom had passed, but how could she know? I did not tell her. No one told her. But at the time Mom passed, apparently, she had been energetically connected with me doing her shamanic healing work. What she said next blew me away.

"Thanks to you, John, your Mom had an amazing transition. It was so beautiful to watch. I considered it a real privilege to witness."

"What are you talking about?" I asked. "I am confused. You totally lost me. How do you know my mother died yesterday?"

"I was attuned to you at the time," she answered. "I witnessed the whole thing. I saw you resting your head on your mother's legs, sobbing as she drew her last breaths, holding on to her like a child."

"Oh, my God!" I exclaimed. "I cannot believe what I am hearing. I knew you were gifted, but I didn't know your gift was this exceptional. Yes, what you saw is true."

"But I saw even more, John," she said. "While I watched, a part of your soul travelled into the other world with your mother as she made her transition. Once you knew she had been greeted by her deceased loved ones and was in good hands on the other side, she touched you on the shoulder in astral form, gently raised you up, beamed love into you and encouraged you to return. You withdrew then and returned to your body."

"No, with all due respect, you're wrong about this," I insisted. "I was in my body the entire time. I never left my body. I did not accompany my mother to the other side. You're right about everything else, love, but so wrong about that."

"No John," she replied. "Apparently you have no conscious recollection or awareness of it, but you did exactly what I said you did. It was so beautiful. She had a very good death and a wonderful transition. She was fully supported in the arms of love the entire time, thanks to you."

"Now listen, dearest, you realize I have great admiration for you, but you are way off-base here," I retorted. "Sorry, but nothing like what you described happened. I should know. I was there. I was in my body the entire time. Yes, I felt terribly discombobulated, but I was firmly in my body. I never went anywhere else."

"You were in two places at once, John," she answered. "Your ability to accompany your mother into the next world arose spontaneously within you in that instant because of the severe emotional pain you were feeling. You wanted to be there for your mother in every possible way and you were. Do not doubt it. I was there too and I saw the whole thing. Think back to when you felt outside of space and time during your guttural sobbing episode. That is when it happened," she explained.

"And, John, you need to know, the mother I saw in the other world was not the weakened suffering mother you described to me in Houston. She was a strong presence, a powerful wise being. She will always be there for you throughout your life. I'm sure of this."

A short while later, I told Raymond about this conversation with my shaman friend. "I have never been out of my body Raymond," I said. "I would not know how to separate from it if I tried."

"Well, it sounds to me like you may have had what I call a 'Shared-Death Experience' John, or at least it sure seems to fit the criteria," Raymond replied. "I have encountered several cases of this unusual phenomenon. I am planning to write a book about it.

"But what's important here, John, for your grief process, is to know that you did everything you possibly could for your mother all the way to the end of her life. Quite possibly, if your friend is right, you helped her on the other side in the hereafter too."

Ever the philosopher, Raymond could not help himself. He was compelled to invoke the spirits of the ancient Greeks. "You know, John, there could be a connection here to Pythagoras," he said. "One of the first documented cases of bilocation or multi-location in history is attributed to him.

"To cite just one well-known instance of his ability, many witnesses were in unanimous agreement that he spoke publicly in two locations at the same time, yet these locations were far apart, a journey of several days by land and sea. He was observed by many witnesses to be both in Tauromenium, Sicily and Metapontum, Italy at the very same time."

A few years later, Raymond published a book about Shared Death Experiences just as he said he would. It is called *Glimpses of Eternity*.

Charles Rodman Lesher

Room S-102 at Hospice by the Sea in Boca Raton, Florida, would yet again become a significant part of my life, over 11 years later, beginning in late April 2018. At that time, it would be serving as the final stop for 91 year-old Charles Rodman Lesher. He was my father-in-law.

Yes, this was the very same room in which my mother died on November 19, 2006. No, I did not request that room for Chuck. It was simply assigned to him at random, one of 30 rooms he could have been given upon admission. It happened to be one of the rooms available, or perhaps the only room available, in a facility that is nearly always 100% full. I must ask again, what are the odds?

When my mother entered this facility in September 2006, it was called Hospice by the Sea, formerly known as Hospice of Boca Raton. But when Chuck was admitted to that same facility in late April 2018, the ownership had changed. My former employer, Hospice of Palm Beach County, acquired Hospice by the Sea and changed the facility's name to the Trustbridge Care Center in Boca Raton. The room numbers changed too as a by-product of extensive remodeling performed after acquisition.

There can be no doubt about it. Chuck had been placed at random in the very same room in which my mother Catherine left this world for the next back in November 2006. The irony here is compounded by the fact that Chuck asked me to arrange his admittance to hospice several times during the last two years of his life. His infirmities were such that he just did not want to live anymore. Like my mother, he too was feeling worn-out.

I understood, but still I refused, selfishly, because I was not ready to lose him, just like my mother. Each time he asked, I prevailed upon him to hang in there and inspired him to have a change of heart. But when his time came, I knew it and could no longer pretend. It happened to be at a time when the same room formerly occupied by my mother was ironically available to accommodate Chuck. How's that for a cosmic affirmation? I can only marvel at the manner in which Spirit works. It is truly awesome to behold.

Chuck was a WWII veteran who saw combat in the European theater. He was involved in the advance on Berlin and in the American occupation there after the Third Reich was defeated.

I was honored to be Chuck's caretaker for the last ten years of his life and to serve as his health care surrogate. He lived with my wife, Vivian, and me for these ten years. He had no assets and only a paltry monthly income, so it was either live with my wife and me or enter a Medicaid nursing home.

The choice was obvious for him. He knew we loved him and he knew we were sincerely delighted to welcome him into our home. Truly, he was not an imposition and never once did we ever make him feel otherwise.

Aside from that, Chuck and I were good buddies. We genuinely liked each other. He was an avid reader and an astute observer of the world scene. He had extensive knowledge of history and geography. He would often impress folks with factoids about one obscure thing or another. He was also a relentless practical joker and a witty comedian. He made up his own jokes constantly and loved getting hearty laughs out of people. Moreover, he was a terrific card player, excelling at pinochle.

Chuck was a skillful chess player too. He and I would hold tournaments weekly, which he would win more often than not. Winning was important to Chuck, but not to me. I would have made a good athlete in competitive sports but for the fact that I intensely disliked watching my opponents lose. I hated how it made them feel, so before long as a young boy, I simply stopped competing.

But when it came to chess, Chuck won on his own merits – that is up until the later years of his life, which is when I would let him win, but without him suspecting it. He hated losing. It made him moody and would ruin the rest of his day. But not so for me. Letting him win was no real sacrifice on my part. I'd rather see him happy over winning than score a meaningless victory for myself by beating him at chess. Sometimes I won just to let him know that I could, at least on rare occasions.

Other than my mother and David Prensky, a friend I will write about in the next section, I cannot recall meeting anyone more generous and selfless than Chuck. He had little, but consistently gave to others what little he had all throughout his life. His generosity extended not just to his four daughters and their kids, but to friends and even strangers. He was always broke because he always gave away what little he had to help others.

On several occasions, my wife and I would learn by happenstance that he gave money to complete strangers, people we never heard of before. For example, at her 50th high school reunion in 2019, my wife reunited with a former classmate who was saddened to learn that Chuck had passed away the year before. He was effusive in his praise of her father. He told her that in 1967 Chuck generously gave him a car, a 1962 Chevrolet Impala. She had no idea her father had done this and was shocked to learn this bit of news.

Chuck died on May 5, 2018. His cremains were interred at the National Veterans Cemetery in Lake Worth in June 2018. His gravestone there reads, "He gave so much and asked so little." Knowing him as well as I did, I attest to the fact that this statement is no exaggeration.

Chuck was a life-long atheist. He was adamant that God did not exist and that life after death was a fairytale. I tried to convince him otherwise time and again, but he was closed-minded on the subject. For someone as learned as he was, I was shocked by his recalcitrance, but on these issues, he would not budge one inch. I kept telling him to expect to be pleasantly surprised when his time came, but he would pay no mind to my advice.

Things changed when Chuck entered hospice. All of a sudden, he became more interested in hearing my thoughts about death and what comes after. I explained the "Welcoming Committee" term to him and told him stories about the deathbed visions I encountered in my work as Executive Director of Hospice of Palm Beach County, the program which was now caring for him as an inpatient.

Chuck refused to let me tell him these stories before, but now on the doorstep of death, he was at last ready to hear me out. But still he did not give any credence to the information I imparted about the deathbed visions and terminal lucidity I witnessed.

One day in early May, Chuck surprised me with a startling revelation. "I've been seeing shadowy figures over there," he said, pointing to those same double French doors where my mother had seen her Welcoming Committee. "I know who they are, but they are all dead people. They are not real."

"Well, who are you seeing, Chuck?" I asked.

"It's Viv's mother, Nonnie, and my sisters Myrtle and Mary, my mother Agnes and my father, Charles, Sr.," he answered. "I think I'm hallucinating. It must be the damn drugs they are giving me. They are not really there."

"That's your Welcoming Committee, Chuck," I explained. "Don't you remember that I told you to expect their arrival?"

"Yeah, I remember," he answered. "But I told you I do not believe in that stuff. I don't believe in God or life after death."

"Well, you are not on morphine Chuck or any drug that would cause hallucinations," I remarked. "Maybe what you're seeing is the real thing. Maybe it is your Welcoming Committee. Are they speaking to you?"

"I see them motioning to me," Chuck replied. "I think they want me to join them. I cannot hear what they are saying, yet I see them talking to me. It must be just a dream, but it's happening every day now, several times a day in fact. I even see them at night in the darkness. They glow in the dark like luminescent beings. They're inside my head, but they are not real. They cannot be real. They are just an illusion, like a mirage or something. They're all dead and buried, long gone."

"Well, Chuck, think of it what you will," I answered. "I won't try to change your mind. But promise me something, please," I asked. "After you die, if you discover that your consciousness continues after death, and that God is real, and that your deceased loves ones are actually alive and well on the other side in the realm of Spirit, would you please send me some kind of unmistakable sign or affirmation from the great beyond?"

"Oh come on!" he exclaimed. "Stop with the bullshit, John. What you're asking is nonsensical. When you're dead, you're dead and that's all there is to it. There's nothing else."

"Fine, Chuck, fine, but just because you don't believe in life after death does not mean that it is not a fact or a reality," I replied. "You could be right. But I say you are wrong. Like I've always told you, prepare to be pleasantly surprised. And keep in mind that your disbelief in life after death does not make it so any more than my belief makes it so. It is going to be what it is going to be regardless of our beliefs. But just forget about it. I should not have asked."

"Sorry, John. I don't mean to growl at you. I know you feel strongly about this. I know you are just trying to help me. You're a good man and I am so grateful to you and Viv for all you have done for me. The least I can do is honor your request, even if it is a fantasy. So, yes, if I discover that life continues after death, and if I am able to send a message to you from the other side as you call it, then I will. You will know it's me. I will think of something clever to let you know it's me…something only I would do."

Dr. David Prensky

Dr. David Prensky was a long-time close personal friend. He was a retired dentist who lived for many years in Palm Beach, Florida. He was an active (and vocal) member of Palm Beach society. We originally met in 1986 when I began my tenure as the Executive Director of the Palm Beach Festival of the Performing Arts, which operated from its main office in the Armour Building on Worth Avenue in Palm Beach. During its heyday, the festival was considered by many to be South Florida's premier cultural event.

Though seemingly indestructible and indefatigable to those who knew him best, David passed away at age 90 in September 2008. He was much loved and deeply mourned by many. To all those who knew him, he was larger than life.

I truly admired David for his love of knowledge. He was an avid life-long learner. He was also a tireless social activist, a relentless crusader for social justice and human rights. He was revered as an expert musicologist, a lover of all the arts and creative expression, as well as a staunch advocate for single-payer health care.

David was a ubiquitous character in the community, much liked and highly respected, best known perhaps for giving lectures at the Kravis Center of the Performing Arts before many classical music performances. He would enthrall concertgoers with his erudite knowledge of classical composers and compositions. Yes, he was a zealous music aficionado with a passion for classical compositions that surpassed most ordinary music lovers.

David was also stubbornly agnostic in all the years I knew him and probably for most or all of his life. He was very much like Chuck Lesher in that regard. David adamantly did not believe in life after death or God. He had no deep spiritual convictions. Yet, the irony is that David lived a life that was one of the most spiritual I have ever had the privilege of observing, but without ever being formally spiritual. It was not a label he would ever apply to himself.

Truth be told, the manner in which David lived his life and treated others would no doubt qualify him for heavenly entrance even by the stiffest standards of the world's major religions, even though he was affiliated with none. So, even without the incentive of other-worldly upside rewards in the afterlife for being kind, caring, loving, compassionate, fair and generous, David possessed all those qualities and more. He truly cared about people and was one of the most compassionate people I knew, akin to Chuck Lesher.

A true humanist, activist and altruist, David devoted even his final days, while an inpatient at Hospice of Palm Beach County - JFK Medical Center Unit, in Atlantis, Florida, to fervent attempts to obtain signatures from every person he encountered on a petition in support of single-payer health care. He was simply an unstoppable man who had no quit in him. For all these reasons, and others, I held the highest respect and admiration for him.

The love of his life, Bryna, was his devoted wife for well over 50 years. She died before him in 2003. Bryna was a gifted artist and avid collector of Mexican artists from the time she and David lived there decades ago. They hung out with Leon Trotsky and budding artists who later became world-renowned. Bryna's death was a devastating blow to David, but still he kept on keeping on with his trademark indefatigable spirit. He asked me to eulogize Bryna at her memorial service held at the stately Society of the Four Arts in Palm Beach. I was privileged to do so and felt greatly honored that David asked me.

In my remarks both before, during and after the ceremony, I tried to comfort David with solid evidence-based reassurance that he would meet Bryna again. I told him the bonds of love are eternal and that he and Bryna are spiritually enjoined forever. But David always brushed off talk of this sort, dismissing it as utter nonsense at worst and wishful thinking at best. I tried my best, time and again, to educate David about the credible evidence supporting the survival hypothesis, but all to no avail.

I visited David as often as I could, but it was emotionally difficult for me for several reasons. First, I knew David was dying and, even with all that I know about death and dying, it is still very hard to say good-bye to such a dear soul whom I loved dearly. Moreover, being the same building where bold visionary plans for COH were born but never realized, made my return after so many years emotionally challenging.

As I walked down the familiar halls at JFK on September 13, 2008, I could only think about what might have been and what could have been in 1984-1985…if only.

As I looked down at my official visitor badge bearing my photo, my name and the names of both of my former employers, I could only shake my head back and forth at the irony of it all. (Please see AffirmingGod.com to see the visitor badges).

But I was there to be with David and so I pressed on despite my weighty thoughts and mixed emotions about the past.

David was in room 4164, hooked up to a BiPAP that pumped oxygen into his failing lungs. A CD player set at a low volume was playing classical selections that were among his favorites. During one of my visits, I sat alone in the room in a chair beside David's bed. He was comatose and unresponsive. I sensed that his time to leave this world for the next was fast approaching.

I sat there silently, holding David's hand, while conveying loving thoughts and guidance to him. I knew full well that patients in this limbo state can often hear the spoken voice as well as perceive the thoughts of others. To my surprise, David's eyes opened wide and bright. He took note of my presence and began squeezing my hand. It was as though he had rallied from death's doorstep.

"You were right, John. You were right!" he proclaimed with great excitement. "We do live on after death!" he said. Then he asked me, "Why is it taking so long for me to cross over? Bryna is there waiting for me," he said. "She wants me to go with her up through the ceiling. She's there right now beckoning me to come. Why can't I go with her now? I want to leave with her now, right now!"

Yes, David had captured a true glimpse of the other side, several times in fact during his final days, witnessed not only by me but others there too including his offspring and a private caregiver. He had multiple encounters with various friends and loved ones who died before him, all while lying there on his deathbed. He told several people about it who were around him during his last week. These mystical encounters at the end of his life gave him great comfort, as well as convincing proof that his true identity was that of an eternal spiritual being, not a temporal physical being headed into nothingness.

For the first time in his life, David no longer thought of himself merely in terms of being just a physical body. He knew he was much more at this point. He realized his body was not even a tiny aspect of his identity any longer because it would soon cease to exist.

Due to his mystical deathbed visions, David discovered for the first time his true larger identity as an eternal spiritual being. For David, it took actual sight of the other side and his "deceased" loved ones over there before he could accept the reality that his body had nothing whatsoever to do with his larger identity as an eternal spiritual being. Knowing David, he would absolutely love it if all of us could learn from his deathbed epiphany and live our lives accordingly henceforth.

Few people loved life more than David. Few could rival his will to live or his prowess at squeezing more juice from life than most ordinary folks. Most of us mere mortals would have to lead ten lifetimes to do as much as David did in his 90 eventful years on earth.

But in David's last few days, as much as he loved life, as wed as he was to the notion that his physical body was the sum total of his being, he could not wait to leave this world for the next. In typical characteristic fashion, he wanted to get on with the task at hand and cross over immediately, at the first sight of his beloved Bryna, with whom he was spiritually reunited, at long last.

This is what it took for David, in the last days of his life, to re-evaluate and re-define his core identity, to make the shift into finally accepting his larger identity as an eternal spiritual being. But David was not alone or unique in re-casting core identity shortly before dying. Many before him and after him have mirrored this same process. The literature is replete with examples of it if one takes the time to do some basic research.

I was honored to join several of David's closest friends in eulogizing him on November 15, 2008 at the Dreyfoos School of the Arts auditorium in West Palm Beach. David made many financial contributions to the school and also donated his vast musical library to them upon his death. In part, this is what I said to David's friends and family gathered on that occasion at his memorial service, including his nephew, Hollywood filmmaker, director and producer Derrick Borte:

"Even during his last days on earth, David continued his role as teacher to those who would listen. In his frail and debilitated state, he mustered the strength he needed to share with us that he was not afraid to die and to tell us that he no longer saw death as the end of existence, but rather as a peaceful transition to an indescribably beautiful divine reality beyond this one.

"Sooner or later, death of the body happens to all of us. When our time comes, we can take heart from David's mystical deathbed encounters. Fear not, he would say today, for our eternal spirit lives on after the body dies. Only the body dies, he would say, and you are not your body. You are just in your body temporarily, but you are not your body, and life does indeed go on after you leave your body. Never mistake your body for your true identity.

"David lived a life entirely devoted to improving the human condition absent the knowledge that eternity awaits us all after death. He did not live a life devoted to human service because there was an upside in it for him.

"Rather, he gave to others and loved others, and left the world much better than he found it because he knew instinctively this was the right way to live one's life. He could not do otherwise, for it was not in his nature to be otherwise. Such was the enormous depth of his intrinsic goodness and beauty. For this, I have no doubt that David was welcomed into the highest reaches of heaven. Once there, I know he felt right at home.

"If David were here with us now, he would urge us to take our grief and channel it into pure resolve to carry on in his tradition. He would beseech us to love one another, care for one another and give to one another. He would ask us to work tirelessly to make this world a better place. We here today are David's legacy, all of us whom he touched. What we do henceforth with our lives, those of us who have been enriched by David, will be a testament to the influence he had on each of us.

"So, in David's memory, in homage to him, go forward from here and immerse yourself in a worthy cause or simply in the cause of being the very best person you can be. Nothing would please him more. Let us keep the spirit of David alive in all we do and say from this moment forward. For, in truth, if ever a person was worthy of emulation, it would be David.

"In my saddest moments, when I miss David most, a little voice inside gently whispers that I have a new angel on my shoulder. In some still quiet moment not too long from now, peek at your shoulder from the corner of your eye and think of David. You just might find you've got a new angel there too. Yes, even from the great beyond, David will keep on giving to us. You see, he simply can't help himself. It's just his nature to be the proverbial gift that keeps on giving. As he was here in life, so too will he be there in the afterlife."

Adam Blakemore Mitchell

Prepare now for the next part of a very curious inter-related story. It happened a little more than two years from the date of David's passing. The date was October 28, 2010. Once more, it became necessary for me to return to Hospice of Palm Beach County's JFK Medical Center Unit. Once more, I was issued a new visitor badge like before when I visited David.

But this time, I was going to visit Adam Blakemore Mitchell, the 26-year-old son of Dr. Edgar Mitchell, Apollo 14 astronaut and sixth man to walk on the moon on February 5, 1971. Adam was born on August 11, 1984 in Jackson, Tennessee. A short 26 years later, he was dying of metastatic testicular cancer. As a close friend to him and his dad, I stopped by to pay respects and give what support I could.

Like before, and again for the same reasons, it was emotionally difficult for me to return to the premises of my two former employers. But all those mixed emotions went away when I walked into Adam's room. To my shock and amazement, I found Adam in the same room where David died just two years before. It was room 4164. I thought to myself again, what are the odds of this happening? I kept both visitor badges to prove it. To this day, I still have them. The badges can be viewed at *AffirmingGod.com*.

During Adam's struggle with cancer, which endured for over two years, we spent a great deal of time together talking about treatment options and the psycho-social aspects of cancer, as well as the basis for my unwavering convictions about life after death.

Adam wanted to be a filmmaker. He graduated Magna Cum Laude from the Film School at Florida State University, College of Motion Picture Arts. His first production was to be a documentary about his father to be called "Man of Science."

Indeed, Adam's famous astronaut moonwalker father was a stoic man of science and also an avowed agnostic. Like Chuck and David, Edgar was stubbornly unconvinced of life after death. We had many discussions about it over the years, but like David, he held fast to his position. He was unmoved by whatever credible evidence I offered to the contrary. And just like David, Edgar was very touchy about the subject, almost combative in response to any efforts I made to offer an empirically grounded spiritual view of reality for consideration.

I never pressed the point too aggressively with Chuck, David or Edgar, despite the strength of my deep convictions, for fear of sounding too much like a proselytizer. I showed the same sensitivity toward Adam. It is important to meet people where they are at.

When I entered Adam's room on that day, like David, he too was near-death and comatose as he had been for several days at that point.

So, instead I spoke with Edgar and Edgar's ex-wife/Adam's mother, Sheilah Ann Sisco Ledbetter Mitchell. They were both present in the room with me at the time.

Within 15 minutes after my arrival, Adam suddenly emerged from his coma, quite astute and alert, seeming quite happy to see me. Then he blurted out, "John Audette! John Audette! I am supposed to ask you for the map. Where is the map? I need to learn about the map!"

Edgar and Sheilah both looked quite astonished at Adam's sudden return to lucid consciousness. They were startled to hear their son forcefully speak those words. My astonishment was greater than theirs, so great it could not be contained. I was beside myself, bursting at the seams with joy.

This was a manifestation of what hospice personnel call "terminal lucidity" in which a comatose patient otherwise disconnected from and dead to the outside world, suddenly regains full alertness and waking consciousness, but only for a short time. It is as though they have returned from the dead to dwell among the living. Episodes like these are frequently reported in the literature.

I knew exactly what Adam was talking about in relation to the MAP. But, not wanting to offend Edgar or Sheilah, I pulled a cop-out and said, "Oh, Adam, I'm so sorry, but I left the MAP in the glove box of my car. I will bring it up with me next time I come to visit you."

Hearing that, Adam cast a look of great sadness and disappointment, then quickly slipped back into a comatose state. I felt I failed him terribly in that moment. His was a classic case of terminal lucidity, but instead of meeting Adam's need then and there, I regrettably chose not to offend his parents.

For her part, Sheilah kept hoping for a miracle right up until Adam's passing and who can blame her. She did not want to lose her beloved son, and certainly not at age 26. She was not ready to let him go. She remained optimistic even until the end that Adam would heal and pull through. I could not deny her that hope or her optimism by actively helping her son transition to the next world. I have seen and read about death-bed miracles. I know that with and through God, all things are possible. Yes, spontaneous remissions do happen.

Anita Moorjani's best-selling book, *Dying to Be Me*, offers one compelling case study to illustrate this point, in relation to her own return from organ failure and clinical death. In Sheilah's presence, I felt it would be wrong in that moment to bring Adam into a guided meditation based on the MAP to hasten and smooth his transition.

For Edgar's part, he was not a believer in the realm of Spirit or the existence of God, or the survival of consciousness after death. Any effort on my part to help Adam leave his body to enter the astral plane to meet his Maker surely would have offended Edgar and made him angry. He would not have welcomed such words from me to Adam at that time. I was absolutely certain of it.

But what I really wanted to say to Adam then was that I did indeed have the MAP he was seeking. I wanted to share it with him to provide the information he was seeking. I did so later, but not at that precise moment for fear of upsetting his parents.

My belief is that Adam was seeking my help with making his transition. He was not overtly spiritual or one who had an unshakable belief in God or an afterlife. But unlike his father, Adam was open-minded about both.

We often talked about the basis for my strong convictions on these subjects, but only in response to questions he would ask me on occasion. Adam liked me and respected me. I am certain our exchanges before his passing helped prepare him for his transition. I am confident I was able to help him during his actual passing.

What neither Adam nor Edgar nor Sheilah could have known at the time was that I was working then with my long-time dear friend Dr. Raymond Moody on a book project about using nonsense exercise techniques to bring about profound altered states of consciousness, peak experiences and epiphanies. These were structured exercises designed specifically by Dr. Moody to induce peak experiences and help the average person experience the greater reality beyond this one in a safe manner.

The working title I suggested for this book at the time was "The MAP." The MAP was an acronym I conceived which stood for "The Moody Awakening Process." The term fell out of favor with Raymond and he never ended up using it in his writings on the subject. But at the time of Adam's death, it was the working title. The eventual title chosen by Raymond was *Making Sense of Nonsense.*

My take about all this was that Adam was already attuned to and connected with the other side. I believe he was receiving information then and there about his pending transition. I believe he was guided to ask me for "The MAP" by his guardian angels or loved ones on the other side. I believe Adam was seeking help to be released from his breath...help in letting go of his body.

My opinion is that he asked for "The MAP" so that it would help guide him to the other side and make his passage quicker, perhaps easier too. Moreover, this was happening in the very same room as David's deathbed visions just two years before. Could this be sheer coincidence? Doubtful. Again, what are the odds? Astronomical, for sure, just like all the other improbable things described in this book.

I was by his side when Adam died two days later on the evening of October 30, 2010 in a private cottage on the grounds of the Hippocrates Institute in West Palm Beach. At his request and with the approval of his family, I remained with Adam at his bedside that night until he passed. Much of that time, we were together alone.

Although Adam never regained consciousness while I was there, I whispered to him the whole time. In hushed tones, I told him the secrets of the MAP. But mostly, I used suggestive guided imagery to ease Adam out of his body and help him make the separation. As his breathing slowed and became shallow, I knew his time of transition had come. It was sad, but sacred too.

His memorial service was held on November 13, 2010 at Bethesda-by-the-Sea Episcopal Church in Palm Beach, where his entire extended family gathered to bid farewell. His remains were cremated and in part buried at a memorial tree planted in his honor on the grounds of the place where he left this world for the next.

Dr. Edgar Mitchell – Apollo 14 Redux

Here we must fast forward a little more than five years to explore the final part of this fascinating interrelated story, which truly adds much more to the cosmic curiosity. The date is January 31, 2016, a little more than five years after Adam's passing.

Once again, I found it necessary to revisit my former employer, Hospice of Palm Beach County/Trustbridge, but this time I went to their main inpatient facility off 45th Street in West Palm Beach, adjacent to the campus of St. Mary's Medical Center.

Much to my deep sadness, this time I was there to visit Adam's father, Apollo 14 astronaut Edgar Mitchell, then 85 years old and soon to depart this world for the next from his hospice bed in room 301. In the weeks and months leading up to his admission, Edgar read several books about consciousness and its disposition after death, some of which I gave him from my rather extensive library on the subject.

These books conveyed the conviction that consciousness is eternal. They all took a responsible scientific and intellectual approach to support that conclusion. This approach appealed to Edgar's intellect and made it more palatable for him to begin to soften his views on the subject of survival, even though throughout the duration of his life he remained agnostic, fully unconvinced that there is any such thing as the continuation of consciousness after the body dies.

Edgar was fond of saying that he could not explore the issue of whether consciousness survives death when no one had yet developed a scientifically acceptable definition of the term 'consciousness.' "How can we know if consciousness survives death when we cannot even define it," he often said.

Edgar was a staunch proponent of the quantum hologram model of nature (QH), which provides a cogent theoretical explanation of how nature gathers, stores, processes, retrieves and applies key information to guide evolution throughout the cosmos.

QH asserts that nature electromagnetically captures the entire experience and event history of all matter, all objects and subjects, animate and inanimate, in order to guide self-organization, self-learning and self-correction in the overall course of evolution of all life in the universe.

He also believed QH gave immortality of sorts to individual human beings by storing their complete event history in the zero point field, much the same way that a computer hard drive stores encoded bits of inputted data. But this was the only kind of immortality Edgar believed in for most of our 34-year friendship.

We agreed about the merits of QH as a theoretical model. I completely shared his enthusiasm for it, as far as it went. We both co-founded a non-profit organization dedicated to QH research and education. It was called Quantrek, Inc. But it was never funded and ceased to be after several years of continuous effort to find funding.

Edgar would often assert that QH was indeed what the mystics referred to as the "Akashic Record" and this could be a plausible hypothesis. However, Edgar would often rely upon QH to quickly explain away all spiritually transformative experiences and all psychic phenomena, reducing them strictly to material terms. That was where he and I parted company.

Like my discussions with David, time and again, I tried my best to educate Edgar about the credible evidence supporting the survival hypothesis, but all such efforts were futile. On this question, he was the proverbial immovable object. Edgar always brushed off talk of this sort with me. He was unwilling to closely examine the evidence.

But even when I would present him with what I considered to be compelling data, he would engage in tautological argument, unreasonably attributing all such phenomena to QH. It was the one single bone of contention between us throughout our 34-year close friendship. This attitude persisted up until the very end of his life, just as it was with David and Chuck.

At the very end, Edgar's stubborn views seemed to relax just a wee bit, nothing earth-shaking, but still a noticeable shift. I pulled a chair up beside Edgar's hospice bed and reached out to hold his hand. There he was comatose in his hospice bed, unresponsive. This giant of a man, my dear friend, who had done so much and survived so many great challenges, had been reduced by the vicissitudes of life to being starkly lifeless and nearly dead. It was a scene I had witnessed so many times before in my hospice work.

Then, like a flash of lightening, I was struck by something out of the ordinary. I took notice with a big smile that Edgar was wearing a curious hospice gown (standard issue as I later discovered). It colorfully displayed a pattern of stars and crescent moons, front and back. The symbolism was not lost on me. I wondered what meaning it could possibly hold beyond the obvious connection that Edgar was an astronaut who traveled among the stars to walk on the moon, one out of only twelve men to do so in all of history.

On impulse, I took a photo of Edgar in this standard issue gown lying in his hospice bed but only to have lasting proof of this coincidence. It was taken shortly before his death and is probably the last photo taken of him. I doubt I will ever share it publicly, but I have it if proof is needed about the hospice gown he was wearing.

Nothing else out of the ordinary happened during my end stage visits with Edgar. There was no major change of heart that he ever communicated to me in the closing months of 2015 or after his hospice admission in late January 2016.

I knew he read the books I gave him, which were later returned to me. I knew they mildly influenced him to rethink his position. He said as much in his final weeks, but sadly he never communicated any substantial change in his outlook to me during the end stages of his life. All he said was that he was ready for where this journey would take him, even in the "unlikely event" that it took him nowhere at all. I took this to mean he was now receptive to survival. That was at least some progress.

I prayed intensely for Edgar and his family as he was nearing the end. I kept them all in the forefront of my daily meditations. During one of these meditations, on or about January 29, 2016, I had a flash of insight which I quickly conveyed to Edgar's immediate family by email. I told them I felt certain Edgar would make his transition either on January 31, 2016, the 45th anniversary of Apollo 14's blast-off from Cape Kennedy, or during the wee hours of February 5th, 2016 which would be the 45th anniversary of the date Edgar first stepped foot on the lunar surface.

Sure enough, on February 4, 2016, at approximately 9:30 pm, Edgar Mitchell drew his final breath in this storied incarnation. He blasted off yet again, but this time bound for the other side, the next world, not the moon. His death occurred just a few hours shy of when he first stepped foot on the moon forty-five years ago to the date. I was nearly spot on in my prediction, off by only a few hours.

It sure seems to me that Edgar David Mitchell attempted to deliberately time his own death to coincide with the 45th anniversary of the Apollo 14 mission, at Hospice of Palm Beach County, just off 45th Street, in West Palm Beach.

By timing his own death in this manner, I believe Edgar intended to send a powerful message to us all about the limitless power of our consciousness to fulfill our intention, even to determine the timing of our own death, which many hospice experts will attest often happens among terminally ill patients. I believe he also meant it as a nudge-nudge/wink-wink to me that his view of survival after death had indeed changed, as evidenced by this last great symbolic feat. He later confirmed this for me through a medium.

There is no question that Edgar applied all the strength and willpower he could muster in those final days and weeks to endure as long as he could in a failing body so that he could lift off from this world once more to explore new worlds in a manner that coincided with his Apollo 14 mission forty-five years earlier, but this time without need of a Saturn Five Rocket. He mystified everyone in his family and those caring for him at hospice by stretching out his life as long as he did under the circumstances, all to demonstrate a very important teaching: *consciousness is at cause and matter is at effect.*

Hospice personnel will attest to the well-known fact that dying patients can and often do exert some degree of control over the timing of the actual physical death, just as Edgar did. One such example very close to home is my father, John Paul Audette. He left this world for the next at around 4:25 a.m. on December 25, 1985 at age 69. A proud WWII vet who fought the Nazis in Europe, he died at the VA Medical Center in Augusta, Georgia.

Dad had terminal chronic obstructive pulmonary disease, (COPD), otherwise known as emphysema. He was a life-long heavy smoker, two packs a day. He was a big fan of Lucky Strike, Camel, Pall Mall and Chesterfield cigarettes. Hard core. No filter. He would not quit smoking despite the constant pleadings of his family. Sadly, he was heavily addicted to the habit.

For some reason unknown to me, Dad really wanted to die on Christmas day. Although it was predicted by his doctors that he would pass much sooner, he did not leave us until Christmas day 1985. I spent most of Christmas Eve with him.

That night, he kept asking me, "Are you sure tomorrow is Christmas, Johnny?"

"Yes, Dad, I'm sure," I said. "Why do you keep asking me that same question? Why is it so important to you?"

"Oh, it's nothing," he answered. "I just want to be sure that tomorrow is Christmas." Soon after his death, I was inspired to write a poignant song about it. I called it "Is it Christmas, Johnny?" Please visit *AffirmingGod.com* to view the lyrics.

But Edgar's timing of his own death was in another league altogether. He clung to life in a greatly diminished deteriorated state for a long time, well past what his doctors thought would be physically possible. That he was able to endure as long as he did was impressive if not miraculous.

This act of willpower was one final great symbolic achievement by Edgar, no less important or substantial than traveling into outer space and landing on the moon. It was one last contribution by Edgar on the occasion of his departure from earth, yet again, 45 years later, a priceless one at that, to help stimulate the evolution of humanity.

I believe Edgar's final act of greatness was meant to remind us all about the power of intention to affect physical reality. It was a dramatic demonstration of mind over matter. I feel certain he did it to convey a clarion call to his fellow human beings — that we should awaken to the boundless power of applied evolved consciousness in service to the greater good of all in the spirit of unconditional love.

After-Death Communication and Contact

Bill Guggenheim, my long-time close friend, wrote a seminal book about after-death communication and contact (ADCs) called *Hello from Heaven!* based on pioneering original research. It is now a classic work. I often give it to bereaved individuals who have recently lost a loved one.

Many find Bill's book to be quite uplifting and helpful. It describes the many ways in which the dearly departed can and do reach out from the other side to their loved ones still in this plane of existence. Another good selection on this topic is Annie Kagan's lovely book, *The Afterlife of Billy Fingers.*

After-Death Communication is a spiritual experience which occurs when one is contacted directly and spontaneously by a deceased family member or friend without the use of psychics, mediums, rituals, or devices of any kind.

After-death contact can include smells like perfume fragrances or cigars, visions, dreams and sightings. Spirit can also use electronic equipment to communicate. We may hear a voice, feel a presence, or even receive a phone call or voice message from our deceased loved one. We might see the lights flicker or have something unusual happen with the radio, cell phone, iPad, TV or computer. We might even witness the movement of physical objects.

The most commonly reported of all spiritually transformative experiences are ADCs. I have been blessed to have several such encounters, four of which are shared here.

Two Misses of Errant Hockey Pucks

On February 16, 2016, a mere 12 days after the passing of Dr. Edgar Mitchell, I had previously scheduled a session with my medium friend, the one from Archangel Michael fame. It was scheduled several months in advance and was not in any way timed to coincide with Edgar's passing. I had several impressive sessions with this medium.

Yet the session that took place on February 16, 2016 was amazing. This time, to my great surprise and delight, instead of communicating with Archangel Michael as I had expected, Dr. Edgar Mitchell came through loud and clear.

I did not ask about Edgar. I actually thought Michael would be coming through again. But this time, it was Edgar and there was much he wanted to say. What he said was quite important, and in typical Edgar fashion, he found a creative way to verify for me that this was indeed a genuine communication from him, not simply my own fantasy. He confirmed it twice, first at a hockey game the night before and second through the gifted medium who relayed his important messages to me the very next day after the hockey game.

During this session, the medium conveyed information to me that only I knew, as well as other information that I did not know but was able to confirm later after the fact. I feel it is best not to share all of the details of this session but suffice it to say that Edgar came through unmistakably and undeniably. He validated many things for me during this session, including his attempt to deliberately time his death as explained previously. So, yes, based on this verification from Edgar after death, I do believe my theory about the timing of his passing is an accurate interpretation of the events that took place and their symbolic meaning.

I will share one other major detail from this session with this medium. It concerns two errant hockey pucks that whizzed closely by my head, as well as a verified after-death communication from Edgar, all during a hockey game between the Florida Panthers and the Pittsburgh Penguins on Monday, February 15, 2016, in Sunrise, Florida. I attended this game with a very close friend from third grade onward, Jimmy Madonna. He was in town visiting from Pittsburgh. He was then and still remains a passionate fan of the Penguins, his hometown team.

I rarely go to sporting events of any kind, and certainly never hockey. My attendance there that night was an exceptional event, done only as a favor to Jimmy. I knew it was really important to him.

During the game, even with terrific home team seats mid-ring 5th row, I was totally bored. As my mind drifted off to cloud nine from boredom, I strongly felt the presence of Edgar Mitchell, who had died just 12 days before. I was not thinking about him beforehand, but he suddenly grew heavy on my mind. I was intensely grieving his loss.

Soon after, I began to receive thoughts that seemed to come from him. They were expressed in my own voice but not formed in or from my own mind that I could discern. I honestly felt like Edgar just popped inside my head for a visit. He wanted to say hello, send love and wish me well, but there were a few other things too. He confirmed what he now knew for certain, that consciousness survives bodily death. He also gave me what I will describe as a crude beginning to define the term consciousness. It is a definition I had shared with him many times before, which he verified for me from the other side during this session.

During our long friendship, we often discussed the seminal role of consciousness and unconditional love as the organizing principle of the universe. We speculated that these factors are the centerpiece of the cosmos, the underlying causal force or "First Cause" of all life within. We often debated the primacy of consciousness, whether consciousness is at cause and matter at effect, yet we fell short of reaching a conclusion or an actual definition of consciousness that we could agree upon.

But to my great surprise, in the spontaneous "thought implants" I received at the hockey game from Edgar, he explained to me what I often shared with him during our many exchanges on the subject. To my delight, Edgar finally agreed with me that consciousness can only be defined as that which is an eternal indestructible aspect or spark of Creator present within all things. He concurred that consciousness is aware, discrete and individuated but also enjoined and entangled with the entire matrix of creation; that it is neither matter nor energy; that embedded in it is an incessant longing or yearning to return to the Source from whence it and all things come; and that it is destined to reunite or reintegrate eventually with the infinitely intelligent origin of all things which we call God or Creator.

Edgar's preferred definition of the term "God" was "ground of being," so I was shocked to hear this interpretation of consciousness from him. I seriously doubted it was coming from him. He had been an avowed agnostic for most of his life. I figured I was imagining what I would like to hear him say, but not what he actually said.

Frankly, it was not a steady flow of words conveyed by him, but more like an imprint in my mind of specific messages from him coming more or less in composite form. They were implanted conceptual impressions that came from him, but fully consistent with the point of view I conveyed to Edgar during many discussions on the subject throughout our long friendship.

As a trained scientist whose doctorate was from MIT, Edgar studied consciousness from all angles and perspectives for many years, but never one that linked it to God or defined it as a God particle. Rather, Edgar repeatedly doubted God's existence during all the years I knew him, so I seriously doubted that this message came from him. It had to be my own fantasy.

Yet, if I heard him correctly, the conclusion he reached after-death was that consciousness could only be defined as a tiny eternal aspect of God that dwells within all things. This had always been my unwavering opinion, but never his.

Nevertheless, based on the information which the medium shared with me on February 16, 2016, I believe I experienced spontaneous after-death communication with Edgar Mitchell in which he defined consciousness as a minute derivative aspect of God that dwells within all things.

I caution the reader to take this for what it's worth. I cannot prove that this was an authentic message from Edgar, or that I heard him correctly, or that I interpreted what he said accurately. But there are certain things I can prove which may legitimize that this was an authentic communication with Edgar.

After his musings about consciousness, he gave me strong encouragement to press on with our work, adding that he would continue to help me from the realm of Spirit. He apologized for not doing more to advance our work while he was alive. He said he wished he had not been so opposed to the spiritual perspective of reality but that his training had strongly molded him in this manner.

These are the messages I thought I heard Edgar convey. I told no one about this. *No one.* Only my wife, father-in-law and friend Jimmy knew I attended the hockey game, but no one knew anything about what happened to me at the game in relation to Edgar, and I never told anyone about my afterlife communication with him.

But during the session with the medium the very next day after the game, Edgar came through unmistakably. This is what he said to me through her on that occasion. He told the medium he wanted to dialogue with me regularly from the other side to convey important information and ideas. He wanted her to inform me that communicating with the other side is quite simple, sort of like "a hockey puck going back and forth from sender to receiver and receiver to sender," akin to a hockey puck whizzing by one's head.

Then the medium said, "John, Edgar is showing me that this metaphor about the hockey puck whizzing by your head has a double meaning for you." I was thunderstruck hearing these words from her. "Yes, it does indeed have a double meaning for me," I said, as my entire body became one huge goose bump.

That was when I told the medium about being at a hockey game the night before. I explained this was a very rare occurrence for me. I told her about the two errant hockey pucks that whizzed by my head during that game. She was startled, amazed and flabbergasted.

Jimmy witnessed the two errant hockey pucks and was impressed that both missed me. Truthfully, I did not dodge them. I was just damn lucky neither one hit me. They flew through the air bullet fast, hardly visible. They travel so fast that they cannot be dodged any more than one can parry a bullet.

Yes, I believe the puck metaphor was Edgar's way of validating the connection with him in real time coming through the medium then and there, but also to authenticate the messages I thought I received from him the night before during the hockey game.

What are the odds that Edgar would mention a hockey puck during the session with the medium the very next day? What are the odds he would also tell me through the medium that the hockey puck had a double meaning for me?

Strangely, I was nearly hit by an errant hockey puck not once but twice during the game, as if to add emphasis, confirming the authenticity of his communication with me in bold-face italics, not just then through the medium, but also the night before during the hockey game.

Somehow, both times, the errant pucks escaped the safety net and whizzed by me on the right side of my head at a high rate of speed. Both times the pucks missed me, thank God! A direct hit from either one probably would have been fatal. And at the time both flew by my head, I was receiving after-death communications from Edgar. What are the odds of that?

I think Edgar was trying to draw my attention to the puck as a symbol to convey the meaning he later explained to the medium about how after-death communication works. I think he wanted me to learn how to do it so we could communicate regularly so he could help to advance our work from the realm of Spirit.

What's more, that night when I told Chuck Lesher, my comedian father-in-law (also from Pittsburgh), who was living with my wife and me at that time, that I was off to watch the Penguins play the Panthers, his humorous reply was, "I don't give a puck!"

Again, the puck symbol surfaced as something I should pay attention to and take sharp notice of, but its meaning did not become clear to me until my session with the medium the very next day when she relayed interesting instructions to me from Edgar about how to facilitate after-death communication.

After the game, I dropped Jimmy off at the Fort Lauderdale home of his brother where he was staying. Then I continued the drive to my home, about 30 minutes away. It gave me time to further contemplate the two errant pucks that narrowly missed me and the meaty messages I received from Edgar about consciousness at the time they were whizzing by me.

As I was thinking intensely about these things, Edgar came through again, prominently, to say more about consciousness. I wrote a summary of what he conveyed to me as soon as I returned home, as much of it as I could remember. As I wrote the summary, more insight flowed into me from him, presumably, which guided my writing.

These were ideas he conveyed to me during this time, and although I had said as much to him in many past conversations, and completely agreed with everything he communicated in that moment, it did not sound like the Edgar I knew during his lifetime.

In addition to what I have already reported, this is what he conveyed to me later that night in a steady flow or stream of information. I believe it was "channeled" to me from him, almost as if to parrot back to me many of the same insights I had earlier shared with him during so many previous discussions in real life. Again, these ideas were conveyed as conceptual impressions in composite form, all of which Edgar was affirming as they came through to me.

Thought and the ability to think, creativity, memory, perception, emotion, cognition and self-awareness are by-products and manifestations of brain processes and the mind, but they do not represent the entirety or whole of consciousness. Consciousness is not the brain and the brain is not consciousness.

Rather, consciousness is core immortal inner essence. It is the God-given capacity for awareness, curiosity, creativity and thought. It is what animates physical form. It is also that which drives the longing and yearning to return to Source from whence all things came. It is what produces the inner craving to be re-united with the Source that brought all things into being in the first place.

All creation and consciousness are derivative of Source/Creator, the one infinite intelligence that has spawned all things. For eternity, they remain inextricably linked to Source/Creator and forever they remain aspects or particles of Source/Creator inter-connected through the zero-point energy field. Therefore, all things are the children or progeny of Source/Creator, which is that from whence all things came and to which all things eventually return.

And because of this fundamental fact, all things are therefore blessed with at least some level of awareness, sentience or consciousness because all things are tiny derivative aspects of the one infinite consciousness which created them, and which blessed them with existence and the sentience that comes with existence.

This is true if only by virtue of the fact that all things are equal participants in quantum processes. All things are comprised of molecules, atoms and sub-atomic particles, collectively referred to as quanta. Through quantum coherence, cohesion and entanglement, as well as quantum non-locality, nothing can be accurately viewed as truly inanimate, not even a blade of grass, or a drop of water, or a piece of wood, or a rock or boulder, for all these things contain quanta and are fully active participants in fundamental quantum processes.

Source created everything including the collective capacity for all aspects of creation to function as co-creators. As integral parts of Source's creation, all things possess a *divine spark* within that qualifies them as participants in co-creation. But as only tiny parts of the whole, they are nowhere near equal to the Source/Creator of the whole. Moreover, they are not the entire whole unto itself except in gross potential, which is only realized when all aspects of creation reintegrate with the whole that is Creator to form a fully God-realized unified matrix, also known as the "Godhead."

This reintegration with the whole occurs when constituent minute parts or aspects of creation match the core signature vibration or frequency of Creator, which is the core vibration and frequency of pure unconditional love.

So, yes, a single drop of water can be removed from the ocean and thus can be represented by that tiny drop. But the drop is not the ocean, and the ocean is not the drop, yet one is both derived and constituted from the other, hence they remain enjoined, interconnected and entangled energetically at the quantum level. Thus, the part is in the whole and the whole is in the part, much like DNA which can re-create the entire form that once originally housed it.

It is true that every individuated, differentiated consciousness takes on unique expression. It is true that consciousness changes and evolves over time. It is also true that consciousness exists as a continuum. The least evolved would be basic awareness and free will without a cognizant connection to the divine. It would be consciousness which is in the dark so to speak, farthest removed from divine light. This is the place where evil springs forth and breeds, because it is devoid of divine light, love and compassion.

At the other end of the spectrum is consciousness that is completely optimized or fully God-realized with maximum connection to and cognizance of Creator in an ideal state of oneness, reunion or attunement with Creator. This is achieved when an individual consciousness reaches a state of pure enlightenment. Such a state of existence is marked by being the perfect expression or manifestation of unconditional love.

In this highly evolved state, the fully God-realized individual, who is a derivative component aspect or spark of divine consciousness, achieves total parity with Source/Creator by achieving perfect alignment or resonance at the same frequency or vibration of Source/Creator.

To exemplify this further, consider the analogy of a radio. When it is tuned perfectly to the right frequency, one receives a perfect and clear connection to the transmitting source. When it is not perfectly tuned to the right frequency, one hears only static.

Another analogy is a musical instrument, any instrument. When it is finely tuned, it produces the perfect expression of musical notes across the entire scale or range of musical notes, thus enabling the performance of beautiful music that is quite pleasing to the ear. When it is out of tune, one cannot make beautiful music, but only a cacophony of discordant sounds.

A perfectly tuned instrument of consciousness is one that is fully enlightened in a constant state of unconditional love and oneness with all things. One goes with the other. One cannot exist without the other. To be in oneness is to be in a state of unconditional love. To be in unconditional love is to be in oneness.

In that highly evolved state of being, a human being can command quanta. This is how Christ was able to perform miracles like walking on water, changing water to wine, and so on. He was the ultimate alchemist because He could command air, water, fire and earth. He could command quanta, and thereby was able to feed the masses from a single loaf of never-ending bread.

Creator engendered the entire cosmos as a laboratory with which to experiment, co-create and spiritually evolve, but also designed it as a sandbox in which to play. All sparks of the divine are empowered to co-create with free will, but the creative choices made of and born by free will produce like and corresponding results or consequences in a cause-effect, action-reaction matrix as designed by Creator.

Loving actions and choices produce loving consequences. Unloving, uncaring and unkind choices create and result in corresponding consequences of the same genre.

In this context, it is important to examine what is evil. It is not some exogenous force that forces people to act or behave in ways that are contrary to divine intent.

Like everything else that manifests in one's personal orbit, evil is a free will choice, one that is born of ignorance, flawed thinking and erroneous perceptions of reality, as well as a false concept or image of oneself.

Evil is merely the absence of love and a denial of the divine. It is a conscious deliberate choice to dismiss, turn away from and ignore the single greatest force in the universe, which is unconditional love. Evil breeds in the darkness where and when divine light has been refused and rejected.

What should be done in the face of evil? First, it must be accurately understood for what it is and there must be clarity about what causes it. Second, it should be met head on face to face with an abundance of overpowering unconditional love to remedy, rectify and transmute it. That is love's mission. That is love's job. No force in the universe is more powerful. And when love fulfills this task throughout the entire cosmos, then all things will achieve singularity in a sublime state of non-duality and total perfect oneness with Source/Creator. This is the destiny of all things.

When this takes place, the reunion and reintegration of all dispersed derivative aspects of Creator will have been completed. All will be returned to its original state of perfection as it was in the beginning, one complete harmonious whole.

This is why mystics say that unconditional love is the primary organizing principle of the universe. There can be no other. And the path toward perfect manifestation of perfect unconditional love is indeed the only path to walk. It is the only path that makes sense. It is the only path that will lead all things back home from whence all things originally came. It is the only dance there is.

Consciousness is the key to everything. It is the primal originating catalyst underlying all of creation. This is why consciousness can only be properly referenced as a spark of the divine, that which is the primordial fundamental creative force in the cosmos. This also explains why consciousness is so hard to define, for it is tantamount to attempting a definition of God. Thus, defining consciousness is no less a formidable task than trying to formulate an accurate definition of Source/Creator, for crudely speaking, consciousness is derived from a tiny aspect of God, its "soul" Source.

Remember, everything that has ever come into being first originated in thought and intention, as an idea or perhaps a dream longing to come true. It is vital to realize that what is seen or observed was first born in the realm of the unseen. The un-manifest becomes the manifest. The implicate order becomes the explicate order. It does not happen the other way around.

Well, there it is. This is the information Edgar imparted to me from the other side, as best as I can remember. But understand that I am not a medium, a channel or a psychic. I am only reporting what actually happened to me on February 15th and 16th, 2016, a short while after Edgar died. From a qualitative point of view, I cannot differentiate between this download from Edgar Mitchell and the one I received in April 1994 to form an international association for the scientific study of spiritually transformative experiences.

Please note that this point of view as expressed by Edgar, or so I believe, completely dovetails with my own personal point of view. While here in physical form, it was never a viewpoint he shared. However, it is quite common for people who have crossed over to the other side and returned to change their perspective about the nature of reality. It is conceivable that Edgar could have had a change in his outlook which is what I personally take away from this communication.

In the session with the medium, she authenticated Edgar's channeling to me. She shared with me things I did not know but was able to verify later. I have had very little communication since then from Edgar. He has occasionally appeared in my dreams, but not in any context that qualifies as meaningful or instructive.

I believe it was a genuine communication from him, but I certainly cannot prove it beyond what I have shared here. In any event, the information about the nature of consciousness is all conjecture until science is able to prove or disprove it. That said, frontier science has already made a defensible and plausible case for the nature of consciousness and its survival after death. It is waiting for traditional mainstream science to catch up, "one funeral at a time," in the words of Max Planck.

In April 2016, soon after Edgar died, I enjoyed an extended visit with Dr. Ervin Laszlo in Tuscany, Italy, near Cecina, as a guest in his lovely home. He and Dr. Mitchell were friends, so I told him about my encounter with the gifted medium, the hockey game, the hockey pucks and the information Edgar imparted to me about consciousness. I also arranged for him to have a session with this same medium, which he considered to be most impressive.

Ervin found the story fascinating. He thought Edgar's remarks about consciousness were "compelling, if not soul-stirring." He said it was "the most original definition of consciousness" he had ever heard. Dr. Laszlo is the author of over 90 books. He often writes about consciousness from a frontier science perspective.

I whole-heartedly believe and propose that consciousness is the elusive missing link Einstein was searching for in the last years of his celebrated life. At long last, frontier science is now equipped to test this assertion in its quest to develop a robust "Theory of Everything" or "TOE." From this effort, a valid unified field theory may emerge and the long-sought "Holy Grail" of science might surface.

The embryonic field of "torsion physics" is the new cutting edge for science in its quest for TOE. Some scientists consider this field to be quackery or pseudo-science. I firmly disagree. Rather, I believe it holds great promise. One day it may help us achieve a better understanding of how consciousness intersects and interfaces with matter through the phenomenon of "torsion waves," or "spin fields," what some call "spirality" or "quantum twisting."

Einstein and French mathematician Elie Cartan first coined the term "torsion wave" in 1913 in the context of their postulation that the entire cosmos is interconnected through quantum entanglement. Their keen observation further expounded on the pioneering work of the Russian scientist N.P. Myshkin, who in the late 1800s, postulated the existence of an embedded matrix or implicate order underlying the whole of creation…an implicate order which interfaces with human consciousness through these scalar torsion waves or spin fields.

Myshkin asserted that these fields facilitate the construction of an etheric bridge which enables cause-effect relationships to arise between thought, intention and matter. Simply put, every atom emits torsion waves as it vibrates, essentially forming small vortices created by the spin fields which are spawned by particle rotation. These small vortices create a sacred geometric pattern or vibrating effect which impacts particle behavior and hence influences the disposition of matter. These waves are not mass or energy. Rather, they are theorized to be information conveying intention.

The essential thesis is that the micro-spin or twisting of sub-atomic particles is what ultimately gives rise to macro outcomes in space-time physical reality, all guided by feeling, thought and intention. Here it is necessary to remember the Fundamental Force in nature, also known as Fundamental Interaction, and nature's Four Basic Forces: Gravity, Electromagnetism, the Strong Force and the Weak Force, all of which govern how objects or particles interact and how certain particles decay.

Heretofore, science theorized that all the known forces of nature could be traced to these four Fundamental Forces. But what has been missing in this equation all along is a hypothesized Fifth Force, conceived initially by Dr. Myshkin: torsion waves. Torsion waves spiral or twist through gravity, creating spin fields which propagate the fabric of space-time. They are engendered by intention, thought and emotion.

Torsion spirals are non-local measurable "carrier waves" of consciousness, which through spin, spiraling or twisting, produce waves that impact matter with a vibrating effect, as if in a fluid-like etheric medium. This phenomenon explains the mechanisms underlying psychokinesis and teleportation, as well as the process through which human intention directs particle behavior, hence matter itself.

In the 1950s, Russian astrophysicist Dr. N.A. Kozyrev conclusively demonstrated that human thoughts, feelings and intentions generate torsion waves. He did so by observing vibrations in an etheric medium. Torsion waves have been experimentally demonstrated convincingly in the constitution of plants and in water, which are decisively influenced by human thought, emotion and intention. The phenomenon has also been demonstrated in studies at the great pyramids of Egypt, whose inherent structure naturally amplifies torsion waves and spin fields within gravity and the fabric of time-space.

Basic internet research will reveal much more about this fascinating subject but understand that science is just beginning to peek through a tiny crack in the tightly closed door of scalar-torsion technology. When work in this area reaches its apex, I believe that the theories of evolution, intelligent design and creationism will be seen not as mutually exclusive competing belief systems, but rather as essential pillars in an overarching holistic explanation of how the cosmos came into being, how it is structured and how it functions.

I also believe that TOE will come into being at this time along with the confirmed triumphant discovery of Einstein's missing link, one that convincingly links general relativity with quantum mechanics. I whole heartedly propose that consciousness is the bridge that will link these two schools of thought.

When science finally embraces TOE, a unique integrative convergent model that marries these three competing schools of thought will become the new order of the day, I predict. Heretofore, they have been in conflict with each other, but arrival at a scientifically accepted TOE will unify them under the same explanatory rubric.

Dr. Edgar Mitchell, speaking to me from the other side, would concur with these sentiments, presumably. Author Nancy Van Domelen conveyed similar and wholly compatible ideas in her 2011 book entitled *A Spark of the Divine,* all based on information she channeled from an extraterrestrial source known as "The Lightbringers." They use the same analogy or metaphor of a "spark" of God or from God to explain consciousness and to define the eternal essence of human beings as an indestructible derivative aspect of the divine which is eternal in nature.

Tangentially and ironically, I learned that Edgar's ex-wife, Sheilah (Adam's mother) died quickly without much warning after rapid onset of a sudden illness, on September 8, 2021 at St. Mary's Medical Center in Saint Louis, Missouri, at the young age of 72. In what I can best describe as a strange coincidence, Edgar died at the inpatient facility for Hospice of Palm Beach County located adjacent to the campus of St. Mary's Medical Center in West Palm Beach.

Perhaps this coincidence, or synchronicity, that they both died at and/or near a facility named after St. Mary has no transcendent meaning. But, on the other hand, perhaps it does suggest something. I do not know, and I am not sure, but it is uncanny and probably worth noting.

Sheilah and Edgar were married in April 1989 but were romantically involved long before that, beginning in 1983. They divorced in July 1998 but remained in close contact with each other, especially during Adam's illness, which was really a rough time for the entire extended family and many close friends.

For many years, Edgar's nephew, Mitch Harkins, was a big part of Edgar's daily life as his housemate, groundskeeper, chef, handyman, auto mechanic and runner of most errands, like frequent trips to the grocery store. He also took care of two beautiful German Shepherd dogs named Hoss and Zeba that freely roamed the five-acre Mitchell estate on Western Way in Lake Worth. Without Mitch's daily assistance with all manner of chores, Edgar would have been lost.

Sadly, on June 28, 2018, Mitch died in Inverness, Florida, at the young age of 50, a little more than two years after Edgar's passing. Now, poignantly speaking, all four are on the other side, sorting it all out. God bless them and may St. Mary, Mother Mary, restore their souls beside the still waters.

Not long ago, Mitch, Sheilah, Adam and Edgar were all here very much alive and well on earth, routinely a part of my life for a good number of years. But now all are departed. Strangely, they left this world in relatively close temporal proximity to one another, which in itself seems quite curious to me.

Critics may say I am reading way too much into these stories about Catherine, Chuck, David, Adam and Edgar. I could describe many more cases I personally witnessed, equally powerful as the ones I shared, but I chose these accounts because they are closely connected to me on a personal level. As such, they have had the greatest emotional impact.

Still, critics might argue that my subjective interpretation of these subjective occurrences proves nothing and over-reaches the data, which reminds me of a famous quote by Mark Twain: "It's not what you don't know that will get you into trouble. It's what you think you know for sure that just ain't so."

Well, at the risk of ignoring Twain's wisdom, in all humility, the interpretation of events is one that I wholeheartedly believe to be valid. It is what I know to be true as a matter of deep abiding conviction based on direct personal experience. Still, there is no generally accepted explanation for them in the current scientific paradigm.

Truth can be very different from that which is perceived to be true. And it is certainly true that when it comes to matters pertaining to the nature of reality, consciousness and life after death, we are just beginning to scratch the surface. At best, we fumble around in our efforts to make educated guesses, using crude scientific methodologies to make discoveries that can be validated by replication under scrutiny of peer review. Still, our knowledge and methods are incomplete and imperfect.

I am not a scientist. I make no claim to be one. But I embrace science and I share the rigor and discipline of scientists in questing for truth. I have no interest in falsehoods, illusions, half-truths, dogmas or pseudo-science. I hold no opinions except those which I believe are defensible and fully supported by credible evidence.

When I come to regard something as true, it is not because I want it to be true or need it to be true, but rather because through a methodical systematic process of rigorous inquiry, I have determined it to be true. Truth, that is scientific truth, can only be found through disciplined observation and rigorous analysis of credible empirical data in a peer reviewed fashion. But truth of the best kind, God's truth, can only be found by going deep within through meditation or *Forest-Bathing* or *Streaming* or some other induction technique described in a subsequent section.

Therefore, all my expressed convictions, views and positions are data-driven and evidence-based. I learned a long time ago through trial and error that chasing butterflies in the field while walking along the primrose path wearing rose-colored glasses is a complete waste of one's time and energy. It serves no purpose to indulge in fiction or fantasy. So, as a matter of disciplined routine, I do my utmost to seek out only truth and represent only truth, objectively speaking. Truth, that is God's truth, is the only thing that interests me. And, yes, I assure you, it is the truth that will set us free.

Marbles the Cat

The second after-death contact I wish to share concerns our deceased cat named Marbles. Vivian Lesher, my spouse since January 1991, is widely known in our neighborhood as the Patron Saint of Feral Felines. The title is most fitting. Vivian is a compassionate, empathetic person who is highly sensitive to the suffering of others, especially homeless hungry animals, hence Eternea's *Distressed Animals Assistance Program*, an outreach initiative, part of our *Love in Action* project.

Ever since I first met her in the fall of 1990, Vivian has made it a practice to feed colonies of feral cats on a daily basis, without fail, wherever we make our home at any given point in time. And even if we move to a new neighborhood, somehow, in short order, the feral colonies find her without fail. It's uncanny, almost as if she has a built-in homing beacon for feral cats.

Most of the time, she feeds these colonies twice each day. She does this quietly and stealth-like, without fanfare or recognition. She does it from the goodness of her own heart and at considerable financial expense. She does it every day without fail, devoting several hours each day not only to preparing their meals, but also washing the dishware she uses to serve their meals, and then she washes out the aluminum cat food cans to prepare them for recycling, complete with removing their labels too.

If that is not enough to impress, well she also traps feral cats to have them spayed, neutered and vaccinated by local veterinarians, and to arrange treatment to those who are injured or ill with one condition or another. She works tirelessly to help these cats who cannot help themselves, emanating from her impressive sensitivity for life, all life. She does what she does because she cannot bear the thought of these animals suffering. The simple satisfaction she gets from her efforts is to see them content after a meal and to see them well again after treatment for any number of issues.

To be sure, the cost of cat food has skyrocketed over the past year but the cost of consulting a veterinarian has become outrageously high. It has reached the level of total absurdity to the point where it is unaffordable except for non-profit shelters with vets on staff. Most of them are operating on overload these days, way beyond capacity. Good luck with trying to get an appointment.

In 1996, one of the feral cats that came to Vivian was pregnant. After she gave birth, when her five kittens could be safely separated, Viv found homes for all but one. He was the runt of the litter, a tiny fellow all black in color with green eyes. We could not find a home for him. So even though we had already reached our maximum quota of "inside cats," we added him to the inside family.

Our four-year old daughter quickly fell in love with him. She named him Marbles. They became fast friends. He instantly became her baby, replacing all the other dolls she had on hand at the time. He would let her dress him in infant clothing with impressive tolerance and did not seem to mind being rolled around the neighborhood in her baby stroller.

Marbles remained very small in size, which is typical for runts of the litter. He was a mellow easygoing cat. He was not territorial and never played alpha male cat games of dominance. He never killed anything, like birds or lizards. He was a "live and let live" animal. Frankly, he almost seemed as highly evolved as cats can get because he had such a pleasant peaceful demeanor.

Sadly, Marbles died in late 2018 at the age of 22, which is quite old for a cat. He hung in there with us as long as he could. He wanted to squeeze in every last minute he could with us. We hated to see him go and he hated to leave. His death left us very sad and mournful. Of all our cats, he was the most loved because he was just that special and unique. Yes, they all are special, but him more so.

The weighty chore of burying Marbles' lifeless body in our backyard fell upon me. It always does whenever we lose a beloved pet. I surveyed the yard, found a good spot and then dug a grave for him, about two feet wide and three feet deep.

When I reached the bottom of the grave, I noticed an odd stone. It was all black in color. I have never seen a stone like that in our yard before. It was peculiar. I placed Marbles' body in the grave and placed the odd stone on top of him, and then backfilled the hole.

After I finished the backfilling chore, much to my surprise, there was that same black stone lying on the ground off to the side of the grave. I was shocked to see it. I know I placed it on top of Marbles' body before I backfilled the hole. I clearly saw it there when I said a parting prayer for him. How in the world this stone ended up on the surface of the ground after I backfilled the hole is a mystery to me, one I cannot explain. So, I put it in my pocket, brought it into our house, washed it and put it on the desk in my study.

In the days that followed, I kept staring at this stone. It seemed to demand or draw my attention. After being nudged intuitively to pick it up and study it more closely, I noticed it was clearly in the shape of a heart. That's an odd shape for a stone, I thought. I also wondered what kind of stone it was because in the many years we've lived here in our home, I have never come across one like it. So, I took it to a gemologist friend the following week.

He examined it closely with a magnifying glass. My jaw dropped when he identified it as a piece of black marble in the curious shape of a heart. He asked where it came from. I told him I found it in my backyard three feet down below grade at the bottom of a grave I dug for Marbles, our black cat who had just died.

My gemologist friend was plainly taken aback. "John, there is no marble here underground in the soil of South Florida, and certainly none near the ocean where you live. It is most unusual and irregular to find this stone where you did." I thanked him for his efforts and then returned home with the stone to tell Vivian what I had just learned. Tears of joy were streaming down my cheeks the whole way. I instantly realized this stone was a bona fide after-death communication from our dearly departed beloved cat.

"Marbles has sent us a clever gift from the beyond," I told her. "Here, hold this stone. Examine it closely."

"It seems to be shaped like a heart," Vivian said. "What kind of stone is it?" she asked.

"Hold on to your hat," I advised. "It's black marble! I found it in our backyard at the bottom of the grave I dug for Marbles, but there is not supposed to be any black marble in our soil."

"What do you make of it?" Vivian asked.

"Marbles clearly sent us a message from the beyond," I replied. "The stone is shaped like a heart. What does a heart symbolize?" I asked.

"Love," she replied.

"Yes, love," I said. "Marbles is sending us love and gratitude from the other side in the only way we could know it was coming from him.

Obviously, Marbles could not convey his sentiments through the spoken word, so how ingenious it was to do it in the form of a stone shaped like a heart…a stone that is entirely black in color and marble in constitution…a unique stone that is not indigenous to our area. I could dig 500 holes in our backyard and never find another piece of black marble. It is not supposed to be here."

"You really think this came from Marbles and that he's sending us a message from the great beyond?" Vivian asked.

"Yes, I do. That's what I believe, dearest. I think Marbles felt our pain over losing him. I think he tried to ease that pain by manifesting this particular stone in the shape of a heart at the bottom of the grave I dug for him. I think he's saying love is eternal. I believe he is sending us reassurance that his life and all life continues on after death. I believe he is saying thank you for taking such good care of me and for loving me so dearly all those years. That's what I make of it."

Vivian formed big crocodile tears of joy when I shared my thoughts with her about Marbles. They grew much bigger still when I told her that the size of the stone closely approximates the size of Marbles' actual heart. It was cathartic for her, as though all the cumulative grief she felt from all the cats she lost to death in the past had suddenly been purged through this surreal manifestation.

The stone remains in her jewelry box. She takes it out and holds it from time to time, especially when she feels overwhelmed by sadness and grief related to the loss of a beloved animal. It is a stone we now cherish as a family heirloom, which we will one day bequeath to our daughter. Maybe she'll make a necklace out of it and wear it faithfully as a reminder of Marbles and of us too, when it becomes our time to leave.

To see the Marbles' stone, please visit *AffirmingGod.com*.

Charles Rodman Lesher

For several months after Chuck's passing, my wife and I deeply grieved his loss. He was such a big part of our daily lives for so long that his absence was a big adjustment for us both. But more than that, we missed his company, his corny jokes and his off-the-wall recital of oddball factoids. We also had lots of extra time on our hands, time we normally would have devoted to caring for Chuck's daily needs.

For quite some time, there was no other-worldly message from him, no sign he was alive and well on the other side enjoying the realm of Spirit. But just before Thanksgiving 2018, I went into what had been Chuck's bedroom to open the blinds and greet the brand new sunny day. I surveyed the room as I always did and took note of a painting that hung on the wall beside what had been Chuck's recliner, his favorite chair. It was hanging crooked, off-center by at least 25 degrees. That's quite odd, I thought. Without dwelling on the cause, I simply straightened it and paid it no further mind.

A few days after that, the same artwork was crooked again, but this time 25 degrees in the other direction. Once again, I straightened it and gave no thought whatsoever to what might have caused it to move off-center. This went on for a few weeks, but I never connected it with Chuck. I never once thought he was the cause of it.

Then one day in early 2019, when I made my early-morning rounds of our household, I noticed several works of art at odd angles in various rooms, including our family room and living room. All of them were off center by 20 to 30 degrees. How strange! I thought. As I went about straightening them, I began to wonder what could be causing this bizarre occurrence. When it started happening two to three times each week, I really started to wonder. I began to take it very seriously.

"Chuck, could this be you?' I thought. "Are you the cause of this? Is this the unmistakable sign you promised to send me from the hereafter to signal that survival of consciousness after death is a reality?" I went into deep meditation about it and my theory about causation began to develop a huge head of steam. I began to receive major intuitive validity that Chuck was indeed the prankster.

"Well, Chuck, if this is you, bravo!" I thought. "Very ingenious of you to signal me in this way. But if it is really you who is doing this, then please confirm it for me by moving off-center my entire collection of framed Palm Beach Festival posters in our hallway, all at the same time," I requested. "If and when I see that, I will know it is you without a doubt. Case closed."

Several days later, I awoke one morning and noticed that each and every one of the nine framed posters in my Palm Beach Festival collection had been moved off-center by 20-30 degrees. Chuck had indeed kept his promise. He sent me an undeniable message from the great beyond. He made it to the other side successfully and was enjoying his existence in the realm of Spirit, still intensely creative and still the practical joker.

Vivian agreed with me. How could she not? I called her attention to each work of art throughout our house that had been mysteriously moved off-center soon after the fact. She witnessed the whole caper from start to finish. She too suspected it was Chuck's handiwork long before I reached that conclusion. She agreed that it was exactly the kind of thing her father would do to send us a powerful message. And once the message was received by us, and acknowledged for what it was, the odd occurrences stopped. Ever since, works of art throughout the entire house have remained perfectly centered. How very boring.

This aspect of Chuck's story is an example of after-death communication or contact, not deathbed visions or nearing death awareness or terminal lucidity, to be clear.

Catherine Cambria Audette

I grieved the loss of my mother intensely. I did not do grief. Grief did me. I did not have any control over the process. It had control over me. I deeply loved and respected her. She had a heart as big as this world. It was really tough to watch her leave. She knew this. She was well aware of my feelings throughout the whole ordeal.

On December 13, 2006, I wrote a long tribute to my mother and sent it to our entire extended family. In it, I described five after-death communication experiences involving my mother.

The first contact occurred two days after Catherine entered the realm of Spirit. It took place at 2:30 a.m. on Tuesday, November 21, 2006. I could not sleep. I was overcome by sadness at my mother's passing. I went into my study to do some work on my computer.

As I sat at my desk, I glanced up at the hutch above my desk to view the photo of my mother taped firmly to the side of the hutch, where it had been securely placed for over eight years. Although it had been there just a few hours before, it was not there at this time. It had fallen face down on the desk in front of where I was sitting. When I spotted it, I saw my mother's handwriting on the back. It read "Miss you Sonny. Love, Hugs & Kisses, Mother."

The tape was still on the back of the photo and still had plenty of adhesive left in it. So how the photo fell is a mystery, and so too is the matter of when it fell, the timing of it. Moreover, how the photo managed to land where it did and to land face down so that I could see my mother's handwriting is an even greater mystery.

I think my mother reached out to me from the great beyond to comfort me and ease my sorrow with the perfect message at that point in time. This would be so much in character for her, always unfailing in her attentiveness to her children's needs, always going out of her way and making sacrifices to accommodate their needs and help them in any way she could.

The second experience took place on the day Catherine was cremated, December 1, 2006. I spoke with a highly respected psychic located in Tampa about my mother on that occasion. This was a different psychic, not to be confused with the shaman discussed earlier or the medium from Archangel Michael fame.

She accurately described the scene in Catherine's hospice room immediately before and after Catherine died, down to precise details about where I was and what I was doing. She described intricate details known only to me and four other people in Catherine's room at the exact time she passed. Her accuracy about the deathbed activities was uncanny, which gave me strong confidence and belief in what she told me during this session, down to seeing a New York Yankees' baseball cap on Raymond Moody's head as he sat behind me in a Queen Anne chair.

This gifted seer told me that my mother had a hard time letting go because of her strong attachment to her children. She refused to die, even though it was her time and even though her body was worn out. She only let go, according to the seer, when Jesus, Mother Mary and Archangel Michael came to beckon her to leave her body, which she then did, but only because of their beckoning.

Once she decided to let go, the psychic said she went softly into death and was granted "the grace of a happy death." She entered a beautiful sacred space under the "blue mantle of Mother Mary," the seer said. According to the seer, Catherine was greeted by her deceased son Frank and by her deceased parents and her deceased brothers and sisters, as well as her deceased former husbands, as well as many other loved ones, friends and relatives who died before her. It was quite a Welcoming Committee.

According to the seer, the blissful reunion Catherine enjoyed with so many wonderful, dear souls mitigated the sorrow of leaving her children behind. That sorrow quickly evaporated in the midst of this joy. She had completed her mission and purpose in this lifetime. It was time for her to move on.

Catherine had a deep, abiding but silent faith in God and Mother Mary. This kept her strong throughout times of great adversity at several points during life. She did not profess to be spiritual, but she walked a spiritual path during her lifetime, one marked by great self-sacrifice, and much more than her fair share of suffering and hardship. She generously gave whatever she could whenever she could to others, especially her children, without regard for her own needs. For this reason, she ascended to a very high place upon death.

This psychic then told me at the conclusion of the session that Catherine had a message for me to give to all her children, her surviving siblings and her friends, as follows:

I am with you all. I have never left your side. I will never leave you. I am with you always. Look for me in your dreams. I will help you all from this high place where my spirit now dwells. I love you all very much and always remember that love is eternal. God loves you all. He loves us all. He blesses us all. Keep your faith. Stay strong in your faith. I am a new angel on your shoulder. Do not doubt this ever. Look for pennies on the ground and rainbows in the sky for now I can and will bring good fortune to each of you. Here I can do things for each of you that I could not do on earth in my physical body. Say the Rosary for me. Honor Jesus and Mother Mary. Thank them for the grace they gave me and are giving you. Leave your sadness behind. Live, laugh and love. Be good to one another and to others. Stay strong and healthy. Do not grieve for me, for now I am one with God and happier than I have ever been. Believe me when I tell you that we will meet again.

The third story concerns another after-death communication from Catherine to me. It occurred at 3:35 p.m. on Saturday, December 9, 2006 at Catherine's condo in Fort Lauderdale. I went there to continue sorting through my mother's personal effects. I was standing in her bedroom closet surveying the contents. My mother's scent was quite strong and evident there in the closet among her purses, shoes and clothes. I glanced at the rack and saw a few outfits I had purchased for her, outfits that really flattered her.

Sadness overcame me, and then tears began to fall. I missed my mother and was feeling the sting of her death. In that moment of intense emotional distress over her loss, I began to hear "electronic music" coming from the living room.

Curious as to the source and nature of this sound, I left the closet and walked into the living room, and then over to the dining room table where the sound was coming from. As I drew closer, I discovered the sound was emanating from a pile of greeting cards lying there on the table. As I sorted through the pile, I found the card that was playing music about midway down in the stack.

It was a Christmas card to Catherine from Bud Wells, her significant other. Bud and Catherine "dated" for many years, from about 1993 until 2004, the year Bud died. There was no date on this Christmas card, so there is no way to know what year Bud gave this card to his sweetheart whom he loved very much. The melody coming from the card was the melody from the song "Santa Claus is Coming to Town."

The card spontaneously began playing electronic music while I was in the closet. No one else was in the apartment at that time. Her first-born daughter, Domenica, who lived right next door, had piled all of mom's old greeting cards on the dining room table to sort through them. Mom kept many of the cards sent or given to her over the years in a keepsake container.

Domenica decided not to throw these cards away after mom died, but rather thought family members might want to sort through them for the memories. So, she piled them on the dining room table for all to examine. This particular card sounded off right then at that precise moment, spontaneously, without being prompted in any way, well not by any one still in physical existence on earth.

I sat the card upright on the table and let it continue to play, even after I left Catherine's apartment that day. The melody stayed in my head long after I left. After a while, I thought about the words to this song: "You better watch out. You better not cry. You better not pout. I'm telling you why."

Then I realized that the card started to play this tune while I was in my mother's closet, crying and grieving. I was standing there in emotional misery because my mother was gone forever. I was hurting all over, but then this music started to play and it suddenly changed my entire mood. I reminded myself that my mother was not gone forever, but still around, only in a different form.

Yes, this could be a strange coincidence, like the photo that fell in my study, but I believe my mother reached out to me a third time from the other side in a very playful way. Given the nature of this incident, I was inspired to slightly modify the lyrics of this song to convey what I thought my mother wanted to communicate to me: "You better watch out. You better not cry. You better not pout. I'm telling you why. Mother is still around."

I think my mother was also trying to tell me that she wants me and her entire family to have a very Merry Christmas and a great New Year, and not to let her death cast a shadow on what would otherwise be a happy time for all.

The fourth story concerns something else that happened in Catherine's condominium at the time I found the Christmas card Bud Wells gave to my mother. As I sat there in amazement for several minutes listening to the melody from "Santa Claus is Coming to Town," I felt a nudging to go through the pile of cards on the table to see what else I might find. I had not planned to do this, as I reasoned it would be too painful for me, but finding the musical card and listening to it play a happy tune changed all of that.

At the bottom of the pile, I found a book I had given to my mother for Mother's Day in 1993. It was entitled *Mothers: An Illustrated Treasury of Motherhood,* by Michelle Lovric. Mother's Day in 1993 fell on the same day as my 41st birthday. The inscription I wrote for her in the inside cover is as follows:

"Dearest Mother,

I hope you'll enjoy this book. It says a lot about how special a mother is to her children. I suppose it's a poetic tribute to all mothers, but the words inside are meant especially for you. I will never be able to repay you for all that you have done for me over the years. You've always been there for me, and all of your children. You've always given freely to us of yourself and your possessions. Most of all you gave me the gift of life 41 years ago today...the greatest gift of all. You're the best, and I love you very much."

As I sat in my deceased mother's living room reading these words I wrote to my mother in 1993, listening to "Santa Claus Is Coming to Town," I thanked her, silently, for comforting me yet again in this most special way.

Then I read through some of the other cards there on the table, cards she had saved for many years from her offspring, her brothers and sisters, and several close friends. What I read in those cards from so many people over so many years in relation to so many different occasions, was truly heartwarming and healing.

Catherine was indeed deeply loved by many people for her kind heart and generous spirit. The inscription I wrote to her in the Mother's Day book in 1993 was just like so many other words of love, praise and appreciation her other children had expressed to her over the years, not to mention the wonderful accolades she often received from friends and siblings.

A tsunami wave of powerful goose bumps overcame me in that instant, the instant I finished reading all of the cards that had been sent to my mother over the years. I believe it was my mother giving me a huge hug from the other side. A strong abiding peace came over me and the acute hurt I was feeling subsided. It enabled me to recompose myself so I could attend to the practical matters at hand.

The fifth and final story concerns a humorous incident that occurred on Sunday night, December 10, 2006 at around 7:30 p.m. at my home in Florida. I heard a loud crash in the garage and went out to investigate. A 13-gallon trash can had fallen over on the floor. This can contained umbrellas, other odds and ends, and two small signs attached to small stakes. These signs are placed out in the yard to mark certain occasions.

The trash can in question had been in the same location in my garage for over five years with essentially the same contents. It was perfectly balanced and had never fallen over before. But this time it did, and for no good reason. No one had been in the garage, to include none of the family pets. So, why it fell when and how it did is yet another mystery…a mystery that I believe I solved when I lifted the trash can upright only to face directly at one of the signs therein, the Halloween sign.

When I read its message, "Beware of Ghosts," I felt certain my mother had reached out to me yet again. Yes, Catherine had a great sense of humor. I am sure that this was another playful communication from her to let me and the rest of her family know that "Mother is still around."

Near-Death Experiences

There are now hundreds of excellent books on the subject of near-death experiences (NDEs), some of which are impressively evidential of life after death. It is a subject that has captured significant global interest for decades now and justifiably so. The near-death experience is defined as a spiritual, transcendental or other-worldly event that can occur during temporary clinical death (no cardiac, respiratory or brain activity), or also during an extremely close brush with death in which imminent physical death seems to be unavoidable.

I have written about NDEs, including a chapter in a book edited by Craig R. Lundahl, PhD, entitled *A Collection of Near-Death Research Readings*, published by Nelson Hall in 1982. The chapter is called, "Historical Perspectives on Near-Death Episodes and Experiences." In it, I provided many examples of NDEs that go way back in history, even as far back in time as Plato, all of which were strikingly consistent with modern accounts.

There can be little doubt that NDEs, both modern and historical cases, offer impressive evidential support for the existence of God and an afterlife. Here, I share one story among hundreds with which I am familiar to illustrate the point I wish to make. It is a remarkable story of not only a powerful NDE, but also about the afterlife, miracles and divine intervention.

Rickie Bradshaw

In late 2015, I received a letter from my long-time friend, Dr. Kenneth Ring, informing me about the passing of our mutual friend, Rickie Bradshaw. He died on November 24, 2015 in Belpre, Ohio.

The news of Rickie's death at age 59 cast a pale shade of gray on an otherwise cheerful sunny day. It was not so much because of his passing, for he had joyously returned to his true home in the life after, a place he knew well due to a profound near-death experience he had as a teenager. Rather, the remorse I felt in that instant was for humanity. Indeed, humanity lost a really good, kind, sweet, giving and loving person. In all candor, his kind are in short supply here on earth at the present time.

Rickie's loss gave rise to a sea of bittersweet grief. Bitter because those who knew him miss the form, his physical form and presence, his gentle smile, his upbeat disposition and his abiding tenderness. Sweet because we also know he happily returned from whence he came, back to Source/Creator, to the place of bliss that is the ultimate destination for all of us when our time comes to cast aside our temporal physical form.

As the result of his extensive NDE in 1975, Rickie had a great deal of invaluable insight to share about the central questions underlying life's meaning and purpose. With impressive certitude and unwavering conviction, Rickie resolutely answered the questions of who we are and why are we here during our initial meeting when he first told me about his intensely powerful NDE. This is the wisdom he imparted back then, which is as timely now as when he spoke these words to me during our first meeting in 1979:

"Heaven is here. Heaven is now. You don't have to die to get there. We need only open our hearts and minds to the absolute magnificence of it all, here and now. Then we would see that everything is a miracle, that all life is sacred and that all things are one. We are dearly blessed with unfathomable grace, love, beauty, abundance and the gift of free will from our Creator. We are free to make of it whatever we choose. Yet, no matter what choices we make, our Creator loves us all equally and unconditionally for all eternity. Now, how awesome is that? For the much we've been given, it is now clear to me that our constant purpose and challenge is to love all things as our Creator loves us."

I first met Rickie in Peoria, Illinois, as part of the world's first ever prospective study of NDEs. I organized and spearheaded the project at two major medical centers together with a team of four medical doctors and a clinical psychologist. It later became known in NDE research circles as "The Peoria Study." The results were never formally published because the final sample size was too small to allow for proper data analysis.

Based on a frequency study we conducted prior to the start of data collection, we estimated that between the two medical centers, we would receive referrals from their combined medical staffs of at least 500 eligible cases from ICU, CCU and the ER…cases that would meet our bio-medical criteria during the year-long duration of the study. But, due to a lack of cooperation from the medical staffs, most attending physicians did not refer their eligible cases to our study, despite glowing endorsements from the institutional review boards, both hospital administrators and the presidents of both medical staffs.

It was 1979 after all. The subject of near-death experiences was largely shunned by most medical doctors at that time. However, a few progressive doctors took note of our worthy effort with an open mind. They referred 57 patients to us, all of whom met the study's criteria for admission, of which eight reported having an NDE.

One among these progressive physicians was Dr. Anthony Carbonelle, a surgeon. Dr. Carbonelle generously took the time to call internist Dr. Michael Gulley, our physician team leader, to tell us about an extraordinary case he encountered a few years before in his practice. It was the fascinating case of Rickie Bradshaw, a young man who nearly died from being crushed by a car on November 14, 1975. Dr. Gulley thanked Dr. Carbonelle for the referral but declined to include it in our study because it was a "retrospective" case, one that happened prior to the start of our study. It was clearly outside of our sampling parameters.

Nevertheless, Dr. Gulley took note of Rickie's contact information and passed it along to me. I was extremely busy at the time managing our research project and managing the association that later evolved into IANDS, publishing its newsletter and answering correspondence as best I could (being a volunteer staff of one), while also juggling my part-time faculty job at Illinois Central College and full-time work as a health planner for the Illinois Central Health Systems Agency.

I was also spearheading the formation of Hospice of Central Illinois at the time with the late Ruth Kopp Holmes, MD and Vickie Lannie, RN. It was one of the first hospices formed in the country, and certainly the first multi-institutional consortium approach to facilitate the provision of hospice care.

Despite being on extreme overload, I decided to contact Rickie to learn more about his case. I was struck by a comment Dr. Gulley made when he called initially to tell me about Rickie. He told me that Dr. Carbonelle was able to corroborate Rickie's NDE. Apparently, Rickie had shared his experience with Dr. Carbonelle shortly after his return from the other side. Rickie spoke to him of actions and conversations that took place in the ER during the resuscitation attempt that ultimately saved his life.

This was an extraordinary bit of evidence, not commonly found in those days. So, the importance of this case for research purposes was obvious to me even then, despite that fact that it was "retrospective" and not eligible to be entered into our formal study. It was sufficient motivation for me to interview Rickie soon thereafter. It was one of the first, if not the first, cases of confirmed veridical perception on record at that time.

Shortly after Dr. Gulley informed me about this case, I called Rickie and we arranged a meeting. I remember that initial meeting as though it happened yesterday. I had interviewed many NDE subjects prior to this encounter, but Rickie stood out in my mind as a very special case for many reasons.

Right from the start, I was impressed by his candor, authenticity, sincerity, expressiveness, compassion and sensitivity. He was forthcoming with all the information he could remember from his experience, eager to get it all on record, delighted to find a sympathetic, understanding, non-judgmental person to share it with enthusiastically and unreservedly. He was also suffering from homesickness, yearning to return to his true home. He was not comfortable about being back in this world. He told me all about his NDE and how it happened.

When it took place, Rickie was a 19-year old teenager who worked as a bag boy for a local grocery store in Peoria. One day at work, while he was loading groceries into the trunk of a customer's car parked parallel to the front of the store, another car that was parked behind him sped forward. It crashed into the car in front of it, pinning Rickie in between the two vehicles.

The elderly woman driving the car that struck Rickie said her foot accidentally slipped off the brake and onto the accelerator, causing her to speed forward into a collision with the car in front of her. The impact crushed Rickie in the middle of the two vehicles just above his knees or lower thighs.

Upon first impact, Rickie fell to his knees in excruciating pain. Then, all of a sudden, Rickie's horrible nightmare went from bad to worse. The elderly woman driving the other car panicked after she realized she had struck Rickie. She quickly put her car in reverse and backed it up.

Then, the unthinkable happened. She unwittingly put her car back into drive and pressed on the accelerator thinking it was the brake. Once more, the car lunged forward to collide again with the car parked in front, this time striking Rickie at abdomen level, pinning him in between the two vehicles, nearly ripping his torso in two and almost killing him. The impact rendered him unconscious and within inches of losing his life.

Rickie was rushed to the ER at St. Francis Medical Center by ambulance, clinically dead on arrival. There to urgently assist with his care was Dr. Carbonelle. Unconscious in full cardiac and respiratory arrest, Rickie had to be resuscitated. Also, there was life-threatening damage to some of his major organs. A major artery had been severed as well. The situation was as grim as it gets.

"Clamp it right there, dammit! Clamp it right there!" shouted Dr. Carbonelle. Hovering above the chaotic scene below, Rickie took note of all the hurried goings-on below in astral form or in an out-of-body state. Soon after, Rickie entered the tunnel and traveled into the realm of light to encounter loved ones who had died before and also a supreme divine being.

He reported being shown an instantaneous review of human history, as well as a review of his life in its entirety. He recalled seeing a vision of the probable future, one most dark and disconcerting, one which could be prevented, he said, if we could learn to love one another.

Rickie was troubled by the lack of love in this world. He was distressed by what people do to one another, to animals, to nature and to the earth. He said he had been sent back to help others develop a better understanding of who we really are and why we're really here in order to create a kinder, gentler, more loving world.

After interviewing Rickie, I also interviewed Dr. Carbonelle. He was awestruck that Rickie was able to accurately recall precise details of what was said and done in the ER throughout the long ordeal to save his life. Dr. Carbonelle confirmed Rickie was unconscious and unresponsive, bleeding profusely and in both cardiac and respiratory arrest.

In this life-threatening compromised state, Dr. Carbonelle could not understand or explain how Rickie was able to "see" or "hear" anything.

Based on his medical training and knowledge, there was simply no way Dr. Carbonelle could explain how Rickie was able to accurately recall what happened around him in the ER during the resuscitation effort.

After some 24 successive surgeries over a two-year period, Rickie regained most of his feeling and function. His resilience was truly astounding. But one cannot say he returned to his normal self, better than ever. To be sure, he made amazing progress. And he made the best of his situation. He did not let his physical challenges weigh him down. He worked hard with tenacity to pick up right where he had left off.

Nevertheless, when I first met him, Rickie was sad and disheartened about the lack of love and kindness in the world. He was bitter about his divorce from his first wife. He alleged that she had somehow managed to legally take possession of the lion's share of his insurance settlement from the personal injury claim against the driver of the car that struck him.

He was having a great deal of difficulty reconciling himself to this world, having experienced the next. He longed, even then, to return to that place, the life after, and be spared the "outrageous slings and arrows" of this place and the life now. But he knew in his heart of hearts he had been sent back for an important reason: to teach people how to love one another and not fear death.

I was so impressed by Rickie's account that I encouraged Dr. Gulley to interview him and record the interview on videotape, which he did. From the standpoint of a researcher, I came to regard Rickie's insights as credible "empirical data" corroborated in part by one of the surgeons who attended to him in the emergency room right after the accident occurred. Rickie had traveled out of his body to another reality, another dimension, and he returned to tell us what he encountered during his journey to the other side.

I liken Rickie's adventure and all scientifically documented accounts of spiritually transformative experiences (STEs), to adventures of the great explorers throughout history who embarked on brave treks to undiscovered places. Upon their return, whether from the new world or the moon, they excitedly shared what they found and learned during their trips to faraway places.

Those of us who are mere spectators to their adventures are beyond eager to learn what we can from them, and we are wise to do so because in simple terms, they have been some place we have not. As representatives of our species, they ventured into places hitherto unexplored, and have come back to share with us the knowledge of what they found.

Dating back to 1974, I have been honored to meet and interview hundreds of near-death experiencers like Rickie, who conveyed highly similar accounts of their experiences on the other side and are deeply transformed by what they encountered. The wisdom Rickie offered in sharing his story with me is impressively consistent from case to case across thousands of recorded NDEs studied by scores of reputable scientists from all over the world. One such database is Dr. Jeffery Long's *NDERF.org* which contains over 5,000 experiences. Kevin Williams also has an extensive NDE website called *Near-Death.com.*

Rickie was well-known to the first generation of IANDS' members and researchers, highly regarded and well-respected by all who knew him. His near-death experience was compelling, complete with most all of the elements in the model described by Dr. Raymond Moody in his classic work entitled *Life After Life,* including a vision of knowledge about the probable future.

Rickie enjoyed learning about the accounts of others who reported NDEs. He was comforted by their stories. He was glad to learn he was not alone. He was delighted to find others who understood what he experienced. He attended many of the early IANDS' gatherings and met other experiencers, some of whom he formed deep lasting bonds with, like the late Tom Sawyer, one of Dr. Ken Ring's research subjects.

One of the last times I saw Rickie was at his home in Waynesboro, Virginia, near Staunton, close to a 500-acre farm in Headwaters, owned by Dr. Raymond Moody back then. I vividly remember taking a long walk with him down a bumpy dirt road in the recesses of the sloping countryside. As usual, we were lost in deep thought and conversation about how to change human nature and hence the world for the better.

Rickie loved having deep conversations with me and others on that subject. After all, it was the only reason for being, his and mine. We both shared this burning fire in the belly to help engender an optimal future for earth and all its inhabitants while we still had the time and opportunity to do so, lest we should fall short and suffer the tumultuous probable future he saw during his NDE.

As we walked down this old dirt road, we passed by a herd of cattle grazing in an adjacent field. They took notice of us and started walking toward us in a herd mentality, not in a menacing sort of way, but rather, we thought, to enjoy some kind of spiritual bonding, resonance or kinship. He and I were both believers in interspecies communication and bonding, so we thought this might be an opportunity for that to happen with the approaching cattle.

Watching the movement of the herd, Rickie commented that he could sense anxiety among them, that it was plainly visible in their eyes, as if to say they were sensing the coming of a storm and were beseeching us to do something about it. Rickie drew a parallel to his own sense of foreboding about the dark future we will be forced to endure in the coming storm if we do not learn to love one another and live as one, as foretold during his NDE.

I never forgot those words from Rickie, and from other people like him who reported NDEs that featured a vision of a potentially dark future for humanity. As I view the events of today, I can only conclude we are inching ever closer every day to the edge of the precipice, about to fall into the abyss of a most dismal future, one foretold by Rickie and other experiencers whose extensive NDEs gave them a flash forward of what might happen on earth in the near future unless we undergo a global spiritual awakening very soon.

It is because I had the good fortune to meet Rickie, and many others like him, who also reported extensive NDEs and the vision of future knowledge, that I was inspired to conceive the *Association for the Scientific Study of Near-Death Phenomena* which later became IANDS and, much later, another similar non-profit organization called Eternea (*Eternea.org*).

In that sense, one could say that Rickie and others like him fulfilled the purpose for which they were sent back into their bodies and back to their earthly lifetimes. In part, their task was to inspire people like me and millions of others around the world to benefit from the insights and wisdom they brought back from the other side.

It is because of Rickie and others like him, that all of the books have been written, all of the movies made, all of the lectures, workshops and conferences organized, all of the interviews conducted and all of the scholarly journal articles published. It is also the reason IANDS and Eternea came into being.

For this, and so much more, we owe Rickie and others like him the deepest debt of appreciation for being brave trailblazers, helping the rest of us to better probe the mystery of death, helping us find our way to collective enlightenment, that one day we might successfully co-create an ideal future for earth and all its inhabitants.

With benefit of their messages from beyond the veil, it is past time for us all to end the mind-numbing debate about whether consciousness survives bodily death. Instead, in their honor, we should promptly turn our attention to the more important realization that it does, and that guiding it all is a magnificent loving God.

A Case Study in Cosmic Choreography

My life has been blessed with many other kinds of divine intervention and providence of a very different genre than what I have described thus far. For instance, I have been fortunate to experience several synchronistic and serendipitous events, but none more magical or of longer chronological duration than the many twists and turns which culminated in meeting Raymond Moody. Raymond and I formed an enduring close friendship and collaboration which impacted the course of my life significantly.

The initial meeting with Raymond took place in February 1974, but the lengthy process which made it possible began in 1960. The long and winding road which led to meeting Raymond and the many amazing things that unfolded afterwards is the best case study I have ever experienced in what I call *Cosmic Choreography*. Others would call it mystical synchronicity or magical serendipity.

In 1960, I was eight years old in the third grade at North Side Elementary School in Fort Lauderdale. A very close friend back then was a terrific guy named Mike Waters. One day as we were walking home after school, Mike told me he was very sad about his mother. I knew his mother well. I often played with Mike at his home after school. His house was the mid-point between school and my home, so I often hung out with him there after school to enjoy the proverbial milk and cookies his mom would serve us. It was most enjoyable. I always looked forward to it after the school day before heading on to my house, only a few blocks away.

A few weeks prior to this, Mrs. Waters suffered a near-fatal heart attack without warning. No one saw it coming. We all thought she was quite healthy. She was rushed by ambulance to a local hospital. Rumors were that she was clinically dead when the ambulance arrived at her home. It had been summoned by a neighbor friend who fortunately was visiting with her when she collapsed. Thanks to the efforts of fast-acting emergency room doctors, Mrs. Waters was resuscitated and later fully recovered. A couple of weeks later, she returned home.

Mike was quite upset about it, not because his mother survived, but because her personality had changed profoundly. He wanted his old mother back. During our walk home on that day, Mike told me he did not know who his mother was anymore because all she talked about was Jesus, God, heaven and angels from on high, and how much we are all loved by God. Mike said his mother told him she had died and had gone to heaven where she met Jesus, God and angels.

Later that same afternoon, I greeted Mrs. Waters for the first time since she had come home from the hospital. I could not wait to see for myself what she was like. I wanted to hear in her own words what happened to her. When she spoke with me about it, I fully understood what Mike was upset about.

She was a different person. I could see the difference. Her face was all aglow. Mrs. Waters told me she died and went to heaven. She was thrilled to tell me she met Jesus, God and the angels. I asked her to tell me more and she did. She went on and on about it with tears in her eyes. Mike thought his mom had become a Jesus freak. He certainly did not like the change in her. He wanted his old mom back.

I never forgot Mrs. Waters' story or the change that came over her. It was indelibly etched in my mind as something of major significance, but

I could not explain why. It was the first time I ever heard someone talk about a near-death experience, but it certainly was not the last, as I would discover many years later starting in 1974.

I lost touch with Mike and his family after elementary school, but I often wonder how he and his family fared later on in life, especially his mom. My feeling was that her experience had a powerful impact on her and likely changed her forever.

The next significant occurrence in this synchronistic chain of related events was my enlistment in the United States Army in June 1970. It happened right after high school graduation. I volunteered to fight in Vietnam as an infantryman. But through a series of serendipitous happenings and mysterious coincidences, I never served "in country" during over three years of active duty.

Despite my desire to train as an infantryman and fight in Vietnam, I ended up in the Signal Corps as an instructor at the U.S. Army Southeastern Signal School (USASESS) at Fort Gordon, Georgia. I was later assigned to the Office of the Commandant, where I served most of my enlistment. My only other duty station was Fort Campbell, Kentucky, where I underwent basic training, home of the "Screaming Eagles," 101st Airborne Division.

But this begs the question concerning why I enlisted to serve as an infantryman in Vietnam in the first place, which is yet another curious link in this curious chain of curious events. Vietnam was an extremely unpopular war and for many good reasons. Many informed critics labeled it immoral and unjust. Hundreds of thousands of Americans boldly protested it. Many young men burned their draft cards or simply refused to serve when drafted.

Dominick Madonna was not among them. He enlisted in the U.S. Army. Upon entry into the service, even though he informed Army officials he was a skilled automobile mechanic, he was ordered to serve as a combat infantry soldier. After he completed his training, Dominick was promptly sent to Vietnam. He was assigned to the 1st Infantry

Division, 2nd Battalion, 18th Infantry, "B" Company. He was awarded the Purple Heart and the Bronze Star posthumously.

Unlike the draft dodgers and war protestors of his time, who in retrospect may have been on the right side of history, Dominick was raised to believe that one must always do one's patriotic duty. He did so at the cost of his life. His attitude was, "My country, right or wrong, my country."

Dominick was the oldest brother of Jim Madonna, my close friend from third grade onwards. Dominick was a handsome guy, on par with Frankie Avalon good looks. He was always very amiable and affable. He was like a big brother to me. I liked him a lot. So, when he was killed on August 22, 1969 during a mortar attack on his position in Binh Duong Province, South Vietnam, it shook his family and me to the core. He was only 21 years old, born on February 25, 1948, a little more than four years before me. His remains were interred at Mount Carmel Cemetery in Verona, a suburb of Pittsburgh, Pennsylvania.

Dominick was a graduate of Fort Lauderdale High School, class of 1967. I became editor of the Fort Lauderdale High School newspaper, *The Navigator*, the year he was killed, so I felt compelled to write a tribute to him, which was published in the September 26, 1969 edition. I included his last letter home to his folks.

I still have that issue of *The Navigator* among my keepsakes. Dom's photo remains on prominent display in my home study. His name is etched in the Vietnam Veterans Memorial Wall in Washington, D.C., together with over 58,279 other fine Americans who lost their lives in that terrible conflict. It can be found on Panel 19W-Line 96. Please see Dominick's photo at *AffirmingGod.com* and also the story I wrote about him for *The Navigator*.

Truth be told, I enlisted in the Army in June 1970 to avenge Dominick's death and to help liberate the poor oppressed people of South Vietnam, or so my government led me to believe. I told the Army recruiter I wanted infantry. I insisted upon being assigned to Dominick's company. I also wanted to be sent to Binh Duong Province where he was killed. I wanted to be a grunt on the ground like he was, fighting the enemy.

But like all recruits, first I had to take an aptitude test. When the results came in, the recruiter told me I had scored too high on the test so he could not assign me to infantry. He said my country needed me to learn about high-speed encrypted computerized communication systems if I could be approved by the FBI for a security clearance, which I later was. So I agreed with reluctance, but only if I was promised duty in Vietnam.

After basic training, I attended Advanced Individual Training (AIT) at Fort Gordon near Augusta, home of the azalea-blossoming Masters Golf Tournament and not far from where Raymond Moody lived at the time, not so coincidentally. He was a medical student attending the Medical College of Georgia.

I was named honor graduate in February 1971, top of the class in the 72F4H/Digital Subscriber Terminal Equipment course (my Military Occupational Specialty Code). Tradition required the honor graduate to stay at USASESS to teach for one year. To honor that tradition, I agreed I would teach for one year and forego orders that would have sent me initially to Germany. My understanding was that I would then be sent to Vietnam one year later in or about February 1972.

After teaching for several months, I was invited to join the staff of the Commandant's office, which was a truly great honor. I agreed to do this provided my orders to Vietnam would be honored. They were not. I was assigned to the command section for the rest of my enlistment at "the convenience of the government."

Now, truthfully, I never thought I was smart enough for college, but the Commandant of USASESS and others encouraged me to take the "CLEP" test (College Level Equivalency Program). They also urged me to apply for admission to nearby Augusta College. They told me the Army would pay my tuition, so I took the test and earned several freshman course credits in this manner, which Augusta College granted when I was accepted for admission. I took two courses per quarter, four nights per week, while serving on active duty during daytime hours.

When I was discharged from the Army in mid-December 1973, I planned to attend the University of Florida back in my home state, but I would have lost too many credits in the transfer. So, instead, I decided to stay at Augusta College to finish work on my Bachelor of Arts degree with a double major in history and sociology.

So, despite my firm intention when I initially enlisted in the U.S. Army, I was never sent to Vietnam even though I had volunteered for that very purpose. In retrospect, I can only view this as yet another clear example of God's grace. I erroneously believed at the time that Vietnam was a just cause. I did not discover otherwise until much later. Still, I was spared the agony and misery of that terrible war by the grace of God. But Dominick Madonna received no such good fortune nor did 58,280 other U.S. military personnel killed in action. Another 153,372 military personnel were wounded in action and another 1,584 are listed as missing in action. Dead and wounded Vietnamese are estimated to be in the millions, including both civilians and military personnel.

There were other related deaths too beyond these figures that do not make it into the official statistics. For example, consider the four Kent State University students who were shot and killed on May 4, 1970 by the Ohio National Guard for protesting the war: Allison Krause, age 19; Jeffrey Miller, age 20; Sandra Scheuer, age 19; and William Schroeder, age 19. Nine others were wounded by National Guard troops who fired randomly into the crowd of unarmed student protestors, fearing for their lives, they claimed.

Moreover, it behooves us to remember the Vietnamese Buddhist monk, Bo Tat Thich Quang Duc, who bravely died from self-immolation on June 1, 1963 in full public view to protest the war and harsh treatment of his fellow Buddhists. He had driven hundreds of miles from his home temple to the site of his self-sacrifice, which was intended to promote change that would serve the good of others.

In a heavily trafficked Saigon intersection, the Bodhisattva sat in a lotus position, still and motionless, chanting Buddhist sutras before he lit aflame the gasoline that had been poured onto him by another monk at his request. As his body burned horrifically, Quang Duc never made a move the whole time, never made a sound, never uttered a word and never cried out in pain. He remained quiet, calm and peaceful throughout the entire brutal ordeal, never flinching.

If that's not miracle enough, here's another one to ponder. Quang Duc's heart survived the self-immolation completely intact. It survived not just the original self-cremation, but also a second re-cremation of Quang Duc's remains at his funeral, which was attended by over 500 of his fellow monks.

The heart was charred but had fully crystalized, almost rock-like. For a time, it was put on public display in a glass container at a local Buddhist temple, the Xa Loi Pagoda. The much-revered relic was offered as a symbol of compassion. It attracted large numbers of people, so many that it was soon seized by the military. Its whereabouts today are unknown.

And then there were other American war protesters who were so disturbed by the atrocities in Vietnam that they too self-immolated following Quang Duc's example: Alice Merz on March 16, 1965; Norman Morrison on November 2, 1965; and Roger Allen LaPorte on November 9, 1965. Reportedly, hundreds of other similar acts took place in several other countries around the world.

What purpose was served by all these deaths? By all this misery and suffering? Nothing. Nothing at all. My heart breaks when I think about all those who died and suffered, along with their loved ones left behind. How great was their pain? How great is it still?

I could have been one among the innumerable tragedies caused by the Vietnam War, but by the grace of God, I was not. It turns out that, in retrospect, enlisting in the U.S. Army had nothing whatsoever to do with going to fight in Vietnam. Rather, it was for another purpose entirely, one I could never imagine or anticipate, but one which was clearly cosmically choreographed.

During first quarter 1974, honorably discharged from the U.S. Army, I re-entered civilian life and became a full-time student at Augusta College. Soon after, I was elected president of the Sociology Club. At our very first meeting, I asked my fellow club members for suggestions concerning interesting speakers we could bring to campus. A fellow classmate and club member by the name of Kathy Tabakian suggested her next door neighbor, Dr. Raymond Moody.

I asked Kathy what Dr. Moody would speak about. She informed us that Raymond earned a doctorate in philosophy from the University of Virginia and could speak on many interesting subjects. But she said that most interesting of all could be a talk about his interviews with people who had been resuscitated following a close brush with death and the mystical experiences they underwent during the time they were unconscious and near-death.

When Kathy said that, I lit up like a Christmas tree. It brought back to mind the ancient memory from third grade concerning Mrs. Waters and her amazing journey to heaven. The resurfacing of this old memory from 1960 ignited a fire within me. I told Kathy I could not wait to meet Raymond. She arranged our initial meeting for the next day. I was overcome with anticipation about this meeting and could hardly sleep the night before, all for good reason.

I met Kathy at Raymond's home late that next afternoon, just before dinner. This is when she first introduced us, and when she did, I heard the ring of destiny. It rang loudly in a sustained manner. I felt then and still feel today it was the major defining moment in my life. It was the single most important event in my personal history. I knew it instinctively when it first happened.

Meeting Raymond was clearly the culmination of a long deliberate process over considerable time, which I can best describe as sacred

Cosmic Choreography. This is a term I coined to give due recognition to a lengthy course of chronological events all seemingly intertwined and related to each other, and all aimed at achieving some greater strategic outcome. Others might call it divine providence, or destiny, or fate.

Raymond and I took an instant liking to each other and we remain close to this day. He was a full-time medical student at the Medical College of Georgia (MCG) at the time. This is where he conducted research that eventually led to the publication of his classic work, *Life After Life* in late 1975, which fast became a global best seller. It remained so for years to come. MCG is also where I later conducted my thesis research for my Master of Science degree from Virginia Tech.

Kathy Tabakian, who introduced me to Raymond, is mentioned in the Acknowledgements section of *Life After Life*. In this work, Raymond coined the term "near-death experience" (NDE) and outlined what is now commonly known as "The Moody Model," which is descriptive of a wide range of phenomena associated with NDEs.

I was most eager to help Raymond with the underlying research that led to the publication of this book. He generously acknowledged my efforts in his second book, *Reflections On Life After Life.*

Now, please carefully consider all the many twists and turns in my life that built to a crescendo and seemingly culminated in meeting Raymond. Undeniably, these events brought me to a place and time where I was blessed to have this good fortune.

What are the odds that all these happenings would occur in my life to deliver me on that day to the doorstep of Raymond Moody's home? To my way of thinking, this is proof positive of divine intervention and providence, which often find expression through synchronicities and serendipities such as these.

But to what end? What purpose did all this serve? April 1974 and what happened afterwards can be viewed as where the rubber meets the road. It gives major significance and obvious transcendent purpose to what would otherwise be meaningless random events.

As the result of Kathy's brilliant suggestion at our first meeting, the Sociology Club invited Raymond to speak on the campus of Augusta College in April 1974 at the Performing Arts Center. It was packed to capacity, standing room only. Students and faculty alike were eager to hear what this young medical student with a doctorate in philosophy would reveal about his research concerning patients who had been resuscitated from cardiac arrest and were brought back to life from death's doorstep.

This talk was one of the first Raymond gave on NDEs. It pre-dated the release of *Life After Life* by well over one year. I was in the audience, of course, hanging on every word. It was then that I received what I can only describe as "divine inspiration" to form an international association that would harvest and harness the enormous power of these extraordinary experiences to trigger profound individual and social transformation on a global level through the vehicle of science.

I was a self-avowed agnostic at that time, but I was deeply moved by Raymond's discussion of his research findings on this occasion, down to the core of my being. I reasoned then, as I do now, that these experiences possess great potential to change human nature and, consequently, the nature of social, political and economic systems, as well as organized religion.

From that point forward, with rapidly waning agnosticism that transformed eventually into the firm convictions expressed in this book, I committed myself to this work and have maintained that commitment ever since. The experience Mrs. Waters shared with me in 1960 as a young eight-year-old boy strongly reinforced in my mind that Raymond's research findings were valid.

Thanks to the hundreds of testimonies I was privileged to research, from impressive people like Mrs. Waters and many others after her, over time I arrived at the solid conclusion that NDEs, as well as STEs generally, have the combined power to transform people, social systems, as well as science and religion.

Taken together, they form a sound empirical foundation upon which to retire materialism, dualism, dogma and egocentrism. Now, just imagine a vastly changed world where these outmoded constructs are no longer valid. I call it utopia, or perhaps "heaven on earth." Another term for it is "an optimal future."

In the Augusta College Performing Arts Center in April 1974 during Raymond's historic lecture, I conceived what was first called the Association for the Scientific Study of Near-Death Phenomena. I am its primary founder, first president and executive director. From 1977-1980, I managed its affairs from my home in Peoria, Illinois. Raymond Moody, MD, PhD; Kenneth Ring, PhD; Bruce Greyson, MD; and Michael Sabom, MD, accepted the invitation to join me as co-founders.

In 1981, this non-profit organization evolved into the International Association for Near-Death Studies (*IANDS.org*), based at the University of Connecticut, Storrs. Dr. Ring managed it from that point onwards. He was succeeded by many other organizational leaders over time. I continued to serve on its Board of Directors until 1985.

IANDS is primarily focused on near-death experiences, whereas I always believed the focus should be on all manner of spiritually transformative experiences, each and every genre, leaving no stone unturned. I believe all roads should be explored to shed light on the mystery of what happens when we die.

Also, my focus then and now, unapologetically, is at the macro level. I view things from a systems perspective. I am interested primarily in applying scientific findings from STE research as a catalyst to engender both social and individual transformation on a global level, in order to help create an optimal future for earth and all its inhabitants. In my view, this is the most important priority and what should receive greatest emphasis.

I am quite proud of the fact that IANDS has done and continues to do a great deal of good globally. Its mission and vision, as they came to be defined by its leadership, is worthy of praise and support. The organization has indeed helped many, especially a great number of experiencers with their unique challenges, as well as several notable researchers who utilize it as a terrific resource.

Years into the future, during the fall of 2011, with strong encouragement from *New York Times* number one best-selling author, Eben Alexander, MD, my download from April 1974 morphed into yet another "reboot" iteration, that being another non-profit organization called Eternea, Inc. (*Eternea.org*). It still exists today but is only minimally operational due to insufficient funding. Dr. Alexander served as its first Chairman & Chief Science Officer. He resigned in May 2013 to focus fully on writing future books, teaching and to pursue research ambitions.

For the record, I am not a medium, channel or psychic. I did not hear any voices in April 1974 or thereafter. I saw no visions back then and certainly no burning bushes. Yet, the whole idea or concept of the association (in all its iterations) formed in my mind back then, whole to part. It was akin to the implantation of a seed inside my mind from elsewhere, but where I do not know, other than to credit the divine.

While I do not know where the idea came from, I can say it came through me, not from me. My mind did not formulate it. Rather, it was a seed that was implanted in my mind from some other source. Who knows where ideas originate and how they form in our minds. I just credit Spirit because I don't have any other explanation for it.

Once planted in my mind during Raymond's lecture in April 1974, this seed quickly germinated as a channeled "download" from Spirit. I was given the association's mission, vision and its seven major program components, which were and are: 1) Research; 2) Education; 3) Outreach; 4) Technology Development; 5) Personal Growth Initiatives, including resources to safely induce peak experiences/epiphanies; 6) The Convergence Coalition, to align science and religion; and 7) SynerGe, for institutional transformation and global alliance development. I was also instilled with a very clear understanding of its potential significance as an impetus to advance civilization by helping human nature to evolve.

In all its iterations, I have always envisioned the "download" I received in April 1974 to be an international association that could serve as a catalyst to help change human nature and the nature of social, political and economic systems, as well as organized religion. I have always regarded it as a potentially powerful impetus for a global spiritual renaissance…a catalyst for a worldwide mass spiritual awakening, not one that is based on unfounded faith in unproven dogma, but rather on critical thinking focused on the scientific study of human consciousness and spiritually transformative experiences.

Surprisingly, from the very beginning, Raymond was expressly negative about the association idea. He said he was not fond of organizations and discouraged me from pursuing it. I hounded him through much of 1974-1976 to fully support the idea but to no avail. However, in mid-1976, with sales of Life After Life soaring, he finally agreed to share some correspondence with me he received from other researchers. They mostly wrote to him to inquire about doing their own investigations. Correspondence from Dr. Ken Ring and Dr. Michael Sabom were among the letters he shared.

With introductions to them arranged through Raymond, in 1976, I drove up to Storrs to meet Dr. Ring, a psychologist at the University of Connecticut and then down to Gainesville, Florida, to meet Dr. Michael Sabom, a cardiologist at the University of Florida, Shands Medical Center. My aim was to learn about their independent research and to interest them in my idea of creating an international association.

I received my Bachelor of Arts degree from Augusta College – Cum Laude in June 1975. Soon after, Raymond earned his MD credential from the Medical College of Georgia. He relocated to Charlottesville, Virginia, to pursue his residency in psychiatry. I enrolled at Virginia Tech in Blacksburg, to earn a Master of Science degree, which was awarded in May 1977.

My move to Blacksburg was fortuitous because it kept me in close geographic proximity to Raymond. Blacksburg and Charlottesville are only a few hours apart by car, a direct drive on I-81. This enabled Raymond and me to continue meeting frequently during this time.

There were various meetings with other key figures around the same period to promote the idea of launching an association. These meetings were mostly arranged by Raymond and included Bob Monroe from the Monroe Institute in Afton, Virginia, as well as Dr. Bruce Greyson, a psychiatrist at the University of Virginia, and his boss at that time, Dr. Ian Stevenson, head of the Division of Perceptual Studies at the University of Virginia, who wrote a classic work about reincarnation, *Children Who Remember Previous Lives.*

But before leaving Augusta, in the spring of 1975, Raymond arranged for me to meet Elisabeth Kübler-Ross, MD. Raymond was having phone chats with Elisabeth in early 1975 to discuss his NDE research findings, and hers too. One day, he asked me to drive him from Augusta to Kennesaw near Atlanta for his first in-person meeting with Elisabeth. It took place at Kennesaw Community College. That is when I first met Elisabeth and had my first opportunity to chat with her.

On impulse, I shared my "download" experience with her from April 1974. In sharp contrast to Raymond, she loved the idea. She was actually excited about the prospect of creating an international association such as what I envisioned. She said she would lend her name to it and some financial support when it got off the ground. She shared my feeling that it could be a powerful impetus for social and individual transformation. This made us close kindred spirits from that point forward.

Like Raymond, Elisabeth had encountered some NDE cases which featured the "vision of knowledge" element, also known as the "flash forward," such as the preview of the future Rickie Bradshaw was shown. She had a strong sense of urgency, like Raymond. Both felt humanity could soon self-destruct unless people learned to transcend ego, dualism and materialism to become one and love each other unconditionally. She saw this shift happening not through religion, but through the efforts of frontier science focused on the scientific study of STEs and consciousness. She thought the association could further this very important cause.

My hope back then was that all the researchers would be moved to contribute some of their earnings or royalties to the association to provide at least a modicum of financial support for it, but that never materialized due in large part to the severe financial misfortune that befell both Raymond and Elisabeth circa 1978-1981 due to the malfeasance of others.

Nevertheless, despite these setbacks, since first meeting Raymond in 1974 and Elisabeth a year later, I have been diligently trying to find a viable way to apply findings from research into spiritually transformative experiences to the overarching goal of fostering profound individual and social transformation on a global level. In this respect, as well as others, meeting Raymond, and later Elisabeth, changed my life's path and primary purpose.

Prior to these meetings, I was determined to enter law school. My plan was to study international law at the University of Georgia under Professor Dean Rusk, former Secretary of State under President John F. Kennedy. I interviewed him in 1974 about the JFK assassination pursuant to my senior undergraduate thesis for my second major, which was history.

After I asked a number of deeply probing questions which he could not answer, Professor Rusk took an interest in me personally. He encouraged me to apply for law school with his blessings when former Chief Justice Earl Warren could not answer some of my tough questions either.

My jaw dropped when Professor Rusk called Chief Justice Warren during our interview to seek his input, thinking he would surely know the answers to my questions. Some questions he answered, but others he could not or would not.

With what I know now on the subject, Chief Justice Warren would be even more hard pressed to answer my questions today if he were still among the living. Even if he were still alive, my guess is he would decline to answer any question that seriously challenged or contradicted the official findings of the Warren Commission.

After meeting Raymond and Elisabeth, all my ambitions to become a lawyer disappeared. Meeting them blessed me with two distinct advantages over most people. First, because of them, I became involved with the embryonic hospice movement from its inception. Through my hospice work, I was privileged to learn a great deal from dying patients.

Secondly, through Raymond and Elisabeth and other notable scientists of that time, I received the opportunity to meet and interview hundreds of people over the years who had STEs of one kind or another. This also enabled me to meet and work with some of the major leaders in the human consciousness/spiritual awakening movement at that time who authored many of the leading books on these subjects, including Dr. Edgar Mitchell.

Edgar was a NASA astronaut who served on the Apollo 14 mission. He was the sixth man to walk on the moon in February 1971. I first met him in 1982 when we both participated in a panel discussion on the subject of world peace. Together, we formed another non-profit entity called Quantrek for similar purposes, but like IANDS and Eternea, it was never funded appreciably.

The distinct advantages of these meetings provided me with an uncommon vantage point. I was honored to be brought into direct relationship with top leaders in the human potential movement. Through my hospice work, I was privileged to be with dying patients as they made their transition to the other side. Through IANDS and close colleagues like Moody, Ring, Sabom and Greyson I was able to meet hundreds of people who reported NDEs and other kinds of STEs. They were my greatest mentors.

If all other human beings on the planet could retrace my footsteps and be exposed to the same information, I have no doubt that most, if not all, would arrive at the same conclusions I have about God's existence and the afterlife.

All these great blessings happened because of the *Cosmic Choreography* which I just detailed that enabled me to meet Raymond in February 1974 and Elisabeth the next year.

Yet, I cannot say that the resultant formation of IANDS or Quantrek or Eternea thereafter justifies all the exceptional experiences I have had or adequately explains why my life was divinely saved so many times.

To be sure, these organizations have done genuine good in the world, but none came close to fulfilling the amazing download I received from Spirit in April 1974. If that ever comes to pass, then I will know why my life was spared so many times. But until then, I will keep wondering. Perhaps writing this book will be a big step in that direction.

But I will say this much. If I had not learned about Mrs. Waters' NDE in 1960, I seriously doubt I would have given Kathy Tabakian's suggestion any credence about inviting Dr. Moody to lecture at Augusta College. And, further to the same point, if Dominick Madonna had not been killed in combat in Vietnam in 1969, I seriously doubt I would have enlisted in the U.S. Army in 1970. This means I seriously doubt I ever would have made it to Augusta to enjoy a fortuitous meeting with Dr. Raymond Moody.

If that meeting had not happened, then all else which flowed from it would not have happened either. So, as I often say in public lectures, knowing all this background information, I am compelled to ask an obvious question: Did I choose this work or did this work choose me.

Solitary Refinement:
Spiritual Communion in the Mojave Desert

The famed poet John Keats said it long ago: "Truth is beauty and beauty is truth." Imbued with the same inspiration that probably brought Keats to this insight, pursuit of truth and beauty became the focal point of my life at an early age.

If ever there was a search for a Holy Grail in my life, it was a relentless, incessant commitment to seek truth and beauty. Finding truth and beauty became my quest. It has been the primary organizing principle of my life and the central purpose of my existence.

It all began when I could no longer look at the ordinary without seeing the extraordinary within. When I first realized that everything ordinary was teeming with that which is extraordinary, I truly became alive. That was when I learned to fathom the difference between form and the essence underlying form. There is much that meets the eye, but much more that does not.

There is observable matter of course, with which we are all familiar, but then there is the energy and information which underlies and supports all matter and brings matter to fruition in a three-dimensional time-space reality. And then there is anima, the realm of Spirit, which empowers and enables all of it.

Once I learned to distinguish between form, essence and anima, the seen and the unseen, I could not focus on anything but essence and anima. I realized that spiritual essence and anima are enduringly real, yet that which is physical-material is transitory. What we see in physical reality perishes with time. That which is unseen endures.

Once I realized that the ordinary revealed the extraordinary, it was only a short while later that comprehending the extraordinary led me into a more profound communion with God. Indeed, it led me to finding, sensing and feeling God as well, all around me and within me and all creation.

From that moment on, with every step and every breath, I walked in one constant state of grace aligned with the divine, with essence and anima, for nothing else really mattered in the bigger picture. I found God deep within the ground of my own being, where the divine is revealed and felt…where God becomes knowable.

Still, despite this illumination, the summer of 1988 was a profoundly sad time for me. I was feeling disconnected, adrift and alone, like a flightless bird. I was also distressed that I seemed to be failing to fulfill my life's purpose, unable to find my life's stride. It was then I decided to embark upon a vision quest in the North American Indian tradition under the guidance of Spirit Storm, a seasoned shaman I had met four years earlier.

My vision quest brought me to the Mojave Desert near Palm Springs, California, specifically Joshua Tree National Park. As it turned out, this quest was all about the nature of light and its relationship to darkness. At its conclusion, Spirit Storm gave me the medicine name, First Light. He told me my task was to be and to bring the first few particles of light, God's light, into places that are persistently and stubbornly dark.

Light for me was not just the absence of darkness, nor was darkness the mere absence of light. Rather, I came to define light as a high frequency form or expression of love, unconditional love, for light shines on all things indiscriminately without judgment. The sun is our principal source of light and the primary life-enabling force in our solar system. Without it, life could not exist.

In my estimation, the vibration of light is one of the most refined manifestations of pure unconditional love in the universe. It is made possible, as all things are, by the grace and beneficence of our Creator/Source/God. It is no mere coincidence that, according to Genesis, God's first command at the first instant of creation was "Let there be light."

Light sustains all life, no less than water and oxygen. Life is not possible without it. Light shines on everyone, good and bad, regardless of race, creed, ethnicity, religion, nationality, gender or net worth. It warms. It soothes. It nurtures. It engenders and enables life. It brings forth growth and makes possible our very sustenance.

Darkness does not engender or sustain life. Therefore, logically speaking, one cannot equate light and darkness. They are not in the same league. What does darkness give? What does it contribute?

Darkness is the time when light is not. When darkness descends, do we not eagerly await the return of light? Yet, when we are in the light, most do not eagerly await the arrival of darkness. When light is not, life is called upon to rest, to be inert, to replenish, to renew, to recharge. Perhaps this is why many things sleep or find repose at night. Yet without darkness, can there be light and vice-versa?

What is light? What is its origin? What is darkness? What is its origin? These were among my questions in the summer of 1988 when I began preparations for my first vision quest. I had read about such quests before in various books, mostly the popular works by Carlos Castaneda. But when the date was set for my quest to commence, despite all my yearning for greater enlightenment and spiritual communion, the truth is that I became mildly apprehensive and reluctant. Nevertheless, I had made a commitment to see this through and I was determined to do so.

At that time, Spirit Storm lived with a girlfriend named Jane in Hollywood Hills, a suburb of Los Angeles. I traveled there from my home in Lake Worth, Florida, to meet with him and prepare for my vision quest under his direction.

Unbeknownst to us, around that same time, in the same general vicinity, none other than Bob Dylan, George Harrison, Tom Petty, Roy Orbison and Jeff Lynne wrote and recorded a great collection of songs by their impromptu band known as the Traveling Wilburys. It all happened close by in Coldwater Canyon in a borrowed house owned by Dave Stewart of the Eurythmics.

Ironically, the house where they recorded their popular tunes was not far away from the Bel Air home of Gavin de Becker where George Harrison died in November 2001 and also the Santa Monica hospital where Tom Petty died in October 2017. Roy Orbison died much earlier on December 6, 1988 in Hendersonville, North Carolina, not long after the Wilburys recorded their songs. As of this writing, Bob Dylan and Jeff Lynne are still with us, thank God.

There I was in close proximity to these guys, musical heroes all, who were writing and recording some of my favorite tunes of all time. I was in the general vicinity fasting, meditating and practicing the Medicine Wheel ritual following Spirit Storm's instructions. What a vastly sharp contrast in personal realities. They were having loads of fun being creative as could be, and I was slugging it out in the spiritual trenches so to speak, seeking greater enlightenment and communion.

All of these musicians were deep thinkers and spiritually awakened people. I often wondered what might have happened if we had somehow met around that time. I sometimes imagine a fictional scenario in which we all meet, have discourse about the scientific study of spiritually transformative experiences joining forces with their wealth and command of popular culture, all to change basic human nature, as well as the nature of social, political and economic systems.

With their combined star-power and massive global following, I dreamt of the enormous potential that could have been realized if only that meeting of minds had taken place. But, alas, it was only a personal fantasy, one that was not meant to be in reality. And to think we were on the same spiritual wavelength was likely my own fanciful projection.

In November 2002, one year to the date after George Harrison died, I attended a musical tribute for him at the Royal Albert Hall in London, England. It was called "The Concert for George." Bob Dylan did not make it to the event, sadly, but Jeff Lynne and Tom Petty did, along with some of the stars from Monty Python and a host of other musical luminaries including Sir Paul McCartney and Ringo Starr. Sitting just in front of me in a section known as "The Stalls" was Sir George Martin, long-time producer of The Beatles at EMI/Abbey Road Studios.

During this bittersweet occasion, I was revisited by the same fantasy I had back in 1988 in connection with the Traveling Wilburys. I kept thinking about the last words George Harrison uttered just before he died in de Becker's Bel Air home. "Love one another" were his final words.

If I could have advised Olivia Harrison, his widow, of one thing about the staging of this memorial tribute to her late husband, it would have been to prominently display those last words her husband spoke in neon lights above the stage where the greats of music were performing and also to imprint them on the orange and yellow confetti that rained down from the ceiling at the end, like ethereal snowflakes or copious tears from heaven.

And in her remarks to the audience, I would have suggested she highlight those words while beseeching the musical greats on that sacred stage to combine their collective vast wealth and star-power to inspire the world to love one another and become one, which was also the central message of Jesus and all of the great sages, mystics and saints throughout history. It was what George advocated too.

In 1992, I fortuitously met George Harrison's older sister, Louise, in Homestead, Florida, in the aftermath of Hurricane Andrew. We helped organize local musical entertainment for the displaced victims of the hurricane who were living in Tent City. We became close friends and worked together on various projects thereafter. She is best described as an upbeat tireless social activist who championed several worthy causes, always giving in its true spirit.

I also had a private meeting with Yoko Ono Lennon in New York City at Studio One, the Dakota, in June 1984, which took place at her invitation. We talked about near-death experiences and the work of the association I founded, among other things. In the wake of her husband's horrific murder just a few years before, I hoped she would find the information about NDEs comforting and become inspired to support our effort. Alas, it was just wishful thinking on my part.

But back to the summer of 1988, instead of entertaining rosy dreams about how to inspire the world to love one another with help from the Traveling Wilburys or inspiring famous people in general to financially support the work of the association, Spirit Storm set my vision quest in motion. He decided that the day had arrived to proceed with my sacred adventure. We loaded up the rental car and drove east a few hours to Joshua Tree National Park in the Mojave Desert.

We arrived mid-afternoon to be greeted by the intense heat of summer. It was oppressive and sweltering. Honestly, it was so damned hot, I was tempted to re-evaluate and re-consider. Nevertheless, we walked around for a couple of hours taking in the sights, smells and sounds of the desert in search for a suitable place to camp for the night.

During that initial walk, I began to sense the spiritual powerhouse that is Joshua Tree National Park and the Mojave Desert. I began to recalibrate my vibration to the intense vibration of this place. I instinctively knew and viscerally felt that this was a place of enormous spiritual power. It truly felt as though I had entered one of the great rooms in God's house. Intuitively, I was certain that I was under microscopic examination by Spirit the entire time. I knew I had to be impeccable in thought, feeling, word and action. I knew my demeanor and my thoughts would shape my vision quest.

It occurred to me that the ground upon which I was walking, without exaggeration, meshed together into some kind of profound motion-sensitive membrane or matrix that was directly interfaced with the realm of Spirit. I sensed that every step, every thought and every emotion was under close scrutiny by Spirit.

I became acutely aware with heightened senses all of a sudden. In a flash of insight, I suddenly understood what the phrase "ground of being" meant, because the ground became alive to me and sacred too. It was a living thing and I was a part of it, and it was a part of me.

We found an ideal place to camp just as the sun was beginning to set in a glorious display of dazzling colors. Spirit Storm and I meditated for about an hour and then he began to chant while offering prayers on my behalf for a good quest that would bring only good medicine to me. Then we climbed into our sleeping bags for a restful sleep.

I gazed up at the magnificent stars above for a very long time until slumber arrived. I remember feeling enormously awestruck by the vast number of brilliant stars on regal display. I was overwhelmed by their indescribable beauty. I could only marvel at the wonder of it all, and that I was a tiny part of this astonishing whole known as creation. I had never seen so many stars in my entire life. It was truly magical. Actually, the entire place was magical. It felt almost like I had landed on another planet. The landscape was so very different from what I was accustomed to in the ordinary everyday world.

Morning arrived in no time at all. Much as I craved a full breakfast, I was fasting both before and during my quest. If I felt weak or lightheaded, Spirit Storm advised me to eat rice-cakes, which I brought along for my journey through the desert. I also brought along plenty of water and salt tablets to stay properly hydrated.

Our goal at this point was to hike at random, in search of a place to create my circle of stones for the Medicine Wheel ritual. It was to be my chosen sacred spot. I was to walk around the desert being led by Spirit to the right place. The entire time, I was to perform what Spirit Storm called "witnessing," which meant I was to be an alert observer of my environment.

I was to take note of everything, no matter how petty or subtle. I was to look for birds of prey, like hawks or eagles. He advised that even butterflies, rodents, gusts of wind, strange sounds or gentle intuitive nudges from Spirit could lead me to the perfect place. I was told these things would guide me to my sacred spot and I should surrender to Spirit for that purpose. Above all, I should have faith.

But the longer we walked, the more irritable and agitated I became. I was hungry, hot, tired and sweaty. Despite my best efforts to calm my mind, these emotions were overtaking me. Spirit Storm knew it too. He was attuned to me. He seemed to know what I was feeling without me speaking a word. In the midst of these contrary feelings, after a few hours into our walkabout, he dropped a major psychological bombshell on me.

He asked me, "Did you bring the tobacco?"

"What are you talking about?" I replied.

"It's on the list of the things you should bring with you," he said. "Did you remember to bring it?"

"Well, yeah, I saw it on the list, but you know I don't smoke, so I ignored it," I answered.

That answer was not the one he wanted to hear and his facial expressions said as much. "No, John, the tobacco is not to smoke," Spirit Storm explained. "It is to seal your circle. It is for your safety and protection. It wards off evil spirits and bad medicine. But you know this. You've read Castaneda. You know about the kind of craziness that can happen during a vision quest."

"Oh boy," I sighed. "Yes, I do know about the potential for craziness. But honestly, none of that ever occurred to me. It never entered my mind when I saw the word 'tobacco' on your list of things to bring. I did not have a clue it would be used to seal the circle for my protection."

In my over-active mind, which often assumes the worst, I grew very worried, so worried I was tempted to call off the whole thing all because I forgot the tobacco. I was looking for a reason to back out of the vision quest anyway without swallowing my pride or losing face. And here it was, the perfect excuse handed to me on a platter. I forgot the tobacco.

But Spirit Storm was not about to let me off the hook, at least not easily or gently. "Don't worry," he said, as if reading my mind. "I will make special provisions in the altar I plan to build near to where you form your circle. It will be sufficient to protect you. I will be nearby anyway, so there really is no valid reason for concern. Let's continue witnessing. Let's find your sacred spot."

I offered no vocal protest or objection. I simply kept walking and witnessing, waiting for the right moment to tell Spirit Storm I had decided to call off the quest this time around and would re-schedule at some later date, maybe.

I led the way at all times during our walk. Per protocol in vision quests, this is how it must be. I had to find my sacred spot. The shaman could not interfere or influence me in any way. It was between Spirit and me. So, I walked and walked in the sweltering heat. I stopped for a time in a shady spot to rest and hydrate, ready to call it off then and there.

After about fifteen minutes of silence so thick it could be cut with a knife, I said, "Spirit Storm, I am thinking about re-scheduling for this fall maybe."

"I know," he replied. "Your thoughts and emotions are plain as day. I can read you like a book, and so can Spirit. Do as you wish. This is your choice. I cannot make the decision for you."

I prayed and meditated for a bit longer on the question of what to do. I received no nudges from Spirit. I saw no signs in the sky or in my environment that would help me achieve clarity. Truly, I was all alone on this one.

Spirit wanted me to make the choice. It would not influence me one way or the other. After a while, I had cooled down a few degrees and decided I could continue walking for a bit longer, how much longer I was not sure, but I decided to keep walking until I had complete clarity about what to do without any further vacillation.

Spirit Storm said nothing as we continued our walk. He remained behind me. But later, he told me how pleased he was that I chose to head in the direction of his favorite spot in Joshua Tree, a place known to him as "Teacher Rock." I had no idea it was his favorite spot. I just walked in that direction randomly or perhaps intuitively.

As we drew nearer to Teacher Rock, I noticed a large hawk flying overhead directly above a formation of large boulders. I pointed to the hawk and suggested we walk over to the boulders. Once there, I was nudged to climb them all the way to the top. Spirit Storm stayed down below chanting and shaking his rattle.

I watched the hawk circle over one particular place atop this formation of boulders. I walked over to where it was directly overhead. My eyes stayed fixed on the hawk, not on where I was walking or on what was below me.

But when I arrived at the place where the hawk was circling, it simply changed course and flew away quickly beyond the reach of my eyesight. Unsure of what else to do at that point, I looked down at the surface of the large boulder I was standing on, which was angled and perched against other boulders of similar size and shape.

What I saw next was hard to believe. I honestly thought I was imagining things. Peeking through a crevice in between the boulders about three feet down below grade, I spotted a red and white flip top box of Marlboro cigarettes. I yelled out to Spirit Storm. "Get up here right away!" I shouted. "You won't believe what I just found! I can hardly believe it myself!"

It took him a good twenty minutes or so to make the climb up to where I was. Once he got there, I pointed down below into the crevice. I was totally relieved when the look of amazement on his face confirmed for me that he saw what I had seen. I needed his confirmation. I also needed him to witness what happened next.

"This is an incredible omen," he said. "It's the best omen I have ever seen in all my years of shamanism. John, you are going to have an amazing vision quest. Spirit just physically manifested a wonderful gift for you. They sent you two awesome omens, the hawk and the cigarettes. Down there lies your tobacco my friend. Spirit just delivered it here right out of thin air and the hawk showed you where to find it. Your circle will be sealed properly now. No harm will come to you, only sweet divine love.

"Spirit loves you deeply. Spirit approves of you. Spirit is your true ally. Right now, you are being cradled in the arms of Spirit. I see it clearly. It is so beautiful. Now, do you still want to call off and reschedule your quest?" he asked.

"No, of course not," I answered. "But let me retrieve the box first. It could be empty. I'm not even sure I can reach down that far."

"Oh ye of such little faith. Of course, you will be able to reach it," Spirit Storm remarked. "No, it will not be empty. There will be more than enough fresh tobacco in that box down there to more than properly seal your circle. I have already seen it. You're going to have a phenomenal quest, all because you mustered enough faith to keep walking and witnessing even after so much doubt had formed in your mind poisoning you with thoughts of quitting.

"You almost threw away what is now going to be the most amazing experience of your life. Now, aren't you glad you persevered? And let this be a lesson to you in perseverance. There will be many obstacles you must overcome in the future. You must learn to persevere, no matter what. You must learn patience and how to triumph over disappointment and discouragement."

I laid down flat in the prone position on the top boulder and then reached down in the crevice as far as my right arm would extend. My fingers could barely touch the top and sides of the box, but I could not grasp it. I then tried to become one with the boulder, pressing my body further into it while calling on my right arm and hand to extend themselves as far as possible. Still, it was no use. I was close but not close enough to retrieve the cigarettes.

Determined to succeed, I repositioned myself and tried again, but this time with my left hand. Once more, I pressed my body into the boulder. Seemingly, I became one with it. Sensing my urgent need, I could swear the boulder somehow minimally reduced its size just enough to enable my reach. After quite an effort, I was finally able to grasp the box of cigarettes sufficiently to retrieve it.

Spirit Storm and I studied it carefully before I opened it. It was real all right. It was indeed a brand-new flip top box of Marlboro cigarettes, red and white in color. I opened it carefully, almost as if to a silent drum roll, like a kid opening a large gift box at Christmas. The smile on my face and Spirit Storm's face could not have been any bigger or brighter. It was an unspoiled full box of cigarettes minus only one.

"Amazing," I said, "Simply amazing." I dropped to my knees there on that big, beautiful rock and gave heartfelt thanks to God for the astonishing show of grace. I looked around to find that hawk to say thank you, but it was nowhere in sight. All the while, I no longer felt the sweltering heat. I was no longer hot.

I was prompted then to ask foolish but obligatory questions to Spirit Storm. "Did you put this box of cigarettes here for me to find?" I asked. "Did you somehow energetically influence me to come to this spot? Did you somehow manipulate my thought process to ignore the tobacco in the first place?"

He looked at me sternly and answered in what was almost an angry if not dejected tone of voice. "Do not defile this blessed sacred moment with your cynicism and paranoia!" he exclaimed. "That is not who you are. Stop being who you are not and start being who you are, one who is devotedly aligned with God's love and light, one who believes in miracles and the workings of Spirit. Skepticism does not suit you. Surely you know better."

He was silent for a few minutes and then launched into a tirade. "How could I have planted these cigarettes when you have been with me this entire time? How could I know you would journey to this very spot where the cigarettes were found? How was I to know you would forget the tobacco in the first place? And how was I to know that you would carry through with your vision quest when the odds were greatly in favor of a decision by you to cancel or reschedule?

"Trust me, John, if I am good enough to manipulate things as you suggested, then I would quickly retire from shamanism and play the lottery weekly to become a billionaire. Please. No more silly questions and no more pathetic self-doubt. You almost threw all of this away by self-defeatist thoughts of quitting. Now, aren't you thrilled you hung in there?"

"Yes, of course. I am thrilled," I answered. "Actually, I am ecstatic. I can't wait to begin my Medicine Wheel ritual." I surveyed the sky and the landscape further in search of the hawk who helped me to say thank you. In the process of doing that, I noticed in front of me yet another similar formation of boulders. But this formation was smaller, not as high as the one I was standing on just then.

And wouldn't you know it? At the bottom of this nearby formation was a cave opening, about three feet wide and five feet high, with at least 15 feet of depth so far as I could see inside of it. Excitedly, I pointed it out to Spirit Storm. "There it is," I said. "There is my sacred spot. That is where I will form my circle of stones. I am ready now to begin. Thank you, God. All glory to God. How great Thou art!"

I walked over to the cave opening as fast as my feet would carry me. Spirit Storm lingered behind. There was no more fear in me, no more agitation, irritation or anxiety. Honestly, I no longer felt the sweltering heat. I was no longer mindful of it. I approached the opening of the cave with child-like glee. I peered inside and saw nothing for 15 feet or so in front of me. It was ideal for my purposes. There was even an abundance of smaller stones or rocks at the rear of the cave, all of which could be conveniently accessed to form my circle within which I would perform the Medicine Wheel ceremony.

What's more, there was a spot on the cave's floor that was ideal for my circle, plenty long and plenty wide to accommodate me. I dropped to my knees again in the center of it and thanked God for the cave and all other magnificent blessings that had been bestowed upon me. My cup was running over with joy and ecstasy.

It occurred to me then to carefully survey the cave in search of snakes, spiders, mountain lions, wolves, bears, or any other critter that could cause harm to me. Thankfully, I was greatly relieved to find nothing, not one sign of any critter or creature. Then, I gathered rocks from the back of the cave and formed my circle with them. I chose them randomly, but to one in particular, I was drawn.

Spirit Storm walked into the cave about twenty minutes later. He quickly began to set up an altar on a large flat boulder just inside the entrance. It conveniently happened to have a smooth surface large enough to accommodate the rather large altar he wanted to create.

He placed all sorts of trinkets on a small ornate colorful wool blanket, which appeared to be hand-sewn. He then opened each of the cigarettes in the box of Marlboros and sprinkled all the tobacco inside around my circle, blessing each one of the stones along the way. As he foresaw, there was just enough tobacco to seal the circle.

I paid no mind to the altar or what he placed on it. I did not inquire about it because I had surrendered fully to Spirit at this point. I trusted Spirit Storm and the process fully, which obviated the need or desire to ask any more questions. From this point forward, Spirit would direct all things and that was just fine with me.

"You are going to have a marvelous quest," Spirit Storm said. "Know that Spirit is very protective of you. I will not need to remain nearby. There will be no weirdness, just the dance of Spirit unfolding. Only good medicine will find its way to you. You are an evolved soul, John, much loved by the divine whom you have faithfully served in many lifetimes. You know what to do. I am going to leave you now. I will return when your quest is over. I do not know how long that will be. Spirit will let me know when it's time and that is when I will return, not before.

"But I will pray for you and check in on you from time to time. Remember, you are not to the leave the circle for any reason except briefly for bathroom functions which you should do outside of the cave. If you leave your circle, you leave behind its protection, so observe this one restriction above all else."

After Spirit Storm left, I laid down a blanket inside my circle and then sat down in the middle of it to meditate and pray, mostly to express reverence and gratitude, but also to declare my intentions for this quest. I sought clarity about how to fulfill my life's purpose in service to the greater good of all things and in strict accordance with God's will.

I remember feeling quite thirsty, so I drank a fair amount of water and took a salt tablet. I brought a journal with me to create a written record of what transpired during my quest. I spent about an hour writing down what had happened up to that point but could hardly believe the words I was writing to describe the events that had already unfolded. Afterwards, I took a much-needed nap.

I awoke from my nap around dusk just as the sun was setting. It was time to assume my power-stance and then perform my power-dance, as Spirit Storm had taught me. This was part of the ritual to summon Spirit and invite Spirit to work its magic. With great anticipation, I began my first Medicine Wheel, the first of five I would perform during this quest.

Native American cultures often referred to the vision quest circle as the Sacred Hoop of Life. It references the four cardinal directions: North, East, South and West. I was to do my power-stance and power-dance at the beginning of each invocation for each direction and then wait for Spirit to send me whatever medicine it wished to send, if any, before proceeding to the next direction.

When addressing the north, I was to focus on guidance concerning mental or mind issues. When facing east, I was to concentrate on spiritual matters. Emotional concerns were the domain of the south. And, finally, looking west I was to seek guidance about physical health matters concerning my body. At each cardinal point in the circle, I repeated the same ritual, over and over again.

Faithfully, as taught by Spirit Storm, I performed the Medicine Wheel twice on that first day, once before sunset and later at night just before going to sleep. But when it came time for me to sit in silence waiting for spirit to guide, I consistently drew a blank. There was only silence.

Yet, the silence inside that cave spoke volumes. I did not have the capacity to hear or understand its messages nor could I benefit from its guidance. Nevertheless, I found the silence nourishing, comforting and alluring, although not instructive. I discovered that in this sacred silence and stillness, God is revealed, felt and experienced. I was to listen closely with my heart for the cry of an autumn leaf on a tree as it poignantly falls to the ground.

I did not have a watch with me per the instructions of Spirit Storm. I was not supposed to focus on time, but rather find a way to transcend it. So, I'm not sure what time it was, but I grew very tired late that first evening after my second Medicine Wheel ritual. So I crawled into the sleeping bag, more than ready for a restful repose.

I was happy to be in that cave. I felt it was sacred space. I could sense the loving presence of Spirit all around me but could not hear it or see it. Still, I had faith that I was safe, right where I was supposed to be. And I knew I was there for a good reason.

I had no idea what time it was, but sometime in the wee hours of the next morning, I was rudely awakened by loud crashing noise inside the cave. Per Spirit Storm, I brought a flashlight with me in case of emergency. I quickly reached for it and turned it on.

There was nothing in the cave except for a newly arrived surprise visitor. It was a cute full size kangaroo rat. It completely demolished the altar Spirit Storm had put in place by hopping back and forth all over it. "There goes my altar," I thought. "So much for my protection." I figured the kangaroo rat was likely a female with a nest or burrow nearby who was totally freaked out by my presence.

When I focused the flashlight beam on her, she quickly hopped away to conceal herself under the cover of the rocks in the rear of the cave. Kangaroo rats are bipeds. They hop like a kangaroo, hence the name. They're cute as can be too. Later, I learned they're mostly vegetarians and can go long periods without water, far more resilient than camels or giraffes.

I began chanting in a soft soothing voice to let her know I was no threat and would not cause any harm to her or her nest or her burrow. After a while, she got the message. She cautiously ventured back to the altar and then went about her business as she normally would, basically ignoring my presence for the rest of the evening. She was no longer afraid. In that moment, a strong resonance formed between us, bordering on a spiritual bond.

I switched off the flashlight and tried to fall back to sleep, but with no success. So, I stood up and performed my third Medicine Wheel ritual in the thick black darkness of night. As I was finishing the third ritual, the arrival of dawn made itself known. It was inexpressibly beautiful, otherworldly in fact. I focused on the interplay between advancing light and receding darkness. There was a mystical resonance and a curious interdependence between them. One needed the other. One could not exist without the other.

As the darkness retreated to make way for the light, the light advanced to illuminate what the darkness had previously concealed. And when the light receded later in the day, the darkness would once again conceal what the light had previously revealed.

It occurred to me that this is how major social change and individual transformation must take place. It must unfold in a slow, patient, gradual, evolutionary manner, not instantaneously or radically, much as I would prefer.

I was then shown the image of a totally dark room with many people seated around a conference table. I walked in through the door and turned on the light switch to fully and instantly illuminate the room. Let there be light, right?

My thought at the time was 'hey, why are you all choosing to sit here in the dark when you can enjoy the light and see better in the light?' And so, thinking everyone should prefer light to darkness, I flipped the switch to fully and instantly illuminate the room. It was not a very good idea despite only good intentions on my part.

Predictably, my action was quickly met with great hostility and resentment. The appearance of full instantaneous light hurt everyone's eyes. It was most distressing for all of the people around the table because they were accustomed to sitting in total darkness. The sudden arrival of full light was vexing. It could only be introduced slowly over time so their eyes could adjust to it gradually and incrementally. To do otherwise would be to invite sure trouble.

That is when I realized there needed to be a dimmer switch installed in the room, not a simple on/off switch. In this way, light could be slowly and gradually introduced by raising the dimmer switch gently and gradually so as not to hurt the eyes or cause serious distress to anyone.

Such was to be my task in service to Spirit when I emerged from the cave in service to the greater good in the outside world. I could only introduce the light to people slowly, carefully and skillfully, but never in a way that would overwhelm, vex or cause them to recoil.

The scene inside the cave was surreal at the finish of my third Medicine Wheel. It did not suddenly change from being pitch black dark to being fully illuminated with bright light. To the contrary, it was a slow, gradual, poetic process, one that was actually awe-inspiring to witness. The light advanced slowly, but only as fast as the receding darkness allowed.

This is the insight I was meant to learn in the cave. All life long, my impatience demanded instant, revolutionary, radical change. I came to regard the state of the world, as it was then and is now, to be totally inexcusable, intolerable and unacceptable. Due to my inherent nature as an empathetic soul, I wanted to see it profoundly transformed once and for all, immediately.

I am and always have been highly sensitive to pain and suffering in the world in all forms. I yearn for all of it to be healed quickly. But that's just me being me again, projecting my personal hopes, dreams and ideas onto others thinking they will feel the same way simply because it is fully aligned with what is right and good. Sadly, this is just so much wishful thinking on my part. Many are too burdened by their own struggles in life to focus on the woeful plight of others.

For just a few precious moments, in the shadows that danced on the east wall of the cave, where the altar had been created, I saw the silhouette of a middle-aged Native American Indian male, but just the outline of his face. It was projected on the surface of the cave's east wall in full color. It was a face I had seen before…the face of the Indian who appeared in my bedroom when I was eight years old.

It was not lost on me that the east direction is the domain of the spiritual. So when I saw the image of this Native American Indian on the cave's eastern wall, I assumed he was one of my Spirit Guides there to watch over me and bring me good medicine. To this day, my conclusion is unchanged. I am sure it was him. I am sure his intentions were to bring me good medicine, as always.

Not long after the image of this Indian appeared, I heard a whisper inside my brain. It was not my internal voice but rather an unfamiliar haunting voice of a soft-spoken male. It was a "thought with a voice" that I can best describe as a "talking thought implant" or the implantation of a "talking thought" inside my head. It was not expressed in my familiar internal voice. The talking thought said, "John, Spirit waits patiently for you and all humanity to stop waiting for Spirit—to accept, know, revere and align with Spirit."

This was all I heard. Nothing else was conveyed to me. I don't know who or what generated this communication, but I took the word "Spirit" to mean Great Spirit, Creator, Source, God. It was all I needed to hear. This was my epiphany in the Mojave Desert.

In that moment, hearing this talking thought, not with my ears, but reverberating inside my head, I understood the significance and purpose of my vision quest. It affirmed my reason for being in this lifetime. I was indeed reminded of my purpose, but yet I still remained unsure about how to fulfill it. How could I help humanity to know, accept, revere and align with Spirit? How could I go about the challenge of being First Light?

I suspect that writing this book, at long last, may be a big part of fulfilling this task. It may be what I came here to contribute or accomplish. If it does any good in this increasingly troubled world by inspiring people to believe God is real, to revere God and align with God, then this will be confirmation enough for me.

If its impact makes any kind of a meaningful positive difference in the human condition, then it may be enough for me to understand why my life was miraculously saved all the times described in this work. It will explain why I was immensely blessed to have so many marvelous miracles.

With the arrival of morning and the new day, I spotted the kangaroo rat again, but this time she came in close proximity to me as my friend and companion. She was not spooked by my company any longer. She looked at me lovingly, projecting a profound peace. I returned the same energy to her. I thanked her for sharing her cave with me. It was a powerful non-verbal expression of spiritual love. To make her a humble offering, I placed two rice cakes in front of her, which she quickly consumed.

I left my circle and the cave briefly to attend to bathroom functions. When I walked back inside, ravenous hunger pains took hold. So, I ate not one or two but four rice cakes. My energy level soared through the roof. I was ready for Spirit Storm to return. My quest had ended. I was bursting at the seams with eagerness to share with him what took place during the night.

Telepathically, I called out to him and asked him to return. While waiting for him, I updated my journal with the events of the night before. Then I prayed and meditated. Soon after, I commenced another Medicine Wheel ritual, and another after that, but this time to convey gratitude, not seek guidance.

Later that afternoon, Spirit Storm arrived back at the cave. The first thing he noticed was that his altar had been greatly disturbed. I explained why it was in such disarray. It gave him a good laugh. Then he listened patiently to me without interruption as I told him everything that had happened, well, almost everything.

For reasons that today no longer seem valid, I decided not to speak with him about the image of the Indian on the east wall of the cave. I wanted to keep that to myself. I really did not know what to make of it and, frankly, I started to doubt that I saw it at all. I began to think I just imagined it.

It was hard enough for me to tell him about the voice I heard inside my head and the message it conveyed. Moreover, I did not want to dilute the central aspects of my quest with what I thought could be a tangential aberration or hallucination. Even though I strongly felt that the vision of the Indian was real, I began to doubt myself about seeing it.

Spirit Storm took great delight in everything I told him. "Yours was a magnificent quest, John, one of the best I have ever supervised. Congratulations. Well done. I give you the medicine name First Light. You are to bring light to places that are dark. You are to be the light that beckons darkness to recede and retreat. This is your life's purpose. Now let's go to Palm Springs, check into a hotel, shower and enjoy a hearty meal to celebrate your remarkable rite of passage."

Some folks might regard the two days I spent in that cave as self-imposed or self-inflicted *solitary confinement.* That would be one way to view it. But, instead, I call it self-liberating and self-affirming *Solitary Refinement*, a term I conceived to aptly describe my vision quest. My experience was one of sacred communion with Spirit in the Mojave Desert, truly one of the great rooms in God's house. I left there feeling far more enlightened and empowered, ready to pursue my life's purpose with vigor.

As we were walking out of the cave, I looked around to bid farewell to my new kangaroo rat friend, but she was nowhere to be seen. I then asked Spirit Storm if I could take one of the stones with me that formed my circle. He gave me permission to do so.

I slowly surveyed the circle stones and chose one out of the many that beckoned. It wanted to come home with me. This one stone stood out among all the others. It was the only one that could stand upright on its own without falling over onto its side. That was the stone I chose, or perhaps it was the stone that chose me.

I still have it on display. It rests on the hutch in my study as a reminder of my time in solitary refinement. I brought the other stones to the rear of the cave where I found them, returning things inside the cave to their original state.

While I waited for Spirit Storm to shower inside our Palm Springs hotel room, I closely examined the stone I brought with me from the cave. At its base on one of its sides were three elevated straight lines that joined together to form the raised outline of a pyramid. I took it outside into the sunlight and rotated it in my hand. There were dozens of tiny crystal particles embedded in it that glistened in the sunlight. It was a beautiful sight.

As I rotated the stone in the sunlight, in its creases, I noticed a curious display of adjoining lines at the bottom on the opposite side of the pyramid. I could detect the appearance of four letters: "J-o-h-n." These adjoining letters spelled out my first name. I showed it to Spirit Storm when he emerged from the shower. He looked it over carefully and agreed that I was not imagining it.

"I've never seen anything like it before," he said. "You were blessed with remarkable grace during this quest because of your steadfast devotion to Spirit. Never doubt the power of your connection to the divine and never deny your mission as First Light. Always stay strong in your spiritual center and never allow sadness or disappointment to overtake you. Just like the Blues Brothers, now you know you're on a special mission from God, but yours is the real deal. Much depends on it. Do not fail."

We left our hotel room and went for a fantastic meal. I had a voracious appetite and ate heartily. After that, we went to a local cinema and watched the movie *Bull Durham*, which was a welcomed distraction from all the intensity of the past few days. Then we drove back to Spirit Storm's house in Los Angeles where I hung out for a while before flying back to my home in Lake Worth.

Looking back on my time in the cave, with all due respect to the Traveling Wilburys, I would not have traded it to join them during those amazing recording sessions. Yes, it was that powerful for me. To this day, I remain thankful to Spirit for the solitary refinement, my new friend the kangaroo rat, and the box of Marlboro cigarettes.

Incidentally, thus far in my life, I have chanced upon three other such red and white flip top boxes: one on the road near my home; another in the parking lot of a local grocery store; and the last one which I found while walking along the Intracoastal Waterway not far from my home. It was the third box that signaled something profound.

Nothing out of the ordinary happened after finding the first two boxes. I left them where I found them thinking they might be meant for someone else. I also regarded them as gentle nudges from Spirit reminding me to stay on the right track and remain strong in the fullness of my spiritual center.

But, in early 2008, shortly after I found the third box, a friend phoned me to suggest that I should have a session with a powerful Apache shaman from Asheville, North Carolina, who would be coming soon for a visit to nearby Pompano Beach. I agreed and a date for our session was set in mid-March.

In retrospect, I now believe that the third and last flip top box I found full of Marlboro cigarettes was an auspicious omen that portended the meeting with this high voltage shaman. Of course, I did not realize it at the time I made the appointment, but my session with him would turn out to be seismic in its spiritual importance.

It would dig up a very old painful wound, a trauma so deep and so long buried I thought it would never surface again to see the light of day. I was wrong about that. He found this old wound at the very beginning of our session and brought it right back up to the forefront of my consciousness. And so, now, it is a story I must share, for it closes and completes the circle.

The Apache Shaman

I should have seen it coming after I found that third box of Marlboro cigarettes near my home, lying there next to the seawall of the Intracoastal Waterway. I should have guessed well in advance that the Apache shaman I was to meet about a week later would be a chain smoker whose favorite brand was Marlboros in the red and white flip top box.

He was the houseguest of a good friend of a good friend. She lived in a high-rise condominium overlooking the Atlantic Ocean. When I arrived for my appointment, I was greeted by his host and escorted to the outside balcony. The shaman, a true Native American Indian of the Apache tribe, was sitting in a nicely cushioned patio chair, enjoying a terrific view of the ocean, calm and smooth as glass that day. He was smoking a cigarette.

On the coffee table next to him was an opened box of Marlboro cigarettes, red and white flip top box. One cigarette was missing, the one in his mouth…the one he was smoking at the time we met. I introduced myself and we exchanged cordialities. Then he pointed to the open pack of cigarettes on the table.

"That's my calling card," he said. "I just want you to know who you are dealing with. Truth in advertising. Full disclosure." How he was able to know my connection to Marlboro cigarettes flip top box, or the flip top box from my vision quest with one missing, or the full flip top box I had just found near my home is a real mystery to me. I mean, really, what are the odds of this happening? But that was only the beginning of what baffled me, or perhaps I should say what blew me away.

He grabbed onto my left shoulder just above the blade near the cervical spine. He pressed into it with his index finger, sending me through the roof in sharp pain. "What's this?" he asked. "What are you carrying or burying here? Ah, yes, a nasty little miasma."

"This is an old painful wound, one goes way back to when you were just six years old. It was quite a trauma. It totally shut you down. Your spirit went off grid. You became the invisible man. Your very bright spiritual light went way dim. You did not croak, but you cloaked. You went into stealth mode. So tell me what you think happened back then," he requested. "I can see it all, the two young boys and the mechanic's dolly, but I want to know how you saw it."

From the time I was a little boy forming the first conscious thoughts, I can remember it was my innate inclination to question why there is so much cruelty in the world. I continually wondered why some people were wholly mean-spirited while others had only goodness, generosity and compassion in their hearts toward others.

I could not understand nor abide man's inhumanity to man. I saw evidence of it everywhere, so much so I began to shelter and insulate myself from it as much as possible. I honestly thought I came to the wrong planet because things here seemed so dark, primitive and barbaric. I wondered how a place of such astounding beauty could be home to so much cruelty and meanness. Truly, I often felt like "a stranger in a strange land." I still do.

Long before I had any religious training or was introduced to the concept of God, it was my inherent nature to treat others with love, kindness, respect and compassion. This was not something my parents instilled in me, nor the church. Rather, it was a naturally occurring personality trait. It always has been my basic character.

I do not for one minute believe that this makes me holier than thou or more pure of spirit or that it should qualify me as a pie-in-the-sky idealist. Rather, I would like to believe that character such as this is a basic signature trademark of all human beings. To me, it encapsulates what it means to be human. I wish everyone shared this point of view. What's wrong with the world is that many do not.

I cannot say I always had God in my heart. I did not, certainly not before I was introduced to the idea of God, and certainly not during my years as an agnostic. But I always had goodness in my heart. I was always highly empathetic. I always cared for the well-being of all others, not just people, but animals, trees and all other forms of life on our planet, even the planet itself as a whole.

I was always sensitive to the suffering of others and wanted to do whatever I could to make things better for everyone and everything. I just never really knew how to go about it. Most of my life, I have been trying to figure out how to achieve this overarching goal, how to make a meaningful difference to improve the quality of life for all.

If ever I hurt someone's feelings inadvertently, it hurt me worse. Even before I knew how to articulate it in this manner, I consistently held firm to the Golden Rule, as well as an important variation of it from the ancient mystics: "What you do to others you do to yourself," which is said I suppose in reference to the accumulation of karma that shapes and determines future incarnations.

When I became the subject or target of meanness by others, it affected me like a festering wound. Of course, I realize that virtually no one gets through life unscathed by the cruelty of others and by the usual vicissitudes of life itself. To think otherwise would be totally naïve. But some have it far worse than others and that is a gross understatement, I am sorry to say.

Yet all forms of mean-spiritedness are traumatic, from the most minor assault to those that are truly the most horrific, whether it is emotional or physical in nature or both. They impact and diminish us adversely. They shock the psyche. They dampen our spirit. They form emotional calluses and scars, if not enduring physical ones, from which we never fully recover. Sometimes they kill us and rob our very lives from us. Other times they place us in bondage and we remain enslaved by the pain they caused for most if not all of our lives. To be imprisoned by hurt such as this is to die slowly from it.

The old wound that the Apache shaman discovered was the first extremely hurtful incident in my life. It occurred in early 1959 at the age of six when I was in the first-grade. My parents gave me a two-wheel bicycle for Christmas 1958, my first. It was a gorgeous red and white Schwinn with training wheels.

Believe me when I tell you that it was the first time in life I experienced love at first sight. My happiness and joy could not be contained. I was full of glee to receive probably my best Christmas present ever. I rode it constantly around the streets of our neighborhood near my early childhood home just west of downtown Fort Lauderdale. Nothing made me happier, not even my prized Lionel train set. If I could have slept with that bike in my bed, I would have.

After a few weeks of learning to ride with training wheels, my father removed them. He declared it was time for me to ride without them. I did so with ease and grace like a fish swimming through the water. It was gloriously liberating. I loved every minute of it.

One morning, just a block or so from my home, as I was riding my new bike down our street enjoying the warmth of the sun hitting my face, I noticed a car parked in the driveway of a neighbor's house. The hood was raised. I presumed an adult was working on it performing maintenance and repair but had gone inside the house or garage momentarily for one reason or another.

This driveway was not flat or level with the ground. It was raised or slightly elevated, sloping from its high point near the garage door to its low point where it met the street. There was a four-wheeled mechanic's dolly near the front tire of the vehicle on the driver's side. Two young boys, one my age perhaps and the other maybe two years older, were squatting down next to it.

The two boys had their eyes fixed on me, watching my every move, looking at me with mean-spirited grins. I have never figured out why. I did not know them. In fact, I had never seen them before, and I never saw them again after the incident. We said nothing to each other. Not one single word was spoken.

As I approached the spot where their driveway met the road, I was traveling in the middle of the street at what was full speed for me then. Without any provocation whatsoever, the older boy suddenly pushed the dolly down the driveway right into the path of my oncoming bicycle. It rapidly descended, picking up speed as it went along due to sloping nature of the driveway's design.

The timing of his shove was perfect, as well as the amount of force he applied. It arrived in the middle of the road at the same exact time as my bike's front tire. I had no time to brake or react in any way and so a terrible collision occurred, much to my dismay.

Upon impact, the rear end of my bike flew up into the air and threw me off my seat like a bucking horse. I sailed off the bike over the handlebars and slid face down on the surface of the road, which was not smooth asphalt, but rather the raised rock kind.

Acting much like a cheese grinder, the sandpaper-rough surface of the road tore and ripped my face to shreds, reducing it to a bloody pulp. To say it hurt like hell would not be doing justice to the pain I felt at that moment. I still have a scar under my lower lip from the incident as a lasting reminder of it, not that I need one.

Fortunately for me, my mother was outside in our yard watering bushes she had planted a few days before. She heard my cries and screams. They were so loud, I think the entire neighborhood heard them. She came racing over to my aid, and with super-human strength, lifted me up from the surface of the road. She carried me home where she and my older half-sister Rosemary applied immediate first aid, starting with cold wet facecloths that they placed delicately all over my battered face.

I was in terrible pain. My face felt like someone set it on fire. I was also in a state of great shock. I could not believe this had just happened to me. I did not know those boys. I did nothing to them. I was minding my own business. I was not bothering them in any way. So, why would they want to harm me, I wondered. To this day I still wonder many decades after my physical wounds healed, which by the way took a good month or so to complete, biologically speaking. Emotionally, I am still wounded by it.

Although my new bicycle was undamaged from the incident, I would not ride it again for many months, well past the time it took me to heal physically. I was so traumatized by what happened that I could not bring myself to ride it again, at least not for a very long time, as irresistible as it was. And when I did finally climb back onto to the seat of my bike, I never again rode past the house where those two boys lived or even in that general direction. For me, it became the forbidden zone.

When my father came home from work as a union journeyman plumber, a proud member of Plumbers and Pipefitters Local Union 719, he became furious when he saw the wounds on my face, but even more so when I told him what happened. He instantly marched down the street to have a word with the parents of the two boys who committed the offense.

They warmly welcomed him into their home, I was told. But rather than an ensuing brawl or fisticuffs, they calmed my father down by apologizing profusely for the incident. They claimed that their sons had not pushed the dolly as I had described, but that it rolled down the driveway all by itself and collided with my bike. The timing was so unfortunate, they said. They called it a freak accident.

My father innocently accepted their explanation. He told me I must have imagined that the boys pushed it. He chided me never to tell tall tales again. He figured I fabricated their involvement to avoid taking any of the blame for it. He firmly and quickly concluded that the incident was my fault. He then scolded me and said I should have maneuvered around the dolly or braked immediately to avoid hitting it. It is no exaggeration to confess that the emotional pain of being falsely accused in this way was worse than the physical pain from the injuries to my face, arms and hands.

The Apache shaman knew exactly what happened back then and how it severely impacted me. He saw it all. He brought that old painful wound right back up to the surface. "They were not little boys," he said. "They were lizards, lower vibration beings from the lower astral planes. They did it intentionally. They were on a mission to shut you down. It worked."

"What are you talking about?" I asked. "What do you mean? Why would anyone want to shut me down? I have no special powers or abilities. And how do you know about this incident and the Marlboro cigarettes? It's mind-blowing. How can you see such things?"

He then put me through an exercise. He told me to close both eyes and extend out both arms palms up. He placed a powerful onyx stone in one and a special high voltage crystal in the other. He asked me to grasp them in my hand and describe the difference between them in terms of their energy. I could not. I could only tell him that one weighed less than the other. He told me to open my eyes and then explained the intense spiritual power of both objects, neither of which I could feel or discern.

"You're dead even to yourself," he said. "You're a dead man walking. You've been dead to yourself since the age of six. You don't even know who you are or the special abilities you have. Yep, I would say those lizards shut you down all right. They did a damn good job of it too. But now it's time for you to come out of hiding. It's time for you to join the battle between light and darkness, good and evil."

How can people like these two boys be so cruel and cold-hearted? I wondered. What possessed them to do such a diabolical thing? Both of them suffered no consequences whatsoever for their terrible behavior. Both went unpunished and unscathed. They skated away scot-free with no admission of guilt or expression of remorse.

After spending nearly a whole lifetime pondering this deed and other dark deeds I have experienced, along with a multitude of global human atrocities of far greater magnitude, I have come to the conclusion that the people who do such things do not carry God in their hearts. If they did, then they would not be capable of such dark behavior and evil. This is why humanity needs God.

Yes, critics will say that all throughout history many atrocities and horrific acts of cruelty were committed in the name of God by those who professed to be true believers and devotees, some even sanctioned by various religions in conducting their holy crusades for instance. But these were unholy crusades and vile acts, not connected with God or ordained by God in any way.

The God I know is a God of pure love and only pure love. The God I know says "Thou shalt not kill" and does not violate that law. The God I know is not vengeful, wrathful, angry, impulsive, mercurial, jealous, inconsistent or judgmental, but rather the constant perfect expression of pure unconditional love and indescribable beauty.

Anyone who truly carries God in their heart is by nature completely incapable of evil or cruelty, not even that which has been sanctioned by religion, or by the state as in the case of war. This is the God I know and aspire to affirm and glorify by exhibiting Godliness as best as I can and as consistently as I can.

"There's no question whose side you're on," the shaman said. "That's totally clear my friend over the course of many lifetimes. But we have to wake you up now and get you into the fight. You're needed. You need to go back into your Medicine Wheel circle. But, this time in order to uncloak, you must do the sweat lodge and take peyote. We must signal your return with a fearless fire ceremony."

"How could those little boys know who I am in the spiritual sense when I did not know myself at that time or even now?" I asked. "At the age of six, I did not know much of anything. I had no awareness of spiritual matters."

"Every soul has a unique signature spiritual frequency," he answered. "Those who are attuned know your spiritual frequency. They can perceive it. Your frequency is off the charts. I knew who you were long before you ever showed up at the door. I knew you were coming and I know who you are in the spiritual sense.

"There are only a few like you on the planet, my friend. You're a Golden One, only one of 46 beings here on earth to help humankind evolve spiritually at this critical juncture. You're here to help usher in the Golden Age.

"The forces of evil and darkness do not want you to succeed. They know who you are, too, and they are determined to neutralize you, as well as all spiritual beacons who are major light-bringers. So, all of your life, you have been effectively thwarted, sabotaged, circumvented, hamstrung and shackled. Am I right? You know I am. Can I hear you say amen?"

"Yes, amen, but I am no one special. I am not what you call a Golden One. You're not the first to tell me this, but I do not believe it. So sorry, but I do not have any unusual talents or abilities. If I did, they are so well hidden from me that even I don't know where to find them. I would not even know where to begin to look. You're right about a lot, for sure, but you're wrong about that. I wish I had great powers, but I do not. So, I must ask you again. How do you know these things? How can you be so sure about it?"

"I am a full-blooded Apache shaman and medicine man. I am directly descended from Geronimo. I am a man of power, a man of knowledge, a seer. Your powers are greater than mine, but you hide from them. You're afraid of them. Those lizards really did shut you down and that's what they aimed to do.

"John, you can do everything I can do and much more, but yet you don't because you don't think you're anyone special. You don't think you have any special gifts. But you do. You just don't realize it.

"My friend, you are seriously blocked. You have not awakened to your power. You are in denial about it. But I see you in the future as gatekeeper and guardian of the light. I see you forming powerful balls from the energy that makes light, molding them with your hands like clay. I see you hurling these huge balls of lights at the lizards, the dark ones, to send them scurrying away fast.

"But you do not see this and you do not accept it. You stubbornly persist in this denial after all these years and all your encounters with Spirit. You keep thinking you are just like everyone else. You think everyone else is just like you. Well, my friend it is you who is wrong, not me.

"Try this one on for size. You are irreversibly in love with God. All you really want to do is honor and serve God. You are constantly thinking about ways to advance human civilization by shifting and improving basic human nature through a global spiritual renaissance or revolution. You imagine it will be one based on the science of consciousness, where it intersects with physics and spiritually transformative experiences, both of which are your favorite subjects for the potential they hold to change the world and shift the global paradigm.

"You cannot help yourself. Every day you wake up thinking about it, and every night when you go to bed, and all throughout the day too. You are incapable of taking a break from it. It is all you really care about. Now what percentage of the human population does such a thing? Any idea? How many are similarly afflicted with this maddening condition?" he asked.

"I think most people want to change the world for the better and often contemplate how to go about it," I replied.

"Wrong, dead wrong," he answered. "Most people don't think about it at all, not ever, and very few are fully obsessed with it like you are. This is the singular driving passion and purpose of your life. It is a forceful wind that blows you along and never lets up.

"My friend, your kind is a rare breed on this planet. You care nothing about material possessions, money, fame or political power. That makes you a rare incorruptible because you cannot be bought or co-opted with the usual trinkets. Those like you in genuine service to the greater good, not themselves, number far less than one tenth of one percent. Wake up and smell the coffee.

"Many pretend to be altruists and speak shallow words about it, but few walk the talk. With each person you meet, ask yourself, 'Are they real or are they Memorex?' Nearly everyone is false, thinking only of themselves and how to feather their own nests. Most come from ego and self-aggrandizement, but not you. You never have. You never will. That mind set is completely foreign to you.

"Time to come out of your shell my friend. The world needs you. This is what you came here to do, First Light. Now get on with it. Oh, don't worry. You'll have plenty of help from the world of Spirit, including your Native American Indian guardian angel, the warrior you met when you were eight years old. He walks with you always. He protects you. He was with you in the cave. He's beside you right now, but you don't even know it, Mr. Dead Man Walking. Time for you to run away from home and join the circus, dude. Stop being Mr. Reliable and Mr. Dutiful."

The shaman went on from there to give me a terrific reading, but mostly he told me things I had already heard before from other gifted seers like him. He too advised me to get on with the great work at hand and to awaken my power without further delay.

Like Spirit Storm, he said the sun was about to set on the human race unless we quickly get our act together. "The Time of Fire is coming soon," he said. "All will be set aflame by humanity's own hand unless a critical mass emerges to fully embrace God. Humanity must stop pretending that God does not exist. We must all affirm, revere and align with Spirit. The hour grows short." Spirit Storm told me the same thing many times. I could not agree more.

The Apache shaman, like many other seers before and after him, consistently revealed not only my spiritual destiny and dharma as First Light, but also this hard to grasp notion that I am somehow divinely appointed, guarded and protected as one whose purpose in life must be fulfilled somehow for the betterment of humankind. Yeah, right. This is my honest reaction to all of these statements.

Please note that I never accept or reject such observations. I merely consider them data points. But adding up all the data points from all the stories shared in this book and others not shared, perhaps there could be some credence to this notion. But this is for others to judge, not me. It is for time to tell.

Tangentially, but further to the same point, consider yet another interesting story from September 2004. At that time, Florida was belted by two back-to-back hurricanes, Frances and Jeanne. We remained in our home to ride out both storms. We chose not to evacuate, even though we were under mandatory orders to do so.

Frances was a Category 4 storm which made landfall in southern Florida on September 5th packing winds in excess of 145 MPH. Jeanne was a Category 3 storm which made landfall in southern Florida on September 26th packing winds of 120 MPH.

The storms delivered considerable damage all around us but left us amazingly untouched. By the grace of God, we were left unscathed. It was rather remarkable to say the least. My neighbor across the street looked out his un-shuttered windows to view our home during both storms.

Afterwards, he told me how astonishing it was that our home was fully spared the ravages of both storms. He said, "It was like there was a divine protective force-field surrounding your house during both hurricanes, John. The fierce winds just seemed to arch or bend around it. Your property was kept safe and left undamaged."

Lucid Dream with Physical Validation

Although I left the Roman Catholic Church in 1970 and never looked back, I kept having the most amazing recurring dreams about Pope Francis dating back to at least 2014. These dreams are mostly consistent variations on the same theme, even though I have never met the man and doubt I ever will.

There is one notable exception to my recurring dreams about Pope Francis. It occurred on September 15, 2017. In my regular dreams, Pope Francis and I know each other very well. We're close friends and confidants. We're always alone, walking side by side. He is dressed in his Papal attire and me in casual attire. We are colleagues of sorts, in intense conversation about how to reform or transform the Roman Catholic Church in a manner consistent with the Seven Statements (explained in Part III) and the Fifteen Elaborations available at *AffirmingGod.com* that were developed as part of the mission of Eternea, a non-profit organization.

As many know, Pope Francis may be the most reform-oriented Pope in all of history. He has expressed a strong desire to overhaul the Roman Catholic Church. But this specific dream is the one Pope Francis dream which stands out above the rest and highlights and underscores this theme of major reform. It is the most cogent, lucid and powerful dream about him by far, one with physical validation that manifested the very same day. The dream occurred around 4 a.m. Eastern Standard Time in the immediate aftermath of Hurricane Irma, just two days shy of what would have been Dr. Edgar Mitchell's 87th birthday had he lived instead of dying the year before.

When the dream ended, I woke up immediately and turned on my computer to write a full account of it so nothing would be lost or forgotten. This is what I wrote back then:

"Pope Francis sent me an invitation to visit the Vatican to attend a gathering of high-ranking church officials. Among them were candidates vying to be chosen as his next chief of staff. He said this person would be his close trusted partner in bringing badly needed reform to the Roman Catholic Church following centuries of unfathomable deceit, hypocrisy and corruption.

I accepted his invitation and went to the meeting in Rome. It was held at St. Peter's Basilica in the Sistine Chapel. The cathedral was filled with church VIPs from around the world. The Vatican Boys Choir opened the meeting singing a sacred hymn. The audience accompanied them in singing the lyrics, but I do not remember what song they sang.

Soon Pope Francis walked on stage appearing quite humble and reverent, almost somber. He said one person in the audience soon would be chosen as his new chief of staff. He said God would choose this person, not him. He said God would send the Spear of Destiny down from the heavens. He said it would land next to the person whom God had chosen to be his new chief of staff. He asked everyone to stand and everyone did, including me.

At the time of this dream, I knew nothing about the Spear of Destiny. I was sitting far in the back of the gathering, alone, off to myself, trying to be totally invisible. I could not even believe I was there, much less at the Pope's invitation.

As I gazed around the room, I wondered who would be chosen. Then, I heard a captivating mesmerizing sound from up above, reminiscent of the glass armonica invented in 1761 by Benjamin Franklin. All those gathered looked up at the ceiling to find the spot from where the sound was emanating.

The ceiling suddenly opened and the celestial regions appeared above. The Spear of Destiny then came into view descending rapidly from the heavens, an awesome sight. Everyone could clearly see it. They were awestruck and spellbound by it, especially me.

The Spear was heading straight for me. My impulse was to move out of its path, but inner guidance compelled me to stand my ground as a show of fearless faith, which is what I did. I could not move anyway. I seemed to be frozen or immobilized right where I stood. I remember being conscious in this dream. I remember consciously choosing to stand my ground motionless as this Spear descended.

To my shock and surprise, the Spear landed right beside me and planted itself into the concrete floor next to my left foot. It was then I realized that if I had moved it would have changed course to follow me and would have landed right next to my left foot regardless of where I went in the cathedral.

The Pope walked over to me all smiles. He kissed my left cheek and then my right. He gave me a warm hug and said, "My dear John, did you ever once doubt it could be anyone other than you? Why would you doubt it could be anyone other than you? You are one who has and will give your life in service to God's truth. You are one who has and will sacrifice himself for God. You are one who has and will die for divine truth."

For what seemed like a long time, I stood before Pope Francis motionless. I remained silent and speechless, overcome with humility and shock. Then I said, "Your Holiness, never once did I ever imagine it would be me. How could God choose me for this great honor? I am the least worthy and the least qualified. Could it possibly have been a mistake?" I asked.

The Pope replied, "God makes no mistakes, my son. This is the will of God. Do not question it. Stay in reverence and gratitude. Now let's go. We have much work to do. We must begin right away."

As we began to walk away, the Sword of Destiny just disappeared. It simply vanished into thin air, as mysteriously as it had appeared out of thin air. The audience was stunned and shocked to see the two of us walk away together, arm in arm, but they applauded politely in a very reserved manner as a show of respect. Nobody knew who I was. They were bewildered that God would choose an unknown person from outside of the Church to be the Pope's new chief of staff.

Then the Pope said, "John, the first thing I must teach you is how to accurately perceive the hearts and minds of people. What do you sense from this audience? Be as honest as you can be." Again, in this part of the dream, I distinctly recall being conscious and making conscious choices.

I told Pope Francis I sensed envy and resentment coming towards me from the audience. The Pope said, "Yes, that's right." Then the Pope asked me to scan the entire audience and focus on one face from whom I sensed these feelings most strongly.

As we walked through the crowded room, I scanned the faces in slow motion. I recognized no one, but there was one man whose face I focused on among all others in a room full of unfamiliar faces. I told the Pope that I found one person in particular from whom I sensed bad feelings much more than envy and resentment. I told the Pope that this person was extremely angry and wanted to kill me.

Then the Pope counseled me to study this man's facial expressions and body language. He said I was correct to single him out. He said this person was the leading inside contender for the chief of staff job and had fully expected to be the one chosen. The Pope said I was correct that this man would seek to have me killed or would try hard to sabotage me. He said this man would be my undoing unless I made him an ally.

The Pope then explained that my first challenge was to find a way to transform this man into a friend. He said this would be my first major test. If I succeeded at this task, our larger campaign to transform the church in accordance with the Seven Statements would be greatly strengthened. If I failed, the Pope said our efforts to bring about serious internal change to the Church would be futile."

When I woke up from this dream, I looked up the Spear of Destiny on Wikipedia. Guess what I found out? It is kept in St. Peter's Basilica! I had no idea. Spooky. I also learned that the spear referred to as the Spear of Destiny is the actual spear used by a Roman solider at the site of the crucifixion to pierce the body of Christ in or around the abdomen, after He died on the cross, to confirm that He was dead.

Later that same day, in real life, a bruise about the size of a half dollar appeared on the top front of my left foot, but I did not injure it in any way. It remained sore and bruised for several weeks. Very strange. How can one explain this physical validation of a lucid dream? I have no idea. I make no claim that it is on par with accounts of the "stigmata" phenomenon, but it is the closest thing that comes to mind.

I meditated about this dream for a few weeks wondering what I should do if anything. I received guidance to write a letter to Pope Francis, the first and only time I ever wrote to a Pope, to propose his involvement with an international conference on the convergence of science, religion and spirituality. I never mentioned the lucid dream. I mailed the letter, but never received a reply.

To me, this dream about Pope Francis symbolized the work of Eternea's proposed Convergence Coalition, which is one of the organization's seven proposed program components. Its purpose is to forge a convergence between science and all religions. It aspires to form a robust collaboration between them to work cooperatively in search of verifiable truth, as well as the advancement of civilization.

Both could learn and benefit from the other. Science could help religion to self-actualize by aligning theologies with valid scientific findings. Religion can enrich science with invaluable insights from ancient wisdom to further reveal hypothetical casual relationships and guide enhanced theory construction.

Inarguably, the world's religions have vast combined resources with extensive infrastructures and established constituencies. If they could unite around the validity of the Seven Statements outlined in the next chaper and champion just those few simple truths, they could greatly accelerate the advancement of human civilization.

If they could unite, the good they could do is incalculable. They could teach people to be beneficent, how to love one another and how to live in harmony as one. They could engage in outreach efforts to help improve the well-being of earth and all its inhabitants. They could help bring heaven to earth by championing such programs as *God for a Day* every day, to be explained in a subsequent chapter.

To be clear, this utopian vision will not happen overnight. It is evolutionary, extremely long range, perhaps best defined in geological terms, realistically speaking. For all religions to align, and then for all religions and all of science to converge, will require a potent catalyst of epochal proportion. Nevertheless, the time to start the process is now, for it is the right course of action to achieve the best possible future.

As for meaningful spiritual progression and full enlightenment of humankind, this too will predictably happen at a tortoise pace, sadly. Despite the rosy intentions of this book and Eternea's idealistic "primrose path" strategies, it may take centuries of sustained efforts as proposed and described herein to fully eradicate materialism, dualism, egocentrism and greed to pave the way for an ideal future.

Could paradigm shift happen sooner, perhaps in this century? Doubtful, but with God, all things are possible, so do not rule it out. Truthfully, I can envision only six catalysts powerful enough in potential to bring about revolutionary, accelerated, seismic change in human nature and the nature of social, political and economic systems. All of them border on fantasy. None are probable. They are:

1. Sweeping individual, institutional and socio-cultural transformation takes place inspired by this book and others highly similar to it, which effectively motivate a critical mass of people to see things from an enlightened perspective due to the knowledge they acquire from such resources;

2. The majority of humankind somehow undergoes profound first-hand individual epiphanies or peak experiences such as those described in this book to evolve into Christ consciousness. This would enable the Golden Rule to become a dominant global practice. Please see the section on Personal Epiphany Induction Techniques to learn more about how to make this happen;

3. Altruistic angelic extraterrestrials land on earth, reveal their presence and teach humankind about their cosmology and ontology to promptly bring everyone into a state of optimal spiritual enlightenment where miracles comparable to what Christ demonstrated can be routinely preformed;

4. Technology development brings new tools or capabilities to openly and accurately communicate with the spiritual realm bringing forth in a reliable manner all the knowledge each individual needs to achieve complete enlightenment;

5. Fulfillment of the Biblical prophecy concerning the "Second Coming of Jesus Christ, not as a lamb but as a lion." If that were to happen as per prophecy, heaven on earth would quickly materialize; and

6. Perish the thought, but should humanity be brought to its knees by global catastrophe or calamity of one kind or another, whether through natural or man-made causes, threatening the very survival of the species, it is conceivable that masses of people would collectively open their hearts to God and embrace God in desperate hope of divine rescue, perhaps unifying like never before to truly love one another.

None of these hypothetical catalysts are likely to happen anytime soon, if ever. Thus, the best we can do will be the best we can do, which is to write books like this and offer grounded wisdom such as the Seven Statements explained in Part III.

PART III

Reflections About God and Divine Emulation

The Seven Statements

In this final conclusion section of the book, emphasis is given to what can be learned from the stories and information presented in Parts I and II. In my opinion, it is the most important part of the book. It attempts to interpret the meaning and significance of the extraordinary spiritual experiences in my life and in the lives of others.

Part III is a humble attempt to explore God's nature and the concept of divine love. Additionally, various methods are discussed to help seekers discover God and develop a closer constant connection to the divine realm. What's more, a structured exercise is introduced to help us evolve into God-centered beings and help transform the world into a God-centered place.

Through my personal experiences, as well as those expressed to me by others, and thousands more that have been studied by serious scientists, several consistent observations have emerged leading to the formulation of Eternea's Seven Statements.

The Seven Statements are evidence-based postulations about the nature of objective reality. They are not new discoveries or insights or original thinking. Rather, they represent a synthesis of generally accepted knowledge based on a three-part convergence model or paradigm which I call "*Integrative Holistic Spirituality.*"

The three foundational pillars of this convergence model are as follows: (1) The timeless wisdom of the ancient mystics, sages and saints; (2) The cornerstone traditional teachings of the world's major religions; and (3) Modern scientific research from the study of spiritually transformative experiences and consciousness.

As such, the Seven Statements may reflect the most accurate comprehension of reality and timeless universal truth formulated by human beings over millennia of reflection, contemplation, mystical experience, scholarly effort and research.

It is conceivable that global acceptance of the Seven Statements could result in the creation of an optimal future for earth and all its inhabitants. The Seven Statements are subject to revision, if or when new scientific evidence emerges which compels their modification.

They are as follows:

1. Consciousness is infinite and eternal, transcending time, space and matter, including the physical body and the brain. Therefore, consciousness does not and cannot die. It is indestructible and immortal. Highly evolved consciousness is the primal causal impetus of all things, through directed focused intentionality in a state of perfect unconditional love fully resonant with zero-point energy, which thereby places all quanta and matter at effect.

2. Consciousness can exist uncontained by form in the realm of spirit, or it may materialize in various physical forms in the dimensions of time and space as needed to evolve spiritually, or to voluntarily serve others altruistically, throughout multiple incarnations during the endless journey of eternal existence.

3. There is an unfathomable yet knowable infinite intelligence or creative Source, which gives rise to all creation, from which all things in the cosmos originate and to which all things in the cosmos return. This Source or Creator is best described as the ultimate in non-judgmental perfection, knowledge, magnificence, beneficence, compassion, kindness, empathy, goodness and unconditional love.

4. All things in the cosmos are one vast interrelated, interconnected, interdependent, interfaced, integrated whole, meaning that all things are one, inextricably linked in the grand matrix of creation.

5. Unconditional love is the organizing principle of the universe. It is the bedrock of all that exists. Unconditional love for all things, including oneself, is the evolutionary imperative underlying all of creation. It is the highest state of being one can achieve and the ultimate evolutionary goal of all spiritual progression.

6. In the cosmic web of creation, there is a vast matrix of cause-effect relationships, meaning that what one does to all other things, one does to oneself. What is sown is reaped. As below, so above. What goes around comes around. Free will is a universally honored and upheld principle and practice, while so too is accountability for all actions or inactions in the exercise or expression of one's free will. Any use of free will which is not consistent with unconditional love and compassion brings eventual adverse karmic consequences.

7. The good of the many is served and upheld by the good of the one. The good of the one is served and upheld by the good of the many. The whole can be only as healthy and strong as its constituent parts. The constituent parts can be only as healthy and strong as the whole itself. Therefore, the whole is dependent on its parts, and the parts are dependent on the whole. A constant symbiotic and synergistic dynamic or gestalt exists between the whole and its parts. A chain can be only as strong as its

weakest link. Any weakness or vulnerability potentially compromises the health, vitality and viability of the whole.

To summarize, the main takeaways from these statements and this book are that first and foremost, based on credible empirical evidence from the scientific study of STEs, we can confidently affirm God is real, meaning the God of love and compassion, and so too are God's angels who watch over us, help us and protect us. Also, our consciousness is eternal and is forevermore tethered to God. It continues beyond death indestructibly, most assuredly. Indeed, the afterlife is real.

Further, we are loved unconditionally by God without judgment, punishment or condemnation. Yet, there is accountability for one's earthly behavior. What exists is an ingenious cause-effect, action-reaction system of karmic accountability and reincarnation. It enables us to rectify actions toward others that were unkind or unloving.

This structure of accountability gives substance to the adage that "what we do to others we do to ourselves." It is a self-directed or self-administered process born of the overpowering desire we all share to become one with God once again. However, this cannot be accomplished until or unless our souls achieve a resonant energy connection with God, or parity with God's signature frequency and vibration, which is that of perfect unconditional love and compassion for all things.

Finally, all things in the entire cosmos are minute aspects of one inseparable whole in the grand interconnected web of creation, destined by the Creator's design to eventually evolve into a perfect expression of unconditional love in full harmony or parity with Creator.

Thus, the ultimate and inescapable destiny of all aspects of creation is to reunite with the Source from which we all came and to which we all will return. In this vein, it is therefore important to remember that the same God who made you made me, including every other human being, fish, bird, animal, tree and plant on earth. Thus, all things are one.

Yes, we are inextricably linked to all other things. Many of the great classical physicists declared this to be a true and valid observation more than a century ago. Consequently, it should be understood that committing evil acts is not just an offense against others, but ultimately a more serious offense against oneself. To choose anything other than love is to make a very foolish choice. Plain and simple, ignorance and evil go hand in hand, for it is ignorant to engage in evil of any kind. And ignorance or denial of the bigger picture is what spawns evil.

But evil cannot be overcome by slaying, conquering or banishing it. Rather, it is our task to transform and transmute it. Pouring God's love and light all over it is indeed the only way in which evil can be truly remedied and rectified. Embracing and affirming God's existence by emulating God's fundamental attributes and qualities effectively transmutes evil by assimilating it into that which is divine.

To rid the world of evil, we must be as love unto all things by mustering all the empathy and compassion we can find in our hearts. We must love all things unconditionally as God loves all of creation. But if we do not know God, or if we continue to deny God's existence, how can we hope to access God's love, the most powerful force in the universe, in order to rectify evil? Simply stated, we cannot and will not.

Many people hold traditional views about evil, believing that it springs forth from Lucifer and his legions of demons. However, an alternative perspective to ponder is that evil is not the result of one singular entity or fallen angel who rules over a domain called hell. Rather, evil is the result of misguided free will choices made moment to moment by sentient beings throughout the universe, including people on earth like you and me. Thus, evil is manifested as a free will choice, not because some supernatural unseen force made us do it.

I define evil as the absence of love, empathy, compassion and kindness. Evil is nothing more than the absence of God. Therefore, God is the antidote for evil. God is the only true remedy or cure. The answer is to discover, embrace and align with God, hopefully soon, while we still have the time and opportunity to do so.

For those like me who are monotheists, there is only one God, who is the Maker, Creator and Source of all things. This is the God I know and refer to in this book, One who is impeccable, all-knowing, all-powerful and omnipresent, the pinnacle of perfection. Therefore, whatever God created, God could un-create if ever God had the desire to do so. Yet, God does not un-create or destroy evil. To do so, I believe would be contrary to God's brilliant design.

My opinion is that God did not create evil, nor is God responsible for evil, but neither does God take sides. Rather, God initiated an evolving creation and embedded free will within it, which God awarded to all sentient beings. Why? Because God has no ego. God did not start creation to populate the universe with brain-dead devotees, robots, automatons or sycophant slaves. Such a view, in my opinion, does a serious injustice and disservice to God through total misrepresentation.

God created free will for all sentient beings. With free will comes the element of choice and, therefore, the capacity for doing good or evil. With free will comes the God-given capacity to choose love, hence Godliness, or to choose the opposite, which is to be unloving or unlike God. Any such choice to be unloving is evil when viewed in the context of evil's definition as the lack of love and compassion, meaning the absence of God. Therefore, evil is where God is not. Evil is where love is not.

Perhaps God's disposition toward evil can be better understood in the context of what happened just after Christ died on the cross. In the midst of one of the most despicable acts of evil in all of history, Christ taught us that we are supposed to love our enemies as we love ourselves. Loving others as we love ourselves is a major theme in the New Testament. It is the central cornerstone of Christ consciousness.

God clearly possessed the ability to destroy all those involved with the persecution, torture and death of Jesus, yet God did not actually harm or punish anyone, especially the guilty. Rather, God extended unconditional love to everyone as Christ exhibited on the cross consistent with the final words He spoke before He died: "Forgive them, for they know not what they do." God displayed unconditional love and tolerance to all despite the worst of all provocations. God chose to love Pilot and Caiaphas, as well as everyone who was complicit in the murder of Christ. God extended mercy and grace to them rather than deliver vengeance upon them.

Now this is not to say that one should turn a blind eye to evil. Far from it. Rather, God and Christ both imparted the clear instruction to us by example that when confronted by evil, we should pour divine love and light all over it in an effort to transform, transmute and assimilate it into divine love and light. Jesus served as the ultimate example of how to confront evil even while He was being horrifically crucified, by extending only unconditional love and compassion to His persecutors.

So how can we consistently engage in the practice of unconditional love? We can do so by making enlightened free will choices about how we behave toward others. To achieve Christ consciousness humans must rise above base emotions like fear, greed, anger and jealously. This is not the easiest thing to do. In the classic words of Somerset Maugham, it is as difficult to lead a fully enlightened life as it is to "walk the razor's edge." The Seven Statements is a helpful roadmap to guide us in this quest.

Thy Will, Not My Will, Be Done

The message I heard in the cave during my vision quest still reverberates within me more than 34 years: *Spirit waits patiently for humanity to stop waiting for Spirit; to affirm, revere and align with Spirit.* This is the central theme for my ongoing spiritual dharma as First Light. I firmly believe this message applies to each individual and to humankind as a whole.

I interpret this profound message to mean that Spirit waits patiently for every human being to stop ignoring Spirit; to stop pretending and acting as though Spirit does not exist; and to honor Spirit by emulating all that God represents each and every day with each and every breath, and with each and every step, in full resonance with divine will.

I can reduce what this all means down to one powerful sentence: *Be as love unto all things at all times—perfect unconditional love.* This was the primary teaching of Jesus, Krishna, The Buddha, Lao Tsu, Confucius, Mohammed, Gandhi, Milarepa and other great sages. To understand love in the spiritual context and what it means in practical terms to love one another, please consult the work of Dr. Leo Buscaglia. He did a masterful job during his life of educating humanity about this most important matter. (Visit *leobuscaglia.org* for more information).

A word that is nearly equivalent to the term "love" is the word "kindness." The two could almost be used interchangeably. So, bravo to CBS News for airing "The Gift: Kindness Goes Viral" on December 28, 2022. Reporter Steve Hartman showcased several wonderful people, young and old, who, from the goodness of their own hearts, performed many selfless acts of kindness in different highly creative ways as a routine part of their daily lives. It is *God for a Day* under a different name. In fact, *God for a Day* could just as easily be called "Project Kindness." Frankly, there can never be enough endeavors of this genre. The more, the merrier, and the faster humanity can realize heaven on earth.

In the program, Hartman queried an MIT professor about devising a mathematical formula which would facilitate the global propagation of kindness. He sought to examine what it would take to make kindness grow exponentially—to make it go "viral." He was looking for a way to describe in mathematical terms what kind of impact might occur from a single act of kindness in terms of its "ripple effects." The professor replied that for kindness to expand exponentially, its purveyors and its recipients would need to dispense it or repay it not on a 1:1 basis, but rather at least on a 4:1 basis. His conclusion was that we should never underestimate the power of just one good deed. There is no telling how much good it will do out there in the world at large.

Giving is another word close in meaning to kindness and love. A December 2022 "Next Door" post on the internet from St. Petersburg, Florida, called for "An Avalanche of Giving" for 30 days, as follows:

> "Every day for 30 consecutive days, *give*. Give joy, smiles, warm words, love, appreciation, and compliments to everyone you meet, including strangers, friends, and family. Speak from the heart, giving the very best of you in every moment of your day, and make it your mission to make every single person's day better with kind thoughts and words. As you *give* the best of you, you will be staggered by the speed that it comes back to you!"

Thus, this book and all the words on its pages mean nothing if they have not decisively inspired much more love in the world. Jesus once said, "By their fruits you shall know them." This book and its author should be held firmly to that sterling standard. What fruits will humankind harvest from this literary effort? My hope is that a much more loving and compassionate world comes about as a result.

Perhaps the effort to bring more love into the world begins with each person embarking on an inner journey of self-reflection where they start to ask questions like: Where will I find ultimate happiness and contentment? What is the point of my existence? How can I make my life count for something positive in the world? If you are not yet asking yourself these questions, perhaps one day you will.

Predictably, there will come a time when fame, fortune, power and possessions leave us feeling empty inside and totally unfulfilled. No matter how much we have amassed or accumulated, we yearn for more and more to gratify the senses. This is precisely the time when we wonder if there is anything greater that awaits us beyond life's usual trinkets.

At the end of life, we come to realize that all glory is fleeting. We discover that all fame, power and wealth is temporary, and so too is the physical body we occupy. We eventually come to view it as a temporary container. Sooner or later, we confront the fact that everything on earth is tomorrow's dust, hence the expression "from dust to dust, from ashes to ashes."

It is upon this realization we come to understand what Christ meant by the statement, "Do not place your treasure where moth and dust doth corrode." In other words, do not place value or emphasis on things that do not matter in any ultimate sense.

But whenever or however the time comes for us to leave this world, it will hasten our search for God and an attempt to reconcile with God. For death is the great common denominator. It levels the playing field. It makes us all equal again as we appear before our Creator. Thus, now is the time to seek God and find a reliable compass that will successfully guide and prepare us for our eventual return home.

In this final section of the book, humanity is called upon to awaken spiritually with convictions that are congruent with the Seven Statements and the Fifteen Elaborations. Readers should consider performing a critical self-examination to find acceptable answers to life's big questions; to look at reality from a higher vantage point; and to formulate an enlightened understanding of God in order to become one with God.

I believe we can best find the answers we seek by imitating, emulating or role-playing God in the form of a structured exercise called *God for a Day*. In this manner, perhaps we can develop a greater appreciation of and stronger resonance with God. By emulating God, we can manifest God in the everyday world. When we attempt to duplicate or reproduce God's love, compassion and beneficence, we can make God real in everyday life to everyday people.

The best way to accomplish this goal is to bring love or be as love unto all things...perfect unconditional love, for many believe that perfect unconditional love is God's primary attribute. It is ultimate sweet surrender when with the utmost sincerity we say, "Thy will, not my will, be done." If this idea achieves broad acceptance, it could be the panacea or solution for everything that ails humankind.

Thus, my recommendation for how to know God and how to form a resonant energy connection with God, is to emulate God by being a living vessel or conduit on earth for delivery of God's perfect love to all things, daily. If *God for a Day* gains traction, perhaps eventually it will gain sufficient momentum to become a mainstay global practice. What better way is there to serve God's will than to love others beyond one's love of self?

It is not unlike the advice given by Benjamin Franklin in his musings about moral perfection. Franklin wrote in his famous autobiography that he was a "thorough deist" who believed in one God, the Creator of all that is, to whom we should express our constant gratitude.

Franklin noted that we can best do this by performing good deeds for others. He was clear that loving and giving to others was the best way to show gratitude to God and to serve God, and that it was far more important than what our varying beliefs might be about God.

In his "Thirteen Virtues," Franklin advocated humble "imitation of Jesus and Socrates." He considered both to be exemplars who had achieved moral and intellectual perfection in word and also in deed. Franklin espoused constant self-improvement through constant self-examination, as well as abiding altruism in service to the greater good. He taught by example that each day should be used to its fullest as an opportunity to do as much good in the world as possible by giving to others in the spirit of generosity and love. Perhaps the best example we have of how to do this is the life of Jesus, who once said to the Sanhedrin, "There is only one law, that we should love one another as God loves us."

Thomas Jefferson preached this same gospel of love. He was equally struck by the fact that Christ confirmed the factual existence of life after death, one that involved accountability for earthly actions, and that He used this doctrine as an incentive to inspire people to behave in a morally proper manner. Jefferson also found it remarkable that Jesus managed to leave behind "fragments of his teachings that were so rich as to constitute the most benevolent and sublime system of morals that has ever been taught by man," one which calls for universal philanthropy for all mankind as one family under the bonds of love, charity, peace and unity.

Please understand that this discussion is not meant to be a "come to Jesus" sermon, but precious few humans have been able to approximate the precedent Jesus set for selfless service to one's fellow man. Mother Theresa and Gandhi are two celebrated examples from the past century. But seldom if ever has anyone come close to that standard of service and unconditional love that Jesus established over 2,000 years ago.

Manifestation of the divine through the *God for a Day* exercise is clearly acknowledged and validated in the Bible, 1 Corinthians 3:16:

"Know ye not that ye are the temple of God and that the spirit of God dwelleth within you?"

Many of us go through life oblivious to the divine charge of serving our fellow human beings. Instead, we are largely a self-preoccupied bunch, caring only for ourselves and our immediate families and friends, or for those who are in a position to do us some good. When we give, it is often conditionally, for social recognition, for certain rewards or privileges, for a tax deduction, or to gain certain favor or advantage.

No doubt, some giving is completely selfless, pure of heart and motivated solely by a God-like desire to serve without earthly reward. But altruism is quite rare these days, not often found, which is a sad indictment of the human race. This is all the more reason to start a movement to bring *God for a Day* into vogue, not just as a trendy thing to do, but as a long-term strategy to co-create an ideal future for earth and all its inhabitants.

The Values, Virtues and Attributes of God

Before the exercise of being *God for a Day* can commence, it is necessary to determine what values, virtues and qualities can be safely and defensibly ascribed to God. We must first find a definition of God we can all embrace. At the present time, sadly God means many different things to many different people.

Humanity faces numerous struggles these days, but one of the greatest among them is a modern day "Tower of Babel" syndrome. There are nearly eight billion people on the planet right now and probably as many different views about God and the afterlife. There is even a growing segment of the population who insist that neither God nor the afterlife exist.

Clearly, we lack consensus about God and so many other fundamental matters of critical importance to humanity's shared future. Coming from so many different perspectives and cultures, and speaking so many different languages, with so much division about cornerstone issues, how can we ever hope to achieve unity, harmony, consensus and coherence? Yet, all of which are necessary in order to realize an optimal future for earth and all its inhabitants.

Thus, it is highly appropriate at this juncture to salute the French philosopher Francois-Marie Arouet, whose pen name was Voltaire, and before him the British philosopher John Locke, for astutely observing long ago that there cannot be understanding among human beings nor any hope of effective communication unless all parties involved in any discussion or exchange first give precise definition to the terms and concepts they intend to use or reference in their conversation. If they cannot agree on basic definitions and facts, then there is no basis or hope for effective discourse. This is timeless wisdom and more relevant in modern times than ever before.

People far and wide often make casual reference to terms like God, heaven, consciousness, soul, the afterlife, and so on, as though there is an abiding broad consensus about their meaning, but nothing could be farther from the truth. There is little or no consensus about these terms and concepts among the global population, and therein lies one of the greatest challenges facing humanity, if not the greatest.

How can we form a shared understanding about the true nature of reality when we have not yet come to any agreement about the definition of key terms? And, without benefit of a solid foundational bedrock of shared definitions for key terms, how can humanity ever create advanced social order? Without advanced social order, how can there ever be an optimal future?

Karen Armstrong, a former nun, wrote a masterpiece best-selling book in 1993 entitled *A History of God*. She takes a scholarly approach to the formidable subject of God in this much-heralded brilliant work, which I highly recommend as one of the most important books I have ever read. It really is a "must-read" for all thinking persons.

Ms. Armstrong correctly explains that humans "invented" the concept of "God" in the Middle East some 14,000 years ago to fill a haunting need or void. She writes:

"Homo sapiens is also Homo religiosus. Men and women started to worship gods as soon as they became recognizably human; they created religions at the same time as they created works of art. This was not simply because they wanted to propitiate powerful forces; these faiths expressed the wonder and mystery that seem always to have been an essential component of the human experience…"

Yet, it was not until the sixth century, A.D. that humans invented the term "God." But God, the actual Creator of the cosmos, never disclosed to humans its existence, its gender, its name, its nature or its laws. For many thousands of years, humans have been left to do this for themselves, and this they surely have done, sparking much debate, divisiveness, conflict and violence in the process among competing sects. Multiple definitions of God continue even now sparking ongoing religious strife. As critic Bill Maher points out in his film called *Religulous,* this conflict among the various religions could very well be our undoing as a species.

No one really knows how the word "God" came into being. Its origin remains a deep mystery and the subject of great debate. But there is general agreement that its roots are probably Germanic and that it first entered the lexicon in sixth century Europe, appearing in the Christian "Codex Argenteus."

There is a plethora of names for the Creator, as well as a wide variety of definitions and interpretations, hence so many different competing religions. There is no unanimity on the subject across the whole of humanity. And most all of these belief systems are based on blind faith in unsupported dogma or theology. Virtually none align themselves with science, evidence, facts and established knowledge. Thus, the landscape as such looks much like a veritable breeding ground for trouble, and surely it is. Religious conflict and divisiveness continue to run rampant.

Since I have only my personal frame of reference to draw upon, I wish to share a bit about my own current understanding of God. It is only right for readers and critics of this book to question my justification, credentials and basis for writing a book of this nature. After all, this book advances a confident understanding of God. It even suggests a strategy for how to find God and develop a stronger connection. It does so audaciously, outside the framework of traditional religion.

Who am I to say things of this nature? What qualifies me to do such a thing? By what authority do I proceed in this manner? And, how have I come to espouse so-called knowledge about God? These questions are all valid.

I claim no special knowledge of or understanding about God other than what has come to me through my own prayer, reflection, contemplation, meditation, study and personal peak experiences as described in this book. I am not God's appointed spokesperson or messenger on earth. I have not heard the voice of God or seen God. I have only "felt" God. I am not a religious person nor am I affiliated with any religion. I neither attend church nor actively study the Bible, although long ago I read major portions of it.

By this, I do not mean to infer that those who do are misguided or mistaken in their journey. To the contrary, I have enormous respect for all persons of faith and conviction who are seeking to find empirically defensible spiritual truth whether through their religion or by some other means. Those with religious discipline, who devote their lives to the study and service of God each in their own manner, are worthy of sincere admiration, provided they do not harm or infringe on others in any way.

All Holy Scriptures and sacred texts deemed authentic could help shine light on ultimate objective truth. I welcome all pieces of the puzzle in our collective quest for a better understanding of and a closer communion with God.

No one has a monopoly on understanding truth or God. At best, each religion might possess a piece of holy parchment, one part or aspect of a grander whole. Perhaps by joining these pieces together, augmented by what science can verify through empiricism, we will find the real truth one day; an objective truth that holds up under scientific scrutiny.

My greatest insights about God came from exposure to people who reported having NDEs, a subject I studied intensely for better than 48 years from the perspective of social science. Through these years of studying and interviewing people who reported having an NDE, I began to form a connection with God far beyond what I had experienced through various religions.

My belief in God transcends faith and is based on both an intuitive inner knowing and also direct experience. For me, I accept the existence of God not as a matter of faith, but as a matter of certainty. My certainty is derived from the extraordinary events I have described in this book, as well as an abiding knowing or inherent personal knowledge that is an intrinsic part of my being.

There is something extraordinary deep inside my psyche which affirms God. It has always been a part of me from as far back as my first conscious thoughts as a young child. It stayed with me even during my time as an avowed agnostic.

While I do believe in Christ, and pray daily to Christ and God, I am not a Christian in the conventional or fundamentalist sense. To me, the notion that "Christ died for our sins" is an incomplete simplistic interpretation. To imply that we all have an eternal ticket to ride because Christ died on the cross to "wash away all of our sins" is a probable misinterpretation of His message and His actions and may be inconsistent with the true essence of His teachings.

In symbolic terms, yes, it is true Christ was crucified because we are all "sinners." If we were not, He never would have been nailed to the cross over two thousand years ago. No one who is God-centered could or would do such a thing. Who would kill pure love except pure evil and pure stupidity? What would be gained by it? Nothing but really bad karma. Those who killed Christ were lost in illusion and ego, intoxicated by power, privilege and wealth, imposters all. Christ threatened their status quo and so they killed Him for it, foolishly.

However, through His crucifixion, Christ showed us a path back to Creator/Source, from whence we all came. Indeed, in this regard, He was and is the Truth, the Light and the Way. The path He showed us is one of loving everyone and everything unconditionally, especially those who do not love you back, like those who nail you to a cross.

Christ's sacrifice on the cross did not wipe our personal slate clean. We must do this for ourselves, one incarnation after another. This is not because God commands us to do so, but because we cannot satisfy the yearning of our souls to become one with God again until we become pure expressions of unconditional love. Until then, we must directly atone for whatever we do that is unloving or unkind, whether in this lifetime or another. Our spiritual progression depends upon it.

This is why our response to evil must be consistent with the example set by Christ on the cross. He taught us that we should only confront evil with unconditional love and non-judgment. This is why he instantly forgave everyone involved in His murder. To do less than this, would effectively reduce us to the equivalent of evil and would only further undermine our own spiritual advancement.

To be sure, Christ did show us how we can keep our slate clean. He also showed us how even in the worst of circumstances, we can remain true to our spiritual convictions. He urged us to love our neighbors as ourselves by seeing through the illusions of the body and this world. Remember His words before Pilate, "My kingdom is not of this world." Moreover, He urged us to forgive those who do us wrong, "For they know not what they do."

Sadly, many people in this world don't ever get the luxury to contemplate spiritual matters such as these because they are too burdened with meeting basic subsistence needs. I weep at the thought of it. In today's world, with current technology available to us, there is simply no excuse for poverty, hunger, homelessness, illiteracy, or lack of access to health care or to formal education.

That these conditions still exist is nothing short of shameful, unconscionable and unacceptable. I am reminded of a bumper sticker I spotted one day driving around Mill Valley, California. It read, "If you are not completely outraged, you are not paying attention!" How very true.

We should be ashamed that these scourges still exist in the 21st century. We should be outraged that these deplorable conditions persist. If you were among those suffering, it is likely you would hope those more fortunate would lend a hand. Is that not the Godly thing to do?

Admission to the human race should at least rival admission to a prestigious club, with all the rights, privileges, benefits and guarantees one should be entitled to receive. Admission to the human race should mean the guarantee of coming to a peaceful, harmonious, loving planet where new arrivals enjoy sound parenting, a wonderful home in a safe community, good food, clean water, clean air, healthy soil, clothing, health care, education, transportation, arts and culture, public safety and public hygiene, as well as ample opportunities upon reaching adulthood to make a good living at a job or vocation that is fulfilling. It is time to make this vision a reality. As a species, we can only be as strong as our weakest link. It is how we treat the least among us which will determine how far human civilization will advance.

After reading the typical horror stories in the typical edition of the typical community newspaper on any typical day, one can only cry tears of sadness over the gross brutality that we find around us constantly on this planet. At times like these, it is prudent to ask God to show us a way to rectify or remedy evil. How should we use our free will to ameliorate evil and co-create the kind of ideal world we deserve?

For this reason, I wrote a prayer that I recite daily from the heart. It is called *Daily Prayer for Divine Alignment*. I invite you to use it or amend it for your own purposes.

Father, Mother, Source, Creator, Almighty God, Maker of All Things, Origin of All That Is, Ground from which all being arises.

All Archangels and Guardian Angelic Guides
All Ascended Masters, Sages and Saints
All Forces of Goodness, Love and Light
All Spiritually Evolved Ancestors
I offer this prayer with heartfelt reverence, humility and gratitude.
Thank You for You and thank You profusely for all the love, beauty, grace and abundance showered upon me this day and every day. May everyone be equally blessed and more so.

Please encircle and surround me in every moment of every day with glorious divine energy, love and light to protect me, heal me and empower me. May it be so for everyone and for all things.

Help me this day and every day to allow only that which is loving and good into my life that I may bring only that which is loving and good to all others that I encounter.

Please help me to align my will with divine will at all times and in all places that I may at this moment and in every moment hereafter be a perfect instrument and expression of divine will in service to the greater good of all things.

Please continually remove and protect me from all energies and forces that do not serve my highest and best good that I may uphold my constant intention to perfectly manifest divine love and goodness in all the things I do and to all those I encounter in my daily life moment to moment.

Please help me to discern how I may best serve all others I encounter on this day and every day to completely satisfy divine will. Please help me to bring to others I encounter that which fully serves their highest and best good and that which totally honors divine intention.

I pray these things with fullness of heart and with my declared commitment to be an instrument in perfect service to divine will at all times and in all places.

Thank You. Amen.

When I say this prayer or ask questions, God does not answer me in discernable words. God never does. Instead, for example, in front of me one day was a desktop calendar with one-liner excerpts from *Conversations With God - An Uncommon Dialogue* by Neale Donald Walsch. The quote for that particular day was "One day of doing nothing but My Will would bring you Enlightenment."

That statement sent supercharged goose bumps through me. It is the essential foundational takeaway of this book. I booted up my computer and the idea of *God for a Day* came into being.

Communication from Spirit is nearly always subtle. It often comes in the form of creative inspiration such as the reaction I had from reading this quote by Neale Donald Walsch. Other times, it takes the form of gentle nudges or intuitive urgings, and even soft whispers. But if our hearts and minds are open to it, we will be touched by the divine many times throughout our lives, one way or another.

Structured Exercise:

God for a Day

One day in the foreseeable future, suppose God were to issue a decree or proclamation to all of humanity. Suppose, for a moment, the proclamation declared that, henceforth, there would be a formal "use tax" levied by the divine on the bodies we occupy, the air we breathe, the earth we dwell upon, the solar system and the universe surrounding us, for the rain that cleanses and replenishes us, the oceans and the soil that sustain us, the forests that provide us with timber for building shelter, the gentle wind that caresses and cools us, and for the very sunshine that comes every day to warm us and make all life possible.

Now suppose this hypothetical "use tax" decreed we should all emulate God by becoming *God for a Day,* a week, a month, a year or a lifetime? Would it be too much to ask in view of the much we are given?

The famous psychologist, Carl Jung, once commented that religion preoccupies its followers with the goal of salvation, and in the process, instills fear in them as the primary motivator to lead a righteous life. But, he observed, if religion were to shift its focus to wonder and marvel at the splendor of nature and all creation, then the primary emotion they would elicit among followers in the process would be one of profound gratitude. Could it be otherwise?

So, for those of us who want to say thank you to God in a pure and selfless fashion, to find meaningful ways to express our gratitude, please consider participating in the *God for a Day* exercise as a voluntary "gift-tax" of sorts to express our appreciation for the many gifts God gives us. Who knows? Maybe our efforts in this regard might one day result in unexpected spiritual dividends. If *God for a Day* becomes common practice, perhaps an ideal future can be the end result.

Rather than view these musings as theological discourse or religious commentary, try to view them from the standpoint of social theory, social change, social psychology, social justice and social organization. They are offered for consideration more in the spirit of Gandhi, who, when asked by a journalist what he thought of western civilization, answered: "I think it would be a good idea."

By the same token, I recommend *God for a Day* as a good idea whose time has come. Is it not a reasonable proposition that we should start giving back to God in some meaningful manner? God has given so much to us, but what have we given back?

If enough people get on board with the idea of practicing Godliness for a Day, the human condition can only be made much better. The intent here is to quicken the evolutionary tempo of higher consciousness. The goal is to bring more kindness, empathy, love and compassion into the world. This could become a reality one day if enough people open their hearts to much greater awareness about, appreciation for and acceptance of God. It could grow into a global social movement.

Thus, *God for a Day* is intended to be an organized campaign to stimulate a global spiritual awakening. If a critical mass of human beings engage in this effort, we could co-create a world in which the Golden Rule becomes the dominant reality. It is conceivable this undertaking could evolve into an urgent rescue plan or crisis intervention strategy for humanity, one that has nothing whatsoever to do with organized religion in the traditional sense, but rather takes its inspiration from the scientific study of human consciousness and exceptional spiritual experiences such as those described in this book.

Indeed, the world is a troubled place. It gets more so by the day. Anything we can do to make it less so would be an important step in the right direction…in the direction of God whom many of us purport to love and serve.

Imagine yourself emulating God's values and virtues fully for one day. Just one day. But one might ask why consider being God-like for one day? What's the point or purpose? Well, this exercise is proposed to motivate individuals to know God more fully and grow more intimately connected to God. It is not for the indifferent or faint-hearted, or for those who prefer to remain safe within the illusions of their own little worlds. Rather, it is for those with a longing to find a path to higher truth and a deeper spiritual awakening. It is for those who are ready to fully immerse themselves in Godliness.

A God-Life is a life devoted to serving God first and foremost by attempting to manifest God's values and qualities on earth during this lifetime as much as one can. This does not mean one cannot also lead the "good life" so long as every other human being is able to enjoy the same good life or even greater blessings.

Personally, I like to think of *God for a Day* as a meaningful way to say thank you to God for the body I occupy, the air I breathe, the earth I walk upon and the sunshine that comes every day to make my life and all life possible.

Please keep in mind that the highest compliment you can pay someone is to emulate them. Thus, by the same token, this exercise is meant to honor God in some substantive, creative manner through imitation.

When should this exercise be done? Once a year? Once a month? Well, my advice is to start by devoting just one day to being *God for a Day* and go from there. Try it once. If it agrees with you, try it again as much and as often as you like. I don't think God will mind, not even if you do it every day for the rest of your life. It will draw you closer to God, and nothing will give you a greater sense of satisfaction.

So, just for one day, stop being who you are and become Godly or God-like instead. Remember, it is a game of pretend. Don't tell anyone that you are going to engage in this exercise. You must do so anonymously with reverence and humility, and without using your real name. Remember, all glory to God here. It is not about you, except the deep personal satisfaction you will experience from doing this exercise.

It is for this reason that I do not share details with anyone about my three *God for a Day* adventures to date, except to say that they were most rewarding and fulfilling. I was blessed by Spirit far beyond what little I gave or did during my service to others. I felt it right down to every fiber in my being each time I became a pure expression of divine love to others. I warn you, though. It could become habit-forming. The "high" one gets from it is impossible to duplicate in any other way.

The whole point of this exercise is to become a living example of God on earth; to transform oneself into a perfect expression of God's love for all things; to become God's representative on earth in physical form. To do good toward others is to make God visible in the world. When we do this, we become a bona fide extension of God in the physical world.

Honestly, I experienced a natural high from my three *God for a Day* exercises, possibly a release of endorphins, or perhaps it was the grace of God, or God's love flowing through me as Virginia Hummel described it in the Introduction. I certainly felt God's presence most of the time, as if God were walking right alongside me. It was truly God's love I was expressing, channeled through me, from God to others. And this was my conscious intent each time I did the exercise.

Trust me when I tell you that it is the highest high I have ever known and the closest I have ever felt to God. It was as though I became one with God. When we are giving love, pure unconditional love, we truly become one with God. It is God at work through us. Relish the vibration and the sacredness of it. Behold bliss itself.

So get into character, as an accomplished actor would prepare for the lead role in an epic movie. Give yourself a new name for the day, one that feels right, but just a first name, something innocuous like Cloudborn or Skybird or Redwood or Starry Sky. Mine is First Light. You could also choose a regular name like Darius or Darlene.

On this special day, you must stop and step outside of all social roles like husband, wife, brother, sister, father, mother, son, daughter, grandmother, grandfather, aunt, uncle, cousin, etc. Step outside of your nationality, your occupation, your assets, your net worth, your possessions, your educational degrees, your self-image, your vanity, your fears, your social standing, etc.

You must forget all about your many normal duties and responsibilities. None of these things matter on this special day, for this is a day you consecrate as sacred in service to the greater good of all things in your capacity as *God for a Day*.

As you do this, remind yourself that when you die – when your voice falls silent forevermore, all your social roles die along with your physical body. So too does your eyesight, your hearing, your breathing and your sense of taste and touch. Your entire social identity melts away like snow in the desert. All of your assets and possessions vanish as well, even the whole of your cherished physical body. What's left? What remains? Only your record of deeds during the last incarnation. That's it. That's all.

And what stands out most prominently before God is the selfless love, kindness and compassion you extend to others. This is what you will be most proud of and most eager to celebrate on the other side. It is the only thing God values during your life review. Thus, if you commit to practicing *God for a Day* every day, you will have a superlative life review with no regrets and nothing to feel ashamed about.

In your life review before God, you will also see what you did that was unloving. This will evoke in you the desire to fully atone or make amends in future incarnations, possibly on earth in human form, or possibly elsewhere in some other form. So, why not get a head start?

Please understand that God is not judging you in your life review. Rather, you are judging yourself, and in this exalted state, all you want to do is please God and become one with God again. It is this yearning that creates within you the desire to compensate or atone for all you did in life that was unkind or unloving, to literally cleanse your soul and purge negative karma in order to achieve full resonance with God.

Also, remind yourself that once on the other side, you will be liberated from all illusions and blessed with absolute knowledge. You will suddenly realize that all things are one and you will see yourself as an integral part of that oneness. You will be blessed with a new definition of your nuclear and extended family. It will be one that includes everything and everyone. Remind yourself too that in this expanded state of awareness you realize that your only purpose always is to be as love unto all things.

Know in your heart that the *God for a Day* exercise is meant to be extreme. It is intended to shake you up and wake you up. It is designed to break you away from normal routines—all those things we think are important but really are not...things we spend our lives chasing that in the end don't really matter...not one bit.

Arise and awaken. They are not important. They never were. They never will be. No need to buy new clothes for the occasion or spend money on a face lift or tummy tuck or hair replacement. All vanity is pointless. This is not about adorning oneself to look glamorous or turn heads or impress anyone.

The point of this exercise is to cultivate greater sensitivity to all other living things apart from yourself—to the sensitivity God possesses as a normal state of mind. Selfless service means to put your own self-interest aside. Put all your own needs, wants, problems, fears, and desires into an imaginary lockbox and set it aside. You can return to it and reacquire all these things when your exercise is finished. Trust that your needs will not be neglected or undermined in the process of doing this exercise. Rather, on a very high level, your needs will be served and perhaps even fulfilled.

God help us if the only time we are interested in opening our hearts and minds to this greater level of sensitivity is when the smoking hand grenade is in the trench or when we stand to gain materially in some way from being kind and generous. It would be quite pathetic if we should only desire to be Godly when it is calculated to be in our best selfish interests to do so.

Many people these days are stimulation junkies scurrying from one fix to the next. It's all part of our need to deny our mortality, to deny who we really are and why we're really here. But these fixes we chase are one big illusion, one colossal fantasy. In the end, they do not matter. They are imposters.

What does matter ultimately is action that will increase and enhance our Godliness or our *God Quotient* (GQ) through extending unconditional love and selfless service to others. This is what our priority should be. GQ is a term I coined to measure our ability to continually emulate God much like the IQ score measures human intelligence. GQ varies from zero to 100%. I imagine that most of us, sadly, have a GQ score of less than 25%.

Why invest in temporary, shallow, fleeting, short-term rushes when what matters most is what happens in the bigger picture after death on the other side? This is where our focus should be, hence the *God for a Day* exercise. This is why I often tell people that I try to live not for the things of this world, but for the next.

Remember, this lifetime is nothing more than a proving ground for the spirit. Life is nothing more than a preparation for the eternal reality that comes after death. Life, if you will, is one big preparation for death.

But if you don't want to grow your GQ in this lifetime, then don't sweat it. You've got eternity. Come back and do it all over again another way, another day. It would be about as much fun as repeating 12th grade in high school when you would have a much more enjoyable time going off to college, but all you can do is all you can do, right?

A famous philosopher and social theorist once observed that if you love without evoking love in return, without producing reciprocal love, then your efforts to love did not amount to very much. His point was that if expressing yourself as a loving person does not result in making you a beloved person, then your love is barren.

However, being *God for a Day* is all about expressing love and compassion toward all things, not expecting anything in return. That is the nature of unconditional love. If the love you give authentically inspires others to reciprocate or to pay it forward to someone else, you will have succeeded beyond measure.

It has been said that God is love and love is God. In previous discussion, an effort was made to define God, but the term love is equally important and worthy of an equal effort to define what it means in this context.

Some prominent physicists, astronomers, cosmologists and astrophysicists have commented that unconditional love is the greatest secret of the cosmos and its central organizing principle. The term "organizing principle" refers to the central reason or purpose anything is brought into being. It is the prime directive or imperative which is intrinsically and innately imbued, incorporated, instilled and "programmed" into anything by its architect or designer, or that which spontaneously arises by virtue of its inherent nature.

So, what exactly does the term "unconditional love" mean? Note that it is comprised of two words which must be understood separately first and then as used together. Unconditional means to exist or to be or to come into being without any requisite, condition or qualification whatsoever. It is defined as a state, situation, circumstance or relationship in which one thing is not dependent on any other thing for its function, being or existence.

For instance, human life is conditional on oxygen. Take away oxygen long enough and human life cannot be sustained. Plant life is conditional on sunshine. Take away sunshine long enough and plant life cannot be sustained.

It is inarguable that oxygen and sunlight are given to all human beings and all other living things unconditionally. They are freely available regardless of any other factor, variable or condition. Oxygen is not given only to highly evolved creatures who do no harm to others. Rather, it is freely given to all regardless of their nature. Likewise, sunshine is given to all plants unconditionally, not just those that are fruit-bearing or edible, for example.

In a circumstance where "unconditionality" exists, there is no reciprocity requirement. There is no quid pro quo. One thing is not dependent on another. Rather, a thing is freely given to all recipients and exists as a law of nature without connection to any other contingency or condition or dependency on something else.

Thus, it seems axiomatic that nature does not judge. Nature has no concept of justice. It does not know injustice. It does not discriminate based on good behavior. Nature simply enables life, all life, to perform its functions in order to maintain its existence, in a value-free manner.

When the wolf kills the hare or the lion kills the zebra or the big fish eats the small fish, it is not murder and there is no penalty imposed by nature. Rather it is nature facilitating the functionality life requires without judgement as it was designed by Creator to enable existence and the exercise of free will.

As for the term "love," it has many different faces or forms of expression. The ancient Greeks identified six different kinds of love, but the one of greatest interest to this discussion is Agape. Agape, the highest form of love, refers to God's unconditional love for all creation. Agape is also known as universal love and unconditional love. It is the greatest force in the universe.

By virtue of the innate intrinsic design of the Creator, all living things in the cosmos are intended to ultimately express this form of love toward one another. By divine design, all things in the universe are intended to love each other as God loves them. Those in agape consciousness have the highest possible *God Quotient.*

By mandate of nature, this kind of love is inherently without condition, obligation or duty. It is complete, whole and total unto itself. It is a love like none other. It has no equal and no parallel. It is a love that only gives and asks nothing in return. It is the overarching love which makes all creation possible. It carries no reciprocity requirement.

Without its presence, existence would not be supported anywhere in the universe. It is the underpinning of all life. It does no harm, but serves only purposes that are good, creative, compassionate and constructive. It is fuel for the engine that drives evolutionary processes inherent throughout the structure of the entire universe.

Thus, it may be inferred that the chief by-product of unconditional love is perfect resonance. The by-products of perfect resonance are harmony, alignment, at-one-ment, super-alignment, attunement, cooperation, collaboration and concordance. Its expressions are found in the curious relationship between positive and negative polarities, or in the curious dance between darkness and light. It is the medium in which electromagnetism is engendered. It is the basis for the relationship between intention and thought and the resultant behavior of quanta. Indeed, it drives the processes and interactions of all quantum particles and the zero point field, as well as the very creation of all matter.

Unconditional love, then, is the love that God expresses toward all creation without exception. Our universe is an infinitely abundant universe. It does not know scarcity of any kind. It does not know boundaries, at least none that can be observed or comprehended. Rather, it is infinitely expansive and boundless. It is the proverbial gift that keeps on giving to creation no matter what it receives back from creation.

For example, no matter what humans do, good or bad, constructive or destructive, loving or unloving, the universe continues to provide abundantly for basic needs in support of continued human existence. It even provides humans with a planet to call home, the terra firma beneath their feet and the life-giving sun above their heads, as well as the very air they breathe and water they drink.

The conclusion we can draw from this discussion is that the organizing principle of the universe is unconditional love. It exists to support life and its evolution. By logical extension, then, it seems that the prime directive of nature to all living things is to learn, grow and evolve into a state of complete, total and continuous unconditional love, which is equivalent to Godliness, or a perfect GQ.

When all which exists in the universe becomes the full, complete, total and constant manifestation of unconditional love, then the perfection of all things will be realized. Once this state is achieved, the universe will fulfill and satisfy its prime directive and reason for being. When this occurs, a state of complete and total perfection will exist. All things in the universe will be in perfect alignment as one with Creator.

When this occurs, some mystics believe there will be a grand unification of all things, marked by complete singularity with Creator. This, they say, is the overarching evolutionary goal of the universe. It is, therefore, the organizing principle and evolutionary imperative of the universe, as well as the purpose underlying the existence of all things in the universe.

The God depicted in the Bible's Old Testament often shows anger, jealousy, vengeance and wrath toward humans who are sinful, unfaithful, cruel and unjust. There are also tales about God intervening in human affairs to vanquish evil, contravening and countermanding the exercise of free will. Take, for instance, God's parting of the Red Sea to allow Moses and the Israelites to escape from the army of King Ramses II's.

But know this, the God revealed in the New Testament is a God of unconditional love. The God of the New Testament grants free will as an act of ultimate grace and does not interfere with its expression even when it runs contrary to divine will.

It appears God never intended creation would be completely perfect and fully evolved at inception, but rather imbued with the innate capacity for total perfection and divinity, as well as the evolutionary processes that would gradually nudge it in that direction over the course of eternity.

In my view, God does not want to be the equivalent of Pharaoh, holding subjects in bondage by force and coercion, rewarding those who do good and punishing those who sin. Rather, in the beginning, God constructed the intrinsic capacity for all aspects of creation to evolve into perfection as flawless expressions of unconditional love.

This was not done by divine edict, but by the exercise of individual free will choices over time, one incarnation to the next. Eventually, this process will enable all aspects of creation to achieve total realignment and reunion with Creator in full resonance with the same frequency and vibration, which is that of unconditional love.

Thus, the goal of all life ultimately is to evolve one's immortal soul through the exercise of free will until one becomes fully resonant with Creator through unconditional love. Sooner or later, one learns that this is the only dance there is. No other path will appease the soul's constant yearning for reunion with God.

It is important to realize that God neither seeks nor wants mindless legions of sycophant slaves who constantly genuflect and sing praises. God has no interest in having an army of loyal automatons who obediently serve, follow commands and mechanically worship. God has no ego and neither needs nor wants monuments erected to glorify or pay homage.

Reducing Creator to a neurotic puppet-master who does little more than pull everyone's strings for entertainment and amusement, or for any other purpose, is the ultimate absurdity. God sanctions free will, not slavery. God is not some kind of twisted concentration camp commandant.

Rather, God is a God of love. So, what does the word "love" mean in this context? It is synonymous with the word "God." It is the Golden

Rule. It is putting the needs of others before your own. It is sacrificing for the benefit and betterment of others. It is altruistic service to the greater good of all things. It is genuine kindness, caring, compassion and generosity without any expectation of reciprocity or even acknowledgment. It is ultimate empathy and sensitivity. It is pure goodness without an agenda. Is this not what God is? Is this not what God does? Thus, to be as love unto all things is to be Godly. This is what the *God for a Day* exercise is all about.

I presume God has no desire but one – that all aspects of creation engage in joyful, unbridled, selfless co-creation in service to the greater good of all things based on unconditional love. To extend unconditional love is the best and highest form of reverence. To emulate God's chief qualities, those which reveal God's true essence, is to honor and praise God in the best way possible.

Indeed, God is unfathomable and defies definition, but there are two hallmark attributes which inarguably reveal God's basic nature. They are infinite creativity and infinite unconditional love for all things. So be as love unto all things anonymously with humility to praise God through emulation. Devote yourself to kindness, goodness, empathy and compassion. Create beauty without limitation in humble service to the greater good of all things.

At the heart of the challenge to be *God for a Day* is the process of recalibrating one's basic character and one's persona to role-play God as much and as genuinely as possible. One's character must exude a divine vibration to the fullest extent possible during this exercise to do it right and make the most of the experience.

More than 500 years before Christ, Lao Tsu offered some sound guidance about how to accomplish this feat. He said: "Watch your thoughts. They become words. Watch your words. They become actions. Watch your actions. They become habits. Watch your habits. They become your character. Watch your character. It becomes your destiny."

I would add one more thought to this profound wisdom: Watch your destiny in this lifetime. It can determine the substance of your future incarnations and even whether any are needed for the growth or progression of your eternal soul.

For the purposes of this exercise, you must choose no other focus than to be *God for a Day* and to emulate God's character as best you can. The day before you begin your exercise, to raise your vibration to a divine frequency, go to your most sacred spot in nature alone. Reflect on how you will change and what commitments you will make as *God for a Day*. Contemplate what you will do to get into character to portray *God for a Day*.

Take time to watch the sunset. As the sun sets, note that it has set on your former self. Go to bed early. Get a good night's sleep. Wake the next morning and watch the sunrise. As it rises, know that it rises on the new you, a special being who now emerges as *God for a Day*.

It is best to perform this exercise away from home, away from family and friends or others who might recognize you. So, some advance preparations need to be made, such as a hotel reservation or transportation. You should also pre-arrange essential appointments, plan your route and your activities.

Make sure you are aware of your surroundings and always conduct yourself in a safe manner in all of your activities. Practice alertness, vigilance and situational awareness at all times. It is okay to inform your family and friends that you are embarking on a spiritual retreat for a specified period of time to perform the *God for a Day* exercise. If you think it is prudent, let your family and friends know where you are going.

The good deeds you perform during your exercise should be focused on strangers, people you have never seen before and likely will never see again. Yes, charity begins at home, but focusing on family and friends is not recommended during the *God for a Day* exercise, although they may sense a shift in you and benefit from your kinder nature when you return.

Before commencing divine emulation, please consider a period of fasting, meditation, silence, prayer and solitude, as well as techniques to release anger, guilt, regret, hurt and sadness. Perform balancing and centering techniques also, along with some kind of ritual in which you sincerely forgive yourself and others.

As you surrender self-identity and the dominance of ego, prepare to smile with your eyes throughout the exercise aimed at everyone you meet. Venture forth in Godliness, dressed comfortably and casually. Here are a few ideas to consider for your *God for a Day* exercise:

• Take a long walk. Look for someone who looks lonely and sad. Invite him or her to lunch. Encourage them to tell their life story.

• Send your favorite charity a donation of what you can afford, or, alternatively volunteer your time.

• Go to a local homeless shelter and help prepare the evening's meal. Stay long enough to help with the dishes.

• If you can afford it, give cash to homeless people you select at random and suggest they buy something for themselves that will make them happy. Alternatively, buy several meals at your favorite fast-food restaurant and distribute them while they are still hot to homeless people you encounter.

• Take a pottery class. Learn to work with clay. Make cups, bowls, vases and other items. Paint them with cheerful designs or with inspiring messages. Fill them with fresh organic fruits or flowers. Give them away at random to strangers.

• Wrap a gift of something you treasure before you leave your home to start the exercise. Give it to a stranger when you feel compelled.

• Send flowers anonymously to a bereaved family at a local funeral home or at their residence...check the obituaries in the local paper that day. Alternatively, send the family a book about how to process grief in care of the funeral home so they receive it at the time of the service.

• Mow a stranger's lawn; paint a stranger's house; wash a stranger's car; bring groceries to an elderly person on a fixed income; pay to fill the gas tank of a car randomly at a gas station.

• Consider becoming a registered/trained volunteer for any number of human service facilities. Places that appreciate trained volunteers include shelters for battered women, hospitals, hospices or nursing homes, senior centers, assisted living facilities or rehab centers. Listen to people tell you their stories, offer words of encouragement, read to them, recite poetry, or engage residents in card games or board games. Offer to read poetry or short stories, comedy appropriate to the group, musical or dance performance, arts and crafts classes, and more. Don't offer advice; don't be holier than thou; don't be smug; just feel their pain and empathize.

• Volunteer at a local animal shelter or humane society. Agree to take home at least two pets that you will adopt, if feasible, or commit to finding them homes.

• Pick up litter wherever you see it.

• Buy groceries for the person behind you at the supermarket.

• Pay tolls for the next three cars behind you on a toll road.

• Where permissible, randomly plant trees and flowering bushes in public spaces.

• Plant a garden and share the fruits of your labor with others.

• Circulate petitions to champion high priority humanitarian causes that will help make the world a better place.

• Smile at everyone you encounter and wish them a pleasant day.

Next day, after the conclusion of your *God for a Day* exercise, write a journal of your experiences. Chronicle everything that happened—what you did; what you said; what others did or said; how you felt; how they felt; what you thought; and how it changed you if it changed you at all.

Consider emailing your experiences as *God for a Day* to *GodforaDay@AffirmingGod.com*. Select stories may be published online or in a future book on an anonymous basis to provide encouragement or advice to others. Feel free to share your own ideas about how to be *God for a Day*, directed to the same email address.

After you complete your exercise, you may wish to contact your family and friends to let them know you are okay and that you just spent a day devoted to doing anonymous good deeds. At your discretion, you can encourage family and friends to do the same thing and give them tips on how to go about it. Attend to any healing that may need to take place within you or among your family, friends, or significant others.

This would conclude the exercise. Go about your normal life as you will, hopefully feeling God more vibrantly, alive and well in your heart. Know that you have made God visible to others in this manner.

Through your kind, caring, compassionate and loving actions in undertaking the *God for a Day* exercise, you have brought God forth more visibly in the world.

As more people undertake this basic exercise of *God for a Day,* the synergy that comes from more unconditional love being expressed in the world could begin to create a shift or change in the world at large and result in new ways people choose to allocate their resources of time, energy and wealth.

Perhaps there will come a time when a sufficient number of people will want to engage in *God for a Day* collectively. A strategically focused brigade of love and light-filled people could smartly combine their love, skills, talents, time, money and energy to bring about an optimal quality of life for everyone and everything, one zip code at a time, or one municipality at a time, until eventually the whole world is transformed.

There are many other variations on the *God for a Day* theme that already exist, including *Habitat for Humanity, Random Acts of Kindness, What Would Jesus Do*, and so forth. A basic internet search will yield many other organizations and initiatives with similar good intent.

Ultimately, it is through us that God is expressed and the magnificence of God is further revealed. By revealing God in this way, we can change ourselves and the world. This honors the advice of Gandhi who once said, "Be the change you want to see in the world."

It is well known that Gandhi took a vow of silence every Monday in order to refine his connection to God. He also frequently engaged in prolonged periods of fasting. By doing these things, Gandhi demonstrated the power of simply "being." In this state of silence and fasting, he entered a sacred state of holiness in which he prayerfully expressed his intentions and goals to bring about positive change in the world. Thereafter, he engaged in "doing" by inspiring large groups of people to achieve declared objectives and become more loving.

In the same manner, the *God for a Day* exercise is focused on doing, but it is also equally focused on being. However, being must precede doing. One must enter a God-like state of mind and therefore be in Godliness before undertaking any specific action.

Yet, it is also true that in a sacred state of "being" during fasting, contemplative prayer, or deep state meditation, a person can bring about positive change without engaging in "doing." The power of prayer and focused intention is enormous especially when large numbers of people concentrate on the same intention. The power of an intensely focused group mind should never be underestimated. It can effect real change in real time. The same is true for an intensely focused individual mind.

The aim of the *God for a Day* exercise is to lose yourself in the process of personifying God. When you achieve this goal, you will not miss your former self, not for one minute, because immersing oneself in the role of a kind, compassionate, loving God is far superior experientially than being one's normal self. The euphoria one enjoys through simulating God's love will serve as evidence of it.

In many places the Bible makes references to Spirit rewarding generosity as much as one hundredfold. Ideally, giving should be selfless and anonymous. It should not be motivated by any expectation of reward or reciprocity. Nevertheless, three popular biblical verses speak to the relationship between giving and receiving:

Luke 6:30, "Give and it will be given to you."

Corinthians 9:6, "Remember this, whoever sows sparingly reaps sparingly and whoever sows generously reaps generously.

Proverbs 11:24, "One gives freely yet grows all the richer. Another withholds what he should give but only suffers want."

Personal Epiphany Induction Techniques

Some people may have no interest in doing the *God for a Day* exercise until or unless they first realize that God exists as a matter of direct experiential fact. But a definitive realization such as this is not likely to occur without a firsthand personal spiritual epiphany.

For many people, nothing would constitute convincing evidence of God's existence other than a direct personal meeting with God/Source/Creator in the higher spiritual dimensions. And, nothing but sacred communion with the divine will suffice to facilitate a spiritual awakening and profound individual transformation.

While intellectual and scientific observations are invaluable as far as they go, there is no substitute for direct personal experience. It is far more powerful and has a much greater impact on the psyche, as well as the intensity and duration of transformative effects.

For those who require a direct peak experience, short of a spontaneous STE, there are many techniques that can safely induce a higher state of consciousness and a life-changing spiritual breakthrough. Collectively, they are referred to as *Epiphany Induction Techniques*. No, they do not include dangerous practices to induce cardiac or respiratory arrest, as was dramatically depicted in the popular film called *Flatliners*. This is not best practice and is definitely not recommended.

Alternatively, a wide variety of safe and gentle induction techniques are available to bring about an STE in a safe and non-threatening manner. They include modalities such as kundalini yoga (for advanced and properly trained individuals); tai chi; fasting; chanting; repetitive trance dancing; contemplative prayer; deep state meditation; rebirthing; sensory deprivation; structured conscious breathing regimens; aural and visual tools; virtual and augmented reality devices; transcendent sexuality through tantric regimens; nonsense exercises; regressive hypnosis; sweat lodge rituals; vision quests; and what is known as scrying or mirror-gazing, often used as a form of self-hypnosis.

The shared goal of all these methods is to achieve a state of deep relaxation; to disengage the mind, the ego and the senses; to remove oneself from thought, stress, anxiety and the routine noise associated with everyday living—all to experience profound stillness, calm, silence and transcendence of one's social identity and the mortal shell.

It is in this sacred altered state of consciousness where one feels the presence of God waiting patiently at the intersection of silence and stillness. There is where God is found, in the holy silence and stillness, existing apart from all else, revealed in a subtle energetic manner, in an unmistakable powerful feeling that signals the presence of the divine. It is a glorious feeling. There is none better.

Yes, for me, God's presence comes in the form of a blissful feeling, one that is quite subtle and ethereal. I have never seen God with my eyes and I have never heard God's voice with my ears. I have only felt God's presence, and when I do, it is ecstatic and euphoric. There's no mistaking it.

Deep state relaxation is essential to bring about an altered state of consciousness, and meditation is one of the most popular methods to achieve this state of being. There are many forms of meditation and many different meditation techniques to explore in order to find what works best for each person. It does not require sitting in a lotus position and chanting "OM" or a personal mantra, although that is recommended in some forms of meditation.

Meditation can occur through painting, sculpting, gardening, sky-gazing, bird-watching, or simply becoming mesmerized by the repetitive motion and sound of mild ocean waves kissing the shoreline. There is no one single best way.

Conscious structured rhythmic breathing can be very helpful to the process, but it too can occur naturally as a consequent by-product of entering a deep state of relaxation. This has happened to me on occasion, even to the point where I have forgotten to inhale and exhale, for how long I do not know, but I suffered no ill-effects from not breathing for a time. Yes, it startled and surprised me when I took note of it after the fact.

Altered states of consciousness can be detected by an EEG device, which measures electrical activity in the brain and the brainwave frequencies of beta, alpha, theta and delta states. Much of the time, most of us operate in a "beta" state of consciousness, which is ordinary hyperactive waking consciousness. In this state our minds are full of chatter, as well as noise, stress, worry and distractions. Occasionally, when we are more relaxed and at ease, we might transition into an "alpha" state, akin to daydreaming.

When we turn in for the night and prepare to fall asleep, we might enter a twilight state where we float in between light sleep and ordinary waking consciousness. This is called the "theta" state, one in which we might experience powerful ideas or insights just before drifting off into deep sleep.

In deep sleep, we normally enter the "delta" state. Here we can achieve major breakthroughs, solve major problems, find answers to our biggest questions, and determine how to realize our greatest hopes and dreams. Also, it is in this state that we are most disengaged from mind and ego and thus more closely connected to the higher realms. We can also facilitate healing of our bodies in this state.

Conscious or lucid dreaming occurs when one awakens deep in the delta dream state to become an actively conscious participant in the dream as it is actually unfolding. When the dreamer awakens within the dream, one can find answers or gain valuable insights or impact physical reality in a manner consistent with one's higher spiritual good. This has happened to me several times, such as in my lucid dream about Pope Francis and the Spear of Destiny discussed earlier.

Before falling asleep, most every night, I consciously program my dreams to facilitate personal healing, seek out the help I need or things I want to learn or desire to accomplish. Keeping a dream journal is also a good idea to aid recall.

To facilitate deep state relaxation, the analogy of an engine may be useful. Through the engine which powers our mind and thoughts, we can move from "beta" to "delta" by downshifting the manual transmission of the mind from high gear or fifth gear, all the way down to first gear and then to neutral or park.

The goal here is to lower the engine's RPMs (revolutions per minute) from maximum to idle and then to turn off the engine completely so that the dominant rational mind is placed in suspension with nothing left to power or stimulate it.

When the dominant rational mind is brought into suspension through deep state relaxation, the ego is parked too, and no longer exercises its normal imperial rule. In this way, we achieve a sublime resonant energy connection with God.

The technique I prefer to lower the RPMs and the one I use most often is what I call *Streaming*. This is a term I coined in 1976 at the Cascades in Jefferson National Forest in Pembroke, Virginia, a short drive from Virginia Tech in Blacksburg where I attended graduate school.

In this location, one will find a gorgeous two-mile uphill pathway steeped in the full glory of nature that leads to a rather sublime sixty-nine-foot waterfall. The downhill portion of the trip back to the parking lot is also two miles, but much less rigorous.

As one hikes up to the waterfall, along the entire path, one can hear the mesmerizing sound of rushing water as it rapidly cascades over many rocks and large boulders in the stream bed. It is glorious and resplendent, blessed with surreal beauty and a sacred vibration. I went there often to relieve the stress of graduate school. But more so, I went there to commune with God in nature, which for me is by far the best cathedral or temple of all.

One day early on in my frequent treks to the waterfall, about halfway along the path that leads to it, I discovered a magical place in the stream where I could step on a convenient sequence of smaller rocks and boulders that led to a large one in the center of the stream. Once there, I would lie down on this large boulder, nicely contoured to the shape and size of my body, using my backpack for a headrest.

Then, with a huge smile of anticipation on my face, I would close my eyes and begin a regimen of structured conscious breathing to help induce a deep meditative state, aided by the hypnotic sound of the rushing water from the alluring stream, hence the name *Streaming*. Sometimes I would fall asleep, but more often than not, the calming sound of the stream, combined with my focus on communing with God, would lead me deep into inner space where the divine awaits. This is indeed my favorite induction technique.

There is another closely related method which is also among my favorite options to lower the RPMs. It is known as *Forest-Bathing*. This technique involves venturing deep within a magnificent forest to find a power spot or sacred space using the powers of one's intuition and prayerful requests to be divinely guided to the right place. For me, it usually involved the discovery of a rather remarkable tree that grabs hold, undeniably and unmistakably, and just won't let go. For me, it would be a special towering tree with a shaman-like persona and a canopy that is irresistibly captivating.

Once there, I settle in at the base of this tree sitting in a lotus position with my back against its magnificent trunk. I then begin a meditative process with the same regimen of structured rhythmic breathing as used in *Streaming*. Before long, I find myself attuning to the tree's awesome inner essence and spiritual energy, which serves as a gateway to the divine realm where God waits patiently, most-assuredly. When the resonant energy connection occurs, there is no mistaking it. It is the most glorious feeling one can imagine.

I found that a grove of stately redwood trees worked well for me in my *Forest-Bathing* adventures. It helped me surrender to the void almost effortlessly. I am especially fond of the majestic redwoods in Stout Grove near Crescent City, California, not to mention the magical allure of Olympic National Forest near Sol Duc falls, which is only one of many power spots in that highly enchanted high vibration place.

There is also another method to consider, but one that should be contemplated only when all other options have failed, and then only under controlled conditions with competent professional supervision. I am speaking here about the careful, judicious use of entheogens, which are psychedelic drugs or psychotropic agents such as ecstasy (Molly), peyote, mescaline, psilocybin, ayahuasca, LSD, ibogaine, huachuma (San Pedro Cactus), 5-Me0-DMT; and other substances of a similar nature.

Use of drugs such as these is extreme and potentially dangerous. I do not recommend it, except under medical supervision to control dosage, allow monitoring and provide safe surroundings. One must exercise due caution and care if this option is chosen. Some have achieved favorable results through this method, so much so that some of these substances are now in greater clinical use by psychiatrists and psychotherapists for treatment of various psychological and emotional disorders with generally positive results. Still, I hasten to add that this is not a technique I have tried personally. I have no need or desire to do so, but others I know feel quite differently and are generally enthusiastic about it.

The use of entheogens to trigger spiritual breakthroughs dates back to at least ancient Greece where it was common practice. Asclepius, regarded by historians to be the first physician, who is often associated with Imhotep (the Egyptian God of Healing), used psychedelic agents at his healing temples to facilitate healing and spiritual awakening. The two often went hand in hand. The most famous of his healing temples was a sacred place in ancient Greece known as Epidaurus.

Entheogens were also widely used during the Hellenistic period in Eleusis, circa 340 to 31 BC, as part of secret sacred rites or initiations practiced by the "Eleusinian Mystery Cult." It is believed that initiates, who were required to take a vow of secrecy, ingested a drink called "Kykeon" believed to have contained LSD-like alkaloids derived from ergot fungi, roughly equivalent to psilocybin mushrooms. This triggered an altered or mystical state of consciousness, which often elevated initiates into the realm of the divine, resulting in profound life-changing spiritual breakthroughs.

Another inductive technique from times of old is the pre-cursor to the modern ritual of baptism. This approach, as applied in ancient times, is not recommended either, for obvious reasons, but warrants discussion simply to convey a fascinating aspect of history.

In Biblical times, John the Baptist is reputed to have submerged the followers of Jesus, their heads under water, in the River Jordan, as a show of their faith and conviction. The purpose of this ritual was to symbolically wash away "sins" and enable people to become "born again" in their acceptance of Christ. Even Jesus submitted to baptism by John the Baptist as a show of faith in and acceptance of this ritual.

Some scholars believe that the modern baptism ritual may have originated in Eleusis. Those who desired to be awakened spiritually participated in secret rites of initiation, which sometimes involved ingesting Kykeon as noted above, and other times involved participating in a pre-cursor to the ritual of modern-day baptism.

Some hypothesize that this highly transformative rite of passage is how the celebrated Greek philosophers became so wise, knowledgeable and insightful, particularly about esoteric and spiritual matters, as well as life after death (see Plato's *Phaedo*).

The Eleusinian rituals were sacred and secret rites of passage cloaked in an aura of mystery and speculation. Initiates reportedly received the great blessing of full illumination and vast spiritual wisdom. Many allegedly separated from their bodies and traveled into the divine realm where they encountered sacred beings and divine deities.

The "baptism" process practiced in Eleusis involved submersion in "the holy waters" until initiates actually lost consciousness, essentially from drowning or holding their breath too long, basically, inducing a state of clinical death. Soon after initiates lost consciousness, they were lifted out of the water by the attendants. Then, some unknown potion, technique or process, supposedly foolproof, was administered to resuscitate them. They returned to full waking consciousness, completely unharmed, having suffered no ill-effects whatsoever from being drowned.

In this manner, initiates "died" and were "born again," totally transformed by the blessing of full enlightenment. By "dying" in this fashion, initiates were able to pierce the veil between this world and the next. They reported discovering firsthand the afterlife, God, infinity, eternity, reincarnation and karma. Much like modern day near-death experiencers, they were able to directly commune with God.

Of course, the obvious difference between the contemporary practice of baptism and the ancient Eleusinian mystery ritual is the length of time the initiate is held under water. Today's practice of baptism is limited to placing drops of water on the forehead or facilitating a very brief submersion of one's head under the water, nowhere near long enough to cause unconsciousness or drowning. However, the practice in ancient Eleusis did exactly that and thereby enabled initiates in those days to essentially have their very own near-death experience in which God and the afterlife became very real to them.

One can only wonder what their fatality rate might have been. Even today's doctors equipped with modern medical technology cannot boast a 100% success rate in resuscitation attempts. What's more, no matter how good the process, antidote or technology, some people may have flatly refused to come back because they liked it too much over there.

Of course, we know from NDE reports that some are not given a choice. They are told they must return to fulfill their destiny and serve some important purpose. But those who are given a choice and who decide to return, always do so entirely for selfless reasons, generally to serve family, friends and the greater good of all things. None come back because they highly prefer this reality to that one.

But the overriding point here is that once Source/Creator is directly experienced, by whatever means one chooses, this is when all wonder and doubt about God disappear. This is when the Seven Statements and the Fifteen Elaborations are no longer viewed as hypothetical propositions, but instead are accepted and embraced as facts reflective of fundamental truth.

A direct experience with God enables a person to outgrow their former self and evolve into Godliness every day. One person at a time, this is how an optimal future for earth and its inhabitants can be achieved, by affirming God and achieving Godliness daily.

Matthew 7:7 seems entirely appropriate and applicable to this discussion. If one seeks a direct connection or communion with God with the utmost humility, earnestness, sincerity, reverence and perseverance, it will happen eventually. "Ask, and it shall be given you; seek, and ye shall find; knock, and it shall be opened unto you."

The Future is All We Have Left

Years ago, I wrote a rock 'n' roll song called "The Twenty-Third Century Shakes." The refrain was "We've got to live up to the future 'cause the future is all we have left." I also invented a new term in that song, "futuretosis," which I describe as "the new psychosis," in reference to anxiety about what future course humanity would choose for itself. The song was a plea for humanity to rise to the occasion of the future by co-creating a remarkable future, one that surpassed our greatest hopes. (Please visit *AffirmingGod.com* to view the lyrics.)

Abraham Lincoln once remarked, quite astutely, that "the best way to predict the future is to create it." He could not have been more right when he made that incisive observation, which still holds true today and will for all time.

The future is not fixed. It exists only as a set of probabilities, permutations and combinations. The future will be whatever we collectively determine it to be through our combined choices, actions and also our inactions. Sometimes doing nothing can have adverse or unintended consequences.

The present moment is our point of greatest power because it represents our time of choosing. It is when we will deliberately choose what we will do going forward from a limitless pallet of options and alternatives. But essentially, they boil down to two basic directions. We can choose to embody Godliness or we can choose to embody its opposite. We have the free will power to move in either direction. And the sum total of all the individual choices we make in each subsequent present moment will combine to form the shape of our future.

So, right now, at this precise moment in time, the present, we have arrived at our time of free will choosing. What choices will we make? Hopefully, we will make only those choices which are enlightened, loving and aligned with God. Hopefully, we will choose Godliness on a global scale.

Armageddon and the apocalyptic scenario described in Revelations need not be our fate, but it can be and will be if we accept that as our fate. It is only one of many possible scenarios for the future, a future still to be determined by us collectively.

The qualities God represents are the very qualities humanity seriously lacks and sorely needs in order to prevent self-destruction or a dark dystopian future. Yes, my considered opinion is that only by embracing the reality of God can we climb out of the muck and mire that threatens our survival as a species. Denying the reality of God and all that God represents is to invite, encourage and empower evil. It is to invite further devolution and dysfunction. It is a move in the wrong direction.

And this is the beauty of God's plan, a plan which is richly infused with free will and unconditional love, granting us the grace to co-create whatever future we choose, preferably one that represents the utmost in beauty and magnificence—one that honors God in the best way we can manage, as only one of many different species of intelligent life in the universe, all created by God for this very purpose.

The observations I offer here represent my best attempts to convey what I believe to be truth, the whole truth and nothing but, so help me God. May it serve as the truth that sets you free from illusion, misperception and flawed thinking. These villains are the enemy, and if we let them, they will surely lead us into the infernal abyss of a dark future.

I cannot think of a better solution to all that ails us as a species, other than to collectively affirm and honor God without further delay, lest we all continue to suffer needlessly from an unspeakable host of self-inflicted wounds. We humans must ascend quickly into Godliness lest we all perish or continue to suffer a grossly sub-optimal existence here on planet earth. A future without God is no future at all.

It is time to write history anew, to make a collective history which merits pride, one that represents the best we can accomplish as a species. We have certainly shown our worst over the past several millennia. I, for one, have had more than enough of that. It is time now to collectively emerge from the tar pits so we can dance and frolic on the clouds.

Does anyone care to laugh, sing and dance? I hope so. Let's be good to ourselves and each other by choosing Godliness. What a wonderful world it could be, and it is collectively within our power to make it so. The present moment is the point of power when we can individually and collectively choose this path. Let us do so while we still have time.

And so, if the outpouring from my heart on these pages about the reality of God has still left you unconvinced, uninspired and unmotivated, it is doubtful you will be moved to engage in the exercises and practices that have been recommended. But perhaps you will be sufficiently curious to try one of the various induction techniques described earlier. Find one that might lead to your own personal epiphany and discovery of God. For your own bliss, and the complexion of our shared future, I hope you will try at least one option or another.

In the last century, we invented nuclear weapons and bio-chemical warfare, thinking we were quite clever to do so. Our leaders believed these weapons were necessary to deter territorial aggression. But these methods of deterrence have not proven to be very sensible, especially today. We have succeeded only in foolishly amplifying the risk of totally destroying ourselves and the earth...what Carl Sagan called "the only home we have ever known," in his classic book entitled *Pale Blue Dot*. These weapons could be our undoing eventually, along with the advent of artificial intelligence if we're not careful.

It seems abundantly clear that we have only two primary choices: mass destruction from nuclear war, or heaven on earth. Will we choose to co-create a magnificent optimal future or to inflict upon ourselves an inconceivable nightmare? There ultimately is no middle ground, and again, it is our choice to make.

Our time of free will choosing is now, right now, this very moment. We will either celebrate or mourn our choices, as the case might be. We also will share individually and collectively in whatever karmic consequences are linked to the choices we make.

Martin Luther King, Jr. said it so beautifully and eloquently in his moving sermon entitled "Unfulfilled Dreams," delivered on March 3, 1968, just about one month before he was assassinated:

> "There is a tension at the heart of the universe between good and evil. It's there: a tension at the heart of the universe between good and evil.
>
> "Hinduism refers to this as a struggle between illusion and reality. Platonic philosophy used to refer to it as a tension between body and soul. Zoroastrianism, a religion of old, used to refer to it as a tension between the god of light and the god of darkness. Traditional Judaism and Christianity refer to it as a tension between God and Satan. Whatever you call it, there is a struggle in the universe between good and evil.
>
> "Now not only is that struggle structured out somewhere in the external forces of the universe, it's structured in our own lives. And in every one of us this morning, there's a war going on. It's a civil war. I don't care who you are. I don't care where you live. There is a civil war going on in your life. And every time you set out to be good, there's something pulling on you telling you to be evil. It's going on in your life.
>
> "Every time you set out to love, something keeps pulling on you trying to get you to hate. Every time you set out to be kind and say nice things about people, something is pulling on you to be jealous and

envious and to spread evil gossip about them. There's a civil war going on. There's a tension at the heart of human nature."

And so, who wins this struggle is up to us, each and every one of us. With each decision we make in each minute of each day, we determine the shape, direction and character of our individual lives. Collectively speaking, our separate individual choices add up into one combined whole, which determines humanity's future.

The operative equation is simple and straightforward. It has nothing whatsoever to do with divine dictates, vengeance, wrath or apocryphal Biblical predictions. Rather, it is governed by basic cause-effect and action-reaction relationships.

The unescapable truth is that the longer humanity ignores God, the longer humanity will endure self-inflicted suffering and a grossly sub-optimal reality. The sooner we embrace God and develop a Godly or God-like approach to life—even for a day, then every day, the sooner we will arrive at heaven on earth.

Ludwig van Beethoven (1770-1827) expressed the same sentiments in his much-heralded Ninth Symphony, which is considered by many to be the greatest symphony ever written. And Beethoven, of course, is often revered as the greatest composer of all time. This symphony and *Loved by the Light* have much in common. Both embrace the same goal. Both constitute a reverent prayer for universal love, peace, harmony and oneness. Both pay devout homage to the Creator of all things, and both urge a closer relationship between humankind and God.

Beethoven was inspired to compose his famous symphony by a poem called *Ode to Joy* written in the summer of 1785 by the German poet, playwright and historian Friedrich Schiller (1759-1805). In this work, Schiller described the joy and magnificence of creation, which he called "a beautiful spark of the divine." He saw it as a cause for celebration.

Schiller also wrote of a Creator, a "loving Father who surely dwells above the stars." He beseeches us to "seek Him above the starry canopy."

He offers his poem as "a kiss" for the whole world and invites us to "be embraced" by the magnificence of creation.

In essence, Schiller's poem is a heartfelt yearning for humanity, which he refers to as "you millions," to feel the powerful presence of God abounding in nature, and to celebrate the joy of God's creation. Poignantly, Schiller implores us to "sense our Creator," and "bow down before Him" in humble gratitude. He invites us to set aside the discordant sounds that divide us and join together harmoniously unified as one. He proclaims this to be our natural state of being as it is in the celestial regions, Elysium, where dwells the one God who made all things.

Beethoven was so moved by the message of *Ode to Joy* that he was inspired to compose the Ninth Symphony to bring Schiller's words to life. He does this in the rousing fourth movement that features a choral section augmented by four soloists, all singing in Schiller's native German tongue. Sadly, Schiller died on May 9, 1805, nineteen years before Beethoven immortalized his poem with heavenly classical music.

Although he never heard it, Schiller was honored by Beethoven's musical composition that showcased his words. And, importantly, Beethoven gave humanity a truly timeless gift, one of the greatest ever. For it can be said that through Beethoven's ingenious composition, God is energetically revealed to all those with souls that are attuned. One can literally feel the presence of God and witness God's handiwork by listening intently to the enrapturing flow of musical notes in the mesmerizing performance.

If one desires to have a veritable spiritual experience, then by all means, attend a live performance of the Ninth by a high-quality orchestra. Hearing a recorded version will suffice, but it is not nearly as impactful. I have attended dozens of live performances of the Ninth. Each one empowered me with greater spiritual voltage. Yes, it is my favorite of all symphonies, but this is beside the point. Most classical music aficionados agree that there is something very special about the Ninth Symphony that puts it in a league of its own.

Not surprisingly, Beethoven credited God with composing this work. He often said that he was merely God's transcriptionist; that the notes simply poured out inside his mind from the celestial regions so fast he could not manage to write the score fast enough to keep pace.

To be sure, one can feel the presence of God when this symphony is performed. God's hand is all over it. Through it, God stirs the soul energetically, summoning a sense of divine presence, as God can be felt in each and every note. For anyone who has not had the pleasure of attending a performance of this work, perhaps you can catch a rerun of the New York Philharmonic's masterful performance that was aired on PBS' Great Performances series in October 2022.

The creation of this special work and the power of its performances are cited as an example of what can be accomplished when we set aside our differences and devote ourselves to a lofty common purpose such as *God for a Day* every day. Truly anything is possible when we align our energies with the flow of unconditional love. If humans can accomplish something as sublime as the composition and inspired performance of this amazing symphony, then surely we can do anything.

The Ninth Symphony was one of God's gifts to Beethoven. For me, God's gifts were a box of Marlboro cigarettes found in the desert to seal my vision quest circle, and then later a rock inside a cave with my first name naturally embedded in it—a rock that stands upright on its own with a raised pyramid on one end. God's gifts to me also included Marbles' rock and the many vigilant angels who came to rescue me from certain death seven times.

As we look to the future, a popular adage comes to mind: "Life is God's gift to you. What you do with your life is your gift to God." I humbly submit that choosing to be *God for a Day* every day would be the greatest gift of all to give in return. Wisdom obtained from the blog, *Jesse's Café Américain,* also applies: "Need little, want less, love more."

A Cure For "The God-Shaped Hole"

The "God-Shaped Hole" concept or metaphor has been much talked and written about since it was first introduced by Blaise Pascal in 1670. It is also referred to as the "God-Shaped Void," or the "God-Shaped Vacuum." But by all of its names, this phrase refers to a conceptual empty space inside the soul, psyche, mind or consciousness of all human beings that can only be occupied or fulfilled by God. It is thought to be inherent within human DNA, pre-programmed by the Creator to serve as the in-dwelling location where humans carry a built-in, hard-wired connection to their Creator at all times, at least in potential.

This phrase was first introduced by Pascal in his book entitled *Pensées,* French for "thoughts." Pascal was a French physicist, mathematician and philosopher. It was later made popular in the writings of Jean-Paul Sartre in commentary about Frederick Nietzsche's bombshell proclamation that "God is dead." This, of course, was in reference to works by Nietzsche which promoted atheism, nihilism and existentialism, most notably *Thus Spoke Zarathustra,* published in 1883.

Pascal had a spiritually transformative experience (STE) in 1654 and later wrote *Pensées* inspired by it. He asserted that filling the "God-Shaped Hole" in the human psyche or consciousness with God and love of God is the only way humans can truly satisfy their incessant, seemingly pre-programmed spiritual hunger.

In other words, Pascal argued that only a dynamic, substantive relationship with God could fill the "God-Shaped Hole." He believed it is the only way to completely ameliorate an intrinsic endless spiritual yearning within all humans, even atheists and agnostics, for an enduring reunion with God. He saw it as the single remedy for the relentless inner void or nagging sense of emptiness many contend with from day to day in their search for transcendent meaning and purpose. It was his STE that made God real to Pascal and that filled the "God Void" within him, which he later wrote about in *Pensées*.

But it was not solely the work of Nietzsche that cast humanity adrift on the subject of God and that caused God to fall from a prominent place in the collective psyche of humankind. The work of Darwin, Descartes and Newton, among other scientists, triggered a serious chasm to form between the sacred and the secular. This ushered in the profane or secular age of materialism, which sadly still remains the dominant paradigm in science today.

Over the centuries, religion certainly did its part as well to contribute to growing public disenchantment with God. Abuses, hypocrisy and corruption within the various sects took a heavy toll over time and caused much attrition and cynicism.

Increasingly, a disconnection between the "God of religion" and public belief or acceptance of the "God of religion" widened considerably, creating deep metaphysical despair and ontological anxiety. Steadily, God was replaced by the trappings of materialism, spawning a pandemic of spiritual homelessness, which has been globally devastating in its consequences. People lost their spiritual moorings and largely suspended their search for cosmic meaning. They largely abandoned their quest to comprehend who they are ultimately and why they are here.

Believing that God was dead or had vanished or never existed in the first place, left people to worship only the physical body and material possessions, which promptly took the place of God. There was nothing left of a transcendent nature that could give meaning and purpose to human striving and suffering. Consumerism and perhaps patriotism became poor substitutes to help people grapple with the shallowness, vicissitudes and vapidity of everyday life.

Indeed, God's fall from prominence in the public mind due to so-called scientific advances and the shameful failings of religion, left a grim prognosis for the future of humanity. Surely, we are seeing widespread evidence of that in today's extremely troubled world, growing more so by the day.

Karen Armstrong writes about this issue in her classic book, *A History of God,* cited earlier. She reflects that "...God has been one of the great human ideas of all times..." and that the major religions invented God to serve various social, political and economic agendas along the way, modifying definitions as and when needed to try to remain relevant. She states that it was "...far more important for an idea of God to work than for it to be logically or scientifically sound."

But, Ms. Armstrong opines that the God of these religions had no enduring objective reality and largely became too mysterious and remote to have any relevance for most people. The God of these major religions, she revealed, was too distant, demanding, controlling, inaccessible, inconsistent and fallible for their faith to be sustained.

And so Ms. Armstrong's excellent book chronicles the way humans perceived God over time and how their concepts of God evolved along the way. In the process, she does a convincing job of showing that man made God more in man's image than the other way around. And in the process of expertly narrating this fascinating history, she also demonstrates rather convincingly how and why the "God-Shaped Hole" phenomenon came into being.

Pascal saw it all presciently in 1670, or perhaps earlier during his STE in 1654. His musings about the advent of a "God-Shaped Hole" in the collective psyche of humanity truly hit the center of the bulls-eye, and so did his recommended solution. He insisted that nothing but God can fill the "God-Shaped Hole" within each person.

In my view, Pascal is spot on in this observation, and this is the primary challenge before us today. How can broad public acceptance of God be globally advanced in a truly credible manner so that Pascal's "God-Shaped Hole" can be fully remedied within every human being? What is the cure for the "God Shaped Hole?" I humbly propose four practical strategies which, if implemented together, could provide the cure for this nagging condition, as follows:

1. In view of the evidence set forth in this book and many others like it, governments, corporations, foundations and private individual philanthropists should generously fund scientific research into consciousness, torsion wave physics, spiritually transformative experiences and the techniques which induce them, as a top priority, enabling the world's best scientists and leading academic institutions to greatly accelerate their efforts in these areas;

2. A comprehensive spirited effort should be made by all concerned individuals and institutions to promote the *God for a Day* campaign world-wide, and other programs like it, to encourage broad public support so that people across the globe will participate enthusiastically. It just might be the best way to form a solid personal connection with God and also co-create an optimal future for earth and all its inhabitants;

3. Spread the word about this book far and wide to encourage as many people as possible to read it, and other books like it, in the

hope that a critical mass of humanity will learn and be inspired to discover God for themselves using one or more of the STE induction techniques that were discussed in a previous chapter, or by undergoing a spontaneous spiritual transformation simply from the information presented herein; and

4. Strengthen support for and participation in Eternea, a non-profit publicly-supported 501.c.3 charity which was created for this very purpose. Through its seven program components, Eternea's very mission and vision are to advance effective remedies for "The God-Shaped Hole."

If these things are done in an expeditious manner, the "God-Shaped Hole" that currently weakens most of humanity will be fully remedied. The "Hole" will be wholly filled. It will become a thing of the distant past and none too soon. When that happens, a seismic turnaround will take place. Humanity will realize its highest and best dreams. It will be the start of building an ideal future for earth and all its inhabitants.

This book represents the best thinking I can offer about the challenges now facing humankind. As you complete your reading of this final chapter, please keep in mind that what you have read is not one man's public profession of faith in God and the afterlife. Rather, you have reviewed grounded observations and firm convictions based on first-hand knowledge gained from a wide variety of direct spiritual experiences throughout my lifetime.

I have candidly discussed my personal journey, from one who thought he believed but really did not, to one who believed in absolutely nothing, to one who finally embraced the reality of God and the continuation of human consciousness after physical death. But what was even more important for me to learn is that we not only survive death, but we must also reconcile direct action-reaction and cause-effect consequences related to our conduct in this or previous incarnations, in a self-directed manner.

Nothing I can do or say or write can come close to repaying God or conveying my gratitude for all I have been given and the awesome grace I have received, not even in small measure. But by writing this book, I will at least go on public record as one who states unequivocally that God is real and the afterlife too, expressed as an objective empirical conclusion, not as a statement of faith.

Why am I so resolute? I assure you, it is not because of hope, wishful thinking or delusional bouts of fantasy, but because of compelling exceptional events in my life. By sharing these experiences and what they have taught me, I hope to help de-mystify God and inspire more people to discover a path which makes God real to them and leads them to practice Godliness every day.

There is one critical question humanity should be repeatedly asking itself right now, one which far surpasses and overshadows all other highly important questions: How can we unify in harmonious cooperation and collaboration to expeditiously make these the best of times, not just for a fortunate privileged few, but for everyone and everything on earth, and for the earth too? And what would bring about change of this magnitude?

In order to answer the question, another question must be asked: What would motivate a critical mass of humanity, as well as governments, societies and cultures, to consider this issue seriously as a top priority with the aim of taking decisive action in the right direction?

A principal catalyst to serve this purpose would be transcendental in nature. It revolves around affirming God and the survival of human consciousness after death in which there is an afterlife that involves accountability and direct consequences related to earthly conduct. Since God really does exist and the afterlife too—one which carries consequences for earthly actions—would this not be a huge factor in shaping the choices we make here and now, collectively and individually?

Since such a profoundly transformative process happened to me, I suspect it can happen to anyone. Imagine what might happen if we were to give respectful consideration to the ample evidence from the vast credible literature on point.

The readily available evidence is overwhelmingly convincing that God truly exists. If enough people around the globe judge the evidence to be credible the same way I did, or alternatively, bring about their own direct experience with the divine through application of a safe epiphany induction technique, then perhaps it will be as life-changing for them as it was for me. If so, then perhaps it could make all the difference in the world, and not one minute too soon.

Alternatively, there is the option of a passive approach. We can simply wait for the vicissitudes of life to bring about a change in our perceptions, behavior, values and attitudes. All it might take is a major trauma or loss to shock an individual into reaching out to God for guidance, help or comfort. It is when we are in crisis situations that we become more inclined to be kind, loving, empathetic and compassionate...more Godly.

In one of the best books ever written on the subject of near-death experiences, *Lessons from the Light*, Dr. Ken Ring cites the NDE of Neev, and on page 177, quotes him as follows: "I wish everyone could have one (an NDE with a life review). It would change the world. Everyone would understand each other and there wouldn't be conflict, and there wouldn't be chaos, and there wouldn't be greed or war...the life review is the ultimate teaching tool."

Regardless of compelling accounts such as this one by Neev and others like it as described in this book and elsewhere, no amount of evidence will convince those who do not wish to be convinced. As the popular adage goes, "For those who believe, no proof is necessary. For those who do not believe, no amount of proof is sufficient." People must find and accept God on their own. I hope this book will inspire more to do so. I believe our future depends on it.

Yes, I firmly believe God is the answer to all that ails us. Yes, I firmly believe that God is the only solution. Yes, I emphatically assert that God is real. Yes, I unequivocally affirm God, the God of love and only love.

Albert Einstein, a man of exceptional brilliance, seems to have arrived at a similar orientation. Near the end of his life, he commented that the two ways to live one's life would be to see that "everything is a miracle or nothing is." By this statement, I believe he concluded that everything is indeed a miracle. He would be right in that point of view, because everything truly is a miracle.

Beyond being the source of all miracles, what is God at the core if not the fundamental qualities of perfect altruism, creativity, love, beauty, truth, knowledge, goodness, kindness, compassion, mercy, grace, generosity, harmony, unity and peace? Is that not what the world needs today? Are these crucial qualities not in terribly short supply nearly everywhere?

History has shown us that the ideological infrastructure of any society which omits a strong prevailing belief in God and the afterlife as its centerpiece cannot be sustained. Moreover, it cannot effectively serve as a healthy springboard for the realization of advanced civilization. But to maintain enduring viability, a society's ideological infrastructure must be based upon facts and truth.

A society's shared ideology is what guides and directs all basic socialization processes. It is what essentially programs or conditions all individual members of that society. It fashions social institutions, the family unit and personal identity. If it is founded on lies, half-truths or false assumptions about the nature of reality, then its members will be correspondingly misguided as well, for they will have been denied the truth about the true nature of reality.

To be sure, we are still looking through a glass darkly trying to make sense of it all. But we know more now than ever before thanks to those who have shared their spiritually transformative experiences with us. And, what they have shared, in the main, has enormous implications for how we view ourselves and reality, and for the nature of social, political and economic systems generally, as well as the whole of human nature.

To quicken the spiritual evolution of humankind, based on this invaluable precious knowledge, is the most critical of all endeavors during these dark times on planet earth. To be sure, the accelerated scientific study of consciousness and STEs, is the key to achieving a better understanding of ourselves and the whole of reality. And, whatever consciousness is, it appears to be manifest everywhere throughout the entire cosmos. It is indeed ubiquitous. In its most evolved state, it appears to be the primal cause that gives rise to all manifest reality, placing all else at effect, hence mind over matter and the primacy of consciousness.

In my opinion, humankind will not make meaningful progress in advancing higher civilization or the cause of social justice to realize a more equitable state of affairs until or unless we collectively evolve spiritually. Until we reach broad agreement about the consciousness issue and other fundamental questions underlying human existence, political, financial and religious revolutions will continue to fail or fall woefully short of achieving their objectives. They will continue to disappoint. They will not deliver the level of reform that is sought no matter how many progressive thinkers enter into key positions of power. In the end, they will become corrupted, too, by the very systems they seek to reform...systems that are inherently corrupt at the core, be they political, social, financial or religious.

As a first order of business, broad agreement on the definition of key terms and issues, must be reached, definitions that are rooted in sound empiricism, following the good advice of Locke and Voltaire. We must build an evidence-based consensus about God, consciousness, the afterlife, the nature of reality...about who we really are and why we're really here...about the true meaning and purpose of human existence.

From this most critical foundation, all else will flow, to include commonly shared values, virtues, ethics, morals, mores, attitudes, perceptions and behavior. This is what will determine the complexion of our future and whether we will have one worth living. If it lacks God as its centerpiece and survival of consciousness after death at its core, then our future will be severely imperiled. I humbly submit that Eternea's empirically based Seven Statements could serve as a great catalyst for this purpose, even if only viewed as a straw dog exercise.

Still, what remains is one overarching question which must be contemplated. Even if frontier science could demonstrate the validity of the Seven Statements, hence both the reality of God and the existence of an afterlife, (one that involves direct consequences for earthly behavior), would this motivate a critical mass of humanity sufficient to modify our conduct here and now in keeping with proven transcendent considerations? It seems probable if humanity were truly convinced.

And to speak directly to that challenge, a wise, wealthy and accomplished man agreed with this conclusion back in the fall of 1976. His name was James S. McDonnell (1899-1980). He founded McDonnell-Douglas Aircraft based in St. Louis. It later merged with Boeing in 1997. He is also the founder of the James S. McDonnell Foundation.

I was invited to attend a personal meeting with him in Charlottesville, Virginia, back then. It was held at the Shasta Court home of Dr. Raymond Moody. Also attending were Bob Monroe of the Monroe Institute and Dr. Ian Stevenson from the University of Virginia. Mr. McDonnell was in town to attend a summit of top thinkers to explore future relations with the Soviet Union. He was at the time deeply concerned about the prospect of nuclear war between the U.S. and the U.S.S.R.

Upon his arrival, Mr. McDonnell walked briskly into Raymond's house and took a seat at the dining room table to join the rest of us. With him was a copy of Dr. Moody's book, *Life After Life*, which had just been published about one year before. It had quickly become a global best seller and still was at the time. Mr. McDonnell raised Raymond's book up in the air and waved it back and forth.

"Dr. Moody, you have written a powerful book," he said. "It can change the world. Trust me when I say that something must do so, quickly. The world is on the brink of extinction-level thermonuclear war between the U.S. and the U.S.S.R. Your little book may have the answer we need. What you have done here is to establish a basis for scientific proof of life after death." Then Mr. McDonnell reached inside his jacket pocket and pulled out his personal check book.

"I am a wealthy man, Dr. Moody. I want you to name the amount, here and now. I am ready to write you a check for any sum you wish if you will assure me that you will provide me with scientific proof of God and life after death. I am not joking. What do you say?"

Raymond looked nonplussed for a moment. He gathered his thoughts and then replied. "I am extremely curious, Mr. McDonnell. Why is this so important to you?" Raymond asked.

"Dr. Moody," he answered. "I am convinced that if we can disseminate proof of God and life after death to most people in the U.S.S.R., we will end communism and the threat of nuclear war once and for all. You see, communism holds no place for a belief in God or life after death. If we can provide scientific proof of both, we will create havoc in their ideological infrastructure and cause it to quickly collapse. It will create unsustainable levels of social chaos."

"Well, Mr. McDonnell, that is a most kind and generous offer, but with deepest apologies, I cannot accept," Raymond replied. "You see, sir, I am a Doctor of Philosophy. We take the word "proof" very seriously. There is no way science could ever prove the existence of God or life after death. I am so sorry."

Mr. McDonnell looked very dejected and disappointed. The meeting then came to an abrupt end. But what most impressed me about this exchange is that Mr. McDonnell, same as me, fully understood the enormous sociological and psychological power of empirically validating both the existence of God and the reality of life after death. He and I totally comprehended their importance in framing social ideology, hence social organization and systems of government.

I often wonder what might have happened back then with IANDS if Raymond had crafted a framework that was acceptable to Mr. McDonnell. Would it have been sufficient to bring about the kind of individual and social transformation Mr. McDonnell was hoping to achieve? And if he had sponsored robust research back then, would we be deeply concerned about the prospect of nuclear war with Russia yet again today?

Truth is the cornerstone of all else, particularly in the formulation of fundamental social ideology, and especially in relation to the matters of God and life after death. The Bible speaks to this observation in John 8:32, "You shall know the truth and the truth shall set you free."

And so, I assert that this book presents the truth about the reality of God and continuation of consciousness after death of the physical body. I hope it provides basis enough to end all cynicism and skepticism about these weighty questions. If it does, the threat of nuclear war with Russia and all war and all violence and all inequities will end.

But each reader must determine for themselves whether the content of this book offers soul-stirring truth sufficiently upheld by personal testimony and corroborative evidence. Each reader must ascertain whether this book's wisdom has validity for them and if it qualifies as a legitimate basis for their own enduring spirituality. If a majority are thusly convinced, as I was, and inspired with a passionate zeal to make things better, as I am, then together we build a much brighter future.

Imagine the transformed nature of a truly God-centered humanity. Imagine the transformed nature of a truly God-centered country. Imagine the transformed nature of a truly God-centered world. This is the reality we should concertedly endeavor to manifest. It is within our collective power to do so if we ever muster the collective will to do so.

It is fair to ask about the specifics of that reality. What would it look like and how would it work in practical terms? What do I mean by the terms "optimal future" or "utopia" or "heaven on earth." This is a subject that warrants another book.

But for now, suffice it to say that these terms refer to the realization of a perfect world in which there is no hunger, homelessness, crime, poverty, illiteracy, inequality, racism, war or weapons of war, violence, abuse, pollution, environmental degradation, exploitation, conflict, religious or ethnic strife, addictions, depression, and so on. Wouldn't a world of this kind be far more preferable than the world we have now? Don't we deserve to have a world like this at long last?

In a perfect world, egocentrism, dualism and materialism would be discarded relics from a bygone era of flawed thinking, replaced by oneness, unity, harmony, altruism and a collectively shared spiritual interpretation of reality that is embedded in all social ideologies and permeates all societies and cultures. It could be one that is as simple and straightforward as the Seven Statements, predicated on a solid empirical foundation. In such a world, we would do no harm to any other living thing, for we would fully understand that by doing so we would only bring equal or greater harm to ourselves.

So, what on earth are we waiting for? Let us climb to the mountaintop and enjoy a "God's-eye view" once there. Let us unshackle God from all past faulty perceptions and concocted definitions. Let us demystify God and cease to think that God is inaccessible to us or has abandoned us. Let us transcend our own limitations, myopia and superstitions in the process so that we can finally evolve from great to greater to greatness by embracing our true spiritual identity.

Perhaps this book will contribute ever so slightly to tipping the scale in this direction. I pray it will. What a wonderful world it could be if we resolve to make it so. Heaven is here. Heaven is now. This very day, we can collectively choose to make heaven on earth our prevailing reality.

The solution could be as simple as *God for a Day*, every day, on a mass scale. Considering all that humankind has suffered since inception, is this not the reality we deserve? Then let us claim it. Let us swiftly act to make it so. Now is a great time to begin to apply this cure for "The God Shaped Hole."

It starts with you and me and every other person on earth. One person at a time, a groundswell of grassroots efforts will build itself into a critical mass crescendo that will eventually transform the whole of humanity. No, seismic global transformation won't happen overnight and probably not even in my lifetime, but the journey of a million miles begins with a single step. It is a step on a journey we all must take for our individual and collective welfare. If we fail to do so, most assuredly, I predict the day will come when we will deeply regret it.

Oftentimes, I ask myself what became of the "Baby Boomer" generation, my generation, the peace and love, flower power generation. What happened to our lofty virtues, dreams and ideals? What happened to our determination to change the world for the better? Well, participating in *God for a Day* is yet another chance for my generation to achieve that goal. We can still make it happen. Perhaps Gen X, the Millennials and Gen Z will rise to the occasion along with us. Together, we can optimize the future, one of indescribable magnificence…one we have been waiting thousands of years to realize. Haven't we waited long enough? Haven't we suffered long enough?

Acknowledgements

Many wonderful people helped to make this book a reality. I am deeply grateful to all of them, especially those who kindly offered glowing endorsements, some of which appear in the opening pages.

Much gratitude is due to Dr. Kenneth Ring who strongly encouraged me in October 2021 to write a book about the many angel encounters and other exceptional experiences I have been blessed to have throughout my life. Were it not for Ken's gentle nudging, this book would not have been written.

Virginia Hummel, a.k.a. "Wonder Woman," made numerous contributions, all invaluable, to editing, formatting and the general organization of this book's content, including the interior and cover design. With joy and eagerness, she devoted countless uncompensated hours to help make this book a reality, all for the glory of God and the enrichment of humankind. She developed a special connection to this book's messages because of her own powerful spiritually transformative experiences related to the tragic death of her son in 2006.

Elizabeth Hare devoted many hours editing and proofreading the manuscript. I am exceedingly grateful to her for the skillful finishing touches. I also thank Joe St. Clair, Bill Guggenheim and Dr. Jane Tobal, among dozens of other good friends and close associates, for ongoing assistance and encouragement. My spouse, Vivian, is due heaps of praise as well for her tireless support and inspiration.

To all of you, I say thank you a thousand times over. To God and all the angels, with all the humility and reverence I can muster, I offer enormous love and gratitude each and every day.

About the Author

John Audette served in several senior executive positions during a long career in hospital and hospice administration, as well as physician practice management, public broadcasting, and the performing arts. He earned a Master of Science degree from Virginia Tech.

Mr. Audette is CEO of Eternea, Inc. (*Eternea.org*), which he co-founded with the late Dr. Edgar Mitchell, Apollo 14 astronaut and Dr. Eben Alexander, Harvard neurosurgeon and best-selling author. Eternea's mission is to facilitate scientific research, public education, outreach and practical programmatic initiatives to help people recognize that eternal existence in some form or fashion is a fundamental reality for all living things.

Mr. Audette is also co-founder of the International Association for Near-Death Studies, Inc. (*IANDS.org*). He contributed several chapters about spiritually transformative experiences and non-local consciousness to various scholarly books in the company of such prominent authors as Ervin Laszlo, Deepak Chopra, Jane Goodall, Gary Zukav, Stan Grof, Jean Houston, Larry Dossey and others. He is also gratefully acknowledged in numerous other books on these subjects by various well-known authors whom he assisted dating back to 1975. *Loved by the Light* is his first solo book.

Mr. Audette is an honorably discharged veteran with over three years of active-duty service in the U.S. Army during the Vietnam era.

Website: *www.AffirmingGod.com*

Printed in Great Britain
by Amazon